W9-BYW-881

NetResults.2
Best Practices for Web Marketing

Rick E. Bruner
Leland Harden
Bob Heyman
with Mia Amato

New Riders

201 West 103rd Street, Indianapolis, Indiana 46290

Net Results.2: Best Practices for Web Marketing

International Standard Book Number: 0-7357-1024-4

Library of Congress Catalog Card Number: 00-103156

Printed in the United States of America

First Printing: December 2000

05 04 03 02 01   7 6 5 4 3 2 1

Interpretation of the printing code: The rightmost double-digit number is the year of the book's printing; the rightmost single-digit number is the number of the book's printing. For example, the printing code 01-1 shows that the first printing of the book occurred in 2001.

Trademarks

All terms mentioned in this book that are known to be trademarks or service marks have been appropriately capitalized. New Riders Publishing cannot attest to the accuracy of this information. Use of a term in this book should not be regarded as affecting the validity of any trademark or service mark.

Warning and Disclaimer

Every effort has been made to make this book as complete and as accurate as possible, but no warranty or fitness is implied. The information provided is on an "as is" basis. The authors and the publisher shall have neither liability nor responsibility to any person or entity with respect to any loss or damages arising from the information contained in this book or from the use of the programs accompanying it.

Publisher
David Dwyer

Associate Publisher
Al Valvano

Executive Editor
Steve Weiss

Product Marketing Manager
Kathy Malmloff

Managing Editor
Sarah Kearns

Acquisitions Editor
Theresa Gheen

Development Editor
John Rahm

Project Editor
Michael Thurston

Copy Editor
Nels Hinderlie

Technical Editors
Freude Bartlett
Michael Chanover

Content Wrangler
Mia Amato

Cover Designer
Aren Howell

Interior Designer
Kim Scott

Compositor/ Proofreader
Scan Communications Group, Inc.

Indexer
Lisa Stumpf

Contents at a Glance

Table of Contents

About the Authors

Rick E. Bruner is vice president of interactive marketing research at IMT Strategies, an e-business strategic advisory firm. Prior to co-founding IMT Strategies, Mr. Bruner was president of Executive Summary, a Web marketing strategy consulting company. Mr. Bruner was instrumental in the marketing launch of "push" software pioneer Marimba, Inc. He is an internationally renowned speaker on Internet marketing topics at conferences and has written extensively for *Advertising Age*, *DM News*, *Wired*, *NewMedia*, and *The Industry Standard*. He has a BA in writing from Columbia University and served as the first editor-in-chief of *Budapest Week*, Hungary's first independent English-language newspaper.

Leland Harden is a telecom veteran who has been working in the online industry since 1985. Mr. Harden is executive vice president of strategy at GiftCertificates.com. An internationally recognized authority on online marketing, he was a founder of Cybernautics and later Senior Partner in USWeb's Audience Development practice. Mr. Harden appears regularly as an Internet expert on radio and television and as a conference speaker. He is published in *DM News*, *Interactive Marketing News*, and *AdWeek*, among others. He serves on the board of Web-Runner Communications, and advises venture capital funds domestically and abroad on investments relating to the internet industry.

Bob Heyman is founder and principal of New Canoe, an online relationship marketing firm focused on delivering long-term customer development strategies for Web ventures, part of the Catenas network of international companies. Mr. Heyman is credited with inventing the field of "Audience Development" in 1994 as the co-founder of Cybernautics, a leading internet marketing firm that merged with USWeb (now MarchFirst) in 1997. In a previous life, Mr. Heyman graduated from Harvard with a Masters in Education and was an entertainment attorney whose clients included Jefferson Starship and Ray Manzarek of the Doors. His rock opera "Rock Justice" is included in the top ten most obscure rock operas in the *Book of Rock Lists*.

Dedications

From Rick Bruner:
  To my one true love, Adrienne.

From Leland Harden:
  To Elise, the love of my life, and my children, Verity and Nathanael.

From Bob Heyman:
  To Jill, Sean, and the new crew at New Canoe.

Acknowledgments

Like all books, this one could not have been written without lots of help and support from many sources. We wish to thank some here.

From Rick: A few proper respects to some of the folks who've helped over the years with lots of insight. Thanks for always taking my calls: Steve Diorio, Dale Kutnik, DDT, Smitty, Steve Carlson, Ken Pasternak, Sue Medrano, Richard Hoy, Steve Roth, Nick Denton, Glenn Fleishman, Brad Aronson, Brent Hall, Molly Parsley, Mike Bernstein, Eric Kuhn, Pam Kulik, Al Miranda, Jason Catlett, Steve Vachani, and NRX.

Leland wishes to thank all of his co-workers at GiftCertificates.com, specifically Michael Ahern, Max Bardon, Tim Barefield, Bob Beck, Bertina Ceccarelli, Mark Hasebroock, Jonas Lee, Julie Mahloch, Doug Nielsen, TK Olson, Cristian Ossa, Nancy Robbins, Adrienne Skinner, and Michael Stephenson, with whom he has shared so many great experiences and learned so much; Keith Schaefer, his mentor and friend; and Thom Moritz, his marketing professor and friend.

From Bob: Many thanks to everyone in Sausalito who contributed their time and expertise to this new edition, especially Alex Guerrero, David McHale, Duncan Murphy, Mike Morrone, Jordan Parker, Todd Patrick, Steve Posner, Alex Thompson, and Cara Ucci; to Bill McVey, for his helpful advice; to John O'Neil, for inspiration; and to Steve Weiss at New Riders, for the support of a superb editorial team.

And finally, the authors must express their deepest gratitude to Mia Amato, without whom this book never would have been written. Working with three very distracted, temformental start-up executives, she managed to pull this project together and contribute much of her own insight, delivering on deadline a book we're all proud of.

A Message from New Riders

As the reader of this book, you are our most important critic and commentator. We value your opinion and want to know what we're doing right, what we could do better, in what areas you'd like to see us publish, and any other words of wisdom you're willing to pass our way.

As the Executive Editor for the Graphics team at New Riders, I welcome your comments. You can fax, email, or write me directly to let me know what you did or didn't like about this book—as well as what we can do to make our books better. When you write, please be sure to include this book's title, ISBN, and author, as well as your name and phone or fax number. I will carefully review your comments and share them with the authors and editors who worked on the book.

Please note that I cannot help you with technical problems related to the topic of this book, and that due to the high volume of mail I receive, I might not be able to reply to every message. If you run into a technical problem, it's best to contact our Customer Support department, as listed later in this section. Thanks.

Email: steve.weiss@newriders.com
Mail: Steve Weiss
            Executive Editor
            Professional Graphics & Design Publishing
            New Riders Publishing
            201 West 103rd Street
            Indianapolis, IN 46290 USA

Visit Our Web Site: www.newriders.com

On our Web site, you'll find information about our other books, the authors we partner with, book updates and file downloads, promotions, discussion boards for online interaction with other users and with technology experts, and a calendar of trade shows and other professional events with which we'll be involved. We hope to see you around.

Email Us from Our Web Site

Go to www.newriders.com and click on the Contact link if you

- Have comments or questions about this book.

- Want to report errors that you have found in this book.

- Have a book proposal or are interested in writing for New Riders.

- Would like us to send you one of our author kits.

- Are an expert in a computer topic or technology and are interested in being a reviewer or technical editor.

- Want to find a distributor for our titles in your area.

- Are an educator/instructor who wants to preview New Riders books for classroom use. In the body/comments area, include your name, school, department, address, phone number, office days/hours, text currently in use, and enrollment in your department, along with your request for either desk/examination copies or additional information.

Call Us or Fax Us

You can reach us toll-free at (800) 571-5840 + 9+ 3567 (ask for New Riders). If outside the U.S., please call 1-317-581-3500 and ask for New Riders. If you prefer, you can fax us at 1-317-581-4663, Attention: New Riders.

Technical Support and Customer Support for This Book

Although we encourage entry-level users to get as much as they can out of our books, keep in mind that our books are written assuming a non-beginner level of user-knowledge of the technology. This assumption is reflected in the brevity and shorthand nature of some of the tutorials.

New Riders will continually work to create clearly written, thoroughly tested and reviewed technology books of the highest educational caliber and creative design. We value our customers more than anything—that's why we're in this business—but we cannot guarantee to each of the thousands of you who buy and use our books that we will be able to work individually with you through tutorials or content with which you may have questions. We urge readers who need help in working through exercises or other material in our books—and who need this assistance immediately—to use as many of the resources that our technology and technical communities can provide, especially the many online user groups and list servers available.

- If you have a physical problem with one of our books or accompanying CD-ROMs, please contact our Customer Support department.

- If you have questions about the content of the book—needing clarification about something as it is written or note of a possible error—please contact our Customer Support department.

- If you have comments of a general nature about this or other books by New Riders, please contact the Executive Editor.

To contact our Customer Support department, call 1-317-581-3833, from 10:00 a.m. to 3:00 p.m. U.S. EST (CST from April through October of each year—unlike the majority of the United States, Indiana doesn't change to Daylight Savings Time each April). You can also access our tech support Web site at http://www.mcp.com/support.

Foreword

By John O'Neil
Internet consultant, founder of the Center for Leadership
Renewal in San Francisco, and author of *Leadership Aikido* and
The Paradox of Success

Books on the New E-Conomy, especially e-commerce,

usually become obsolete as the writers produce them.

This new edition of an e-commerce world classic fol-

lows the trend-setting idea of treating a book like soft-

ware. What you hold in your hand has been thoroughly

updated and upgraded in its reissue.

As a student and writer on the subject of leadership,

I am always alert for ideas, concepts, and values that

can strengthen a leader's hand, head, and heart. *Net

Results.2: Best Practices for Web Marketing* promises

to do all of that. Here's what the reader can gain:

- Clear and honest reports from the field. How leaders are using the emerging technology of the Web to reach vast new audiences, with everything from sales messages to customer services, using art forms and incentives that are fresh and intriguing.

- Actual techniques and tools that can be tested and tried almost immediately. Many of these practical ideas cost the developers sweat, tears, and dollars, and the reader gets all the benefits.

- Deep insights expressed through antidotes and case studies that can serve as Michelin-like guides for the veteran and the novice alike. Students and professors should be especially pleased with such material.

Net Results.2 is amazingly hands-on as well as prescient. It moves from the mundane fundamentals—you *still* have to get your Web site right—to the larger strategic issues. I will be recommending this book to leaders because most of them are too removed from the actual battleground of e-commerce. They have frequently left their company fortunes in the hands of specialists and vendors who "talk the talk"—a strange tongue of bit babble, with little concern for profitability, franchise development, alliance formation, or satisfied customers.

Wisely, this edition focuses on business-to-business Web development. It has not left out the audience development (B2C) aspects that made the earlier editions so useful, but mature companies, and especially those just now moving into e-commerce, are in need of lots of help.

As someone involved in start-ups, venture capital, and advising leaders of large global enterprises, I am fully aware of how large the gaps are between the old and new economics. It is somewhat fashionable for CEOs to proclaim that there is no New E-Conomy, just the same old economy with more technology. That may comfort them and their shareholders, but the truth is the old economy is on its way out. The old economy (pre 1995) was local, or at best multinational; competitors were known, and rules of engagement were clear; the bigger, low-tech firms could erect massive barriers to entry. None of that is true today. Everything is morphing:

- Stealth competitors arrive from anywhere (like Nokia from the woods of Finland).

- Technology is not only disruptive, it is downright unruly.

- Alliances, especially in e-commerce, are like talent—they are mission critical.

- Leadership requirements are changing faster than technology.

Information and knowledge is so plentiful that knowledge maps are required to keep track of such things as customer preference, product lines, and value-added analysis of each business unit.

Net Results.2 is one of the powerful tools that leaders and marketing people must have at their ready. The race is just beginning, the New E-Conomy is still open for all contenders, and the winners will be those who blend knowledge, good values, splendid intuition, and constant learning.

John O'Neil
September 2000

Introduction

The More E-Business Changes, the More It Stays the Same

Futurists have a rule of thumb about the impact major new technologies have on societies: We overestimate change in the short-term but underestimate change in the long-term. The Internet has already demonstrated a tremendous impact on the whole world. But rest assured, we ain't seen nothing yet.

So much has changed with the Internet since we wrote the first edition of this book in 1997. Back then, it seemed unthinkable that a dot.com startup like AOL could swallow up a time-honored media empire like Time Warner. And, as we learned in April 2000, e-business has not completely reinvented business. Little things like profitability do still matter after all.

According to research from Morgan Stanley Dean Witter, of the 354 companies that had gone public in U.S. stock markets since Netscape in August 1995, only 12 percent were profitable as of the first quarter of 2000. Yet that's not the last word on the Net's viability as a business opportunity.

The better news is that thousands of companies, large and small, have applied good fiscal management and business principals to the Net, and have realized tremendous corporate value in terms of increased revenue, productivity, sales margins, and new markets. The Direct Marketing Association (DMA), for example, surveyed its 4,500 corporate members in 1999 and found that 96 percent had Web sites, of which 45 percent were using the Internet for e-commerce; of that number, 66 percent were already profitable.

Why You Should Read This Book

After writing the first edition of this book, the three of us, true to our dot.com credentials, each founded a new Internet company. Rick Bruner moved from being a contributing editor for *Advertising Age Interactive* to co-founding IMT Strategies, an advisory and research firm focused on e-business and the impact of technology on sales and marketing strategy. Leland Harden—who, with Bob Heyman, had previously co-founded the pioneering audience development Net marketing agency Cybernautics, which they subsequently sold to USWeb, which is now called MarchFirst—has since taken a domain name he registered in 1995, turned it into equity in an established gift certificate company, and joined to help launch **GiftCertificates.com**, one of the leading e-commerce destinations online today. And Bob Heyman remained true to his calling and launched New Canoe, an online relationship marketing company, which is now part of the Catenas network of companies, located in the same Sausalito marina office building as the original Cybernautics.

Among the three of us, we have more than 20 years of online marketing expertise (yes, that's human years, not Internet years). During that time, we've helped hundreds of companies develop strategies, build and rebuild Web sites, and execute online campaigns. These include America Online, American Airlines, American Express, Barnes & Noble, Birkenstock, Bristol Myers Squibb, Brooks Brothers, Gillette, Home Depot, Hyatt Hotels, IBM, Macy's, and Time, Inc. However, we don't think we have all the answers—far from it—but for better or worse, we're probably as battle-scarred of Internet marketing veterans as you'll find in this galaxy.

We are tremendously gratified by the thanks we have received from hundreds of readers of the first and second printings of this book. The most common theme they expressed was that *Net Results* struck a chord because, although it showed enthusiasm about the potential benefits of the Web, it was solidly grounded in business fundamentals. Now, in its second, fully revised edition for 2001, we strive to balance idealistic vision with executive strategy and actionable programs for success (along with a few snide opinions here and there for good measure).

Make no mistake—we are as bullish as ever about the incredible effectiveness of the Internet for corporate sales and marketing objectives. This is not a matter of speculation; we know of hundreds of companies experiencing phenomenal value from Internet marketing initiatives they've put in place.

The majority of the readers of *Net Results* are not employees at those 300-or-so unprofitable NASDAQ dot.coms struggling to justify preposterous stock valuations with desperate TV ad campaigns. Readers of the first edition of the book did include many netrepreneurs and dot.com professionals, but more were marketing executives and managers of large, medium, and small traditional corporations, looking for practical advice on how to integrate the Net into their businesses.

Readers of this revised edition of *Net Results* will find that, like the development of e-business itself, much is new. A few old strategies, such as seeding newsgroup discussions, have proven less effective over time, while many new strategies have taken their place, such as permission email marketing, addressed in detail in Chapter 6, "Word of Web: Viral Email, and Permission Marketing."

Part I of the book, "Get the Site Right: Web Fundamentals," is focused on strategy and offers readers a framework for evaluating objectives of online marketing programs in Chapter 1, "Return on Investment Goals." Chapter 2, "Web Value Propositions," analyzes how companies can capitalize on the unique set of value propositions that the Web offers both customers and marketers. Chapter 3, "Design Optimization," focuses on optimizing the design and customer "usability" of the site, which can easily be the most critical factor between success and failure with online customers. Chapter 4, "Domain Brand and Market Penetration," has much fun at the expense of the amazing number of companies that continue to commit obvious and humiliating blunders with regard to their domain-naming strategies.

In Part II, "Audience Development," we get down in the trenches and elaborate on the practical details of how to execute cost-effective, customer-friendly online marketing campaigns. Chapter 5, "Find and Be Found: Strategies for Search Engines and Directories," is devoted to one of the best investments in guerilla Web marketing resources—optimizing your ranking in search engine results—and we get under the hood with meta tags, registration techniques, and the secrets to getting listed quickly with Yahoo!

Chapter 6, "Word of Web: Email, Permission, and Viral Marketing" examines how companies can tap the incredible power of email marketing, without upsetting customers, by using viral and permission marketing techniques. Chapter 7, "Building Online Audiences: Affinity Sites and Affiliate Programs," discusses the importance of partners for success, notably in the form of affinity sites and affiliate networks. Chapter 8,

"Media Savoir Faire: Public Relations for a Digital Age," addresses critical do's and don'ts for what remains one of the most efficient uses of marketing resources—public relations—targeting both online and offline media and influencers. Finally, in Chapter 9, "Paid Media: Making Dollars and Sense with Web Advertising," we cut through the hype and explain how to get the biggest bang for your buck in the high-flying world of online advertising.

If your goal in selecting this book is to use the Internet to promote your company, build your brand, generate sales leads, sell direct online, or buy or sell Web advertising, we are confident you will find lots of value in the pages to follow. Whether you work for a Fortune 100 global giant or you run a one-man brand out of your garage, the Net almost invariably needs to be a key part of your sales and marketing mix. Success online requires—as it usually does in all cases—hard work, focus, and imagination. This book, we hope, will help you get there faster, and with fewer mistakes. Good luck, and good marketing.

Rick E. Bruner

Leland Harden

Bob Heyman

Part I

Get the Site Right: Web Fundamentals

IN THIS CHAPTER

chapter 1

Return on Investment Goals

BELIEVE THE HYPE. A good Web site is good marketing.

If you still have any doubts that Net marketing is an asset to your business, you definitely have a place in the marketing history books. There's no question that within a span of a few years, the Internet and the World Wide Web have become the most important communications tool since television. If one of the most-evoked clichés on the Web is that no one is making any money, this book, now in its third edition, stands as an emphatic refutation of that fallacy.

This book contains online audience-development techniques that can succeed in attracting visitors to your site, but it's much more important to first spend time and resources to understand what people will do after they get there. With over nine million commercial "dot.com" destinations to choose from, you'd do better to stay offline than to slap together a site that only tells customers, competitors, and potential investors that you are totally clueless. Or if, after two or three years since its launch, your Web site is still licking the great lollipop of mediocrity, you're just wasting time and money.

Getting to Know ROI

Before worrying about what visitors think of their sites, however, organizations are answerable first to themselves. The first step toward getting their sites—along with the rest of the online marketing mix—right is to set clear objectives for a return on their investment online. Far too many organizations spend substantial sums on the Web without a clear articulation of what they are getting for their money.

Part of the problem, perhaps, is that so many sites that crashed and burned did so with other people's money. The business model that seemed most apt in the last few years went something like this: "Get an idea for a Web site, get started with loans from a venture capitalist, spend it all, raise an IPO, get bought out for millions of dollars, and retire to Tahiti." While this actually happened a few times —BlueMountain Arts, the online greeting card company started by a husband and wife team and sold to Exite@Home for $780 million, comes to mind—a great many more businesses have made substantial profits on the Web by simply viewing the Internet as a new and powerful venue for their company's marketing strategies.

The difference is paying attention to Return on Investment (ROI). When it's your own money, as many Web entrepreneurs know, financial statistics take on an abiding interest. Many Web businesses that were started with outside venture capital have since learned that their investors now fully expect to see a profitable return on *their* investments, *their* ROI.

Old ROI versus New ROI

Traditional business models created to measure ROI went down the toilet in the Web's first flush of success, in part for good reasons. There didn't seem to be anything to measure success against. Such MBA-school measurements as Net Present Value (NPV) models require predictable cash flows, discounted and evaluated over 3 to 10 year periods. Another useful yardstick, Customer Lifetime Value (LTV), could only be calculated over years of experience that might reasonably predict customer behaviors.

During the Web's first big boom year, 1998, most Web businesses hadn't been in existence longer than twelve months, and most customers had even less experience in Web transactions that involved cash. No one knew which buying behaviors were the norms. Revenues from online businesses also did not appear to be aligned with future values, measured by the only measurable numbers: stock prices, which rose to amazing heights and have since fluctuated wildly.

As Web businesses have matured (as much as any two- or three-year old ventures might be said to be mature), marketers have begun to measure success by looking at a different set of numbers, a company's profit and loss (P and L) sheets. The most popular of these metrics is Customer Acquisition Cost, which is simply the cost of any specific marketing campaign divided by the number of prospective customers whose behavior met the campaign's goal (made a purchase, filled out a survey, signed up for a promotional newsletter, and so on).

Tracking customer acquisition costs has become popular as it has become easier, thanks to server log analysis and other forms of online tracking software that make the Web so elegantly quantifiable. It is possible to get precise numbers as to how many visitors surfed a site's pages, how many stopped to purchase something, what they bought, and how much they spent. While the privacy issues surrounding customer tracking features must be addressed, the fact remains that even with simple software tools, organizations can learn an amazing amount about online customer patterns, segmentation, and profitability, compared to all forms of marketing that preceded the Web.

Getting a handle on accountability by measuring customer acquisition costs might not be crucial to business profits, either in business-to-business (B2B) or in business-to-consumer (B2C) Web sites. But it's better than nothing. A year 2000 study of 50 "Best-in-Class" Web companies by IMT Strategies/META survey revealed only five of these popular Web destinations used any ROI measurements at all to track their customer relationship management (CRM) costs, although about a dozen had the available numbers and did not employ them. The most astonishing news was that 30 of the 50 firms had no metrics in place, and were spending their money in what can only be described as a "leap of faith" that profits might occur.

It's extremely unlikely that companies marketing on the Web will continue in this fashion, without availing quantifiable and available data used to measure brand equity, growth of market share, and operational efficiencies. Start-ups are already finding it harder to raise capital without advance market research and CRM projections (see *Due Diligence and the Business Plan* sidebar).

Good Web marketing involves optimizing the Company's Web site elements by studying statistics that give intelligence about customers, and comparing the profitability of certain expenses, such as email advertising (see Chapter 6, "Word of Web: Email, Permission, and Viral Marketing") to Web banner ads,(see Chapter 9, "Paid Media: Making Dollars and Sense with Web Advertising") and to paybacks to affiliated sites that send customers to the site (more in Chapter 7, "Building Online Audiences: Affinity Sites and Affiliate Programs") directly against the revenues they each deliver.

Those who are more patient and forward thinking also compare the Web-related costs of acquiring customers against a continuum of repeat sales or sales over a customer lifetime, or compare across other marketing, sales, and service channels. If you think this sounds a lot like what you've heard before from veterans of catalog or direct marketing campaigns, you are correct.

Bad Web marketing, sadly, is legion. In the ROI-less dawn of the new age, negative revenues were something to boast about, and major players such as **Amazon.com** were permitted to coast for years before displaying a profitable quarter. New customer acquisition costs on some sites are still admitted to be $100 or more per transaction, many times more than what would be tolerated from the results of any direct mail campaign. In the frenzied holiday shopping season of 1999, it was not unheard of for a new Web site to spend $20 million on a month's worth of television advertising, and congratulate itself for ending the year with $12 million in revenue.

If you want to know how to use Customer Acquisition Costs as one ROI method to trim expenses and raise revenues, Chapter 9 includes some useful tables. Customer acquisition metrics, however, are not the only way to look at ROI.

Six Useful Online ROI Models

The Web can be an economical arm of a company's overall marketing efforts, or it can be a money pit if the company doesn't have a clear and measurable marketing objective in mind. The business goals of each company depend on different factors, but most successful online ventures, even those that have no direct e-commerce function, find that the Internet offers marketers a return on investment in one of these six models:

- Brand-Building

- Lead Generation

- Online Sales (E-Commerce)

- Customer Support

- Market Research

- Content Publishing

Content publishing includes Web content management sites such as Yahoo! and MSNBC, as well as digital content sellers such as *The Wall Street Journal* and **MP3.com**. While many early content sites were originally set up to distribute information for free, even those created by amateurs are now pursuing profit. The ROI can be measured as revenue through advertising sales, subscriptions, micropayment transaction commissions, and similar means. Similarly, the online sales and e-commerce models aim for revenues in the form of direct sales or growth of market share. For many other businesses, however, the Web is an expense in return for a competitive advantage in the form of brand promotion, customer support, or market research.

In practice, of course, companies overlap several of these six ROI models. To determine how each model might work best for any particular company requires a full understanding of the Net's core marketing values, discussed in more detail in Chapter 2, "Web Value Propositions." This chapter, however, looks at examples of how companies are realizing ROI today with these six models. (See Figure 1.1.)

Brand-Building

The Web can play an important and cost-effective role, alongside television, print, billboards, and other advertising media, in building consumer awareness of an offline brand. Ongoing research by Millward Brown Interactive and other researchers, argues that even standard ad banners can measurably increase brand awareness for advertisers and compared favorably to television in brand recall studies.

Figure 1.1
The Hershey Foods Web site tries to be all things to all visitors, and successfully juggles all six ROI models while addressing the interests of investors, vendors, candy-loving kids, and their parents.

In an increasingly global marketplace, it is entirely possible that the only way a potential customer might discover a company's product is through cyberspace, and for many organizations that is reason enough to be there. Awareness also has a tangible value in brand equity when a business is merged or sold.

Although it is hard to measure branding by itself, it is possible to correlate branding efforts with increased interactions, lower costs of lead generation, or growth of market share. (See Figure 1.2.) For business-to-business Web sites, early and expensive online advertising might not be as important to building the brand as co-branding. If nobody in cyberspace knows the company's name, the banner ad or the placement of its logo on the Web site of a better-known partner lends credibility. As discussed in Chapter 7, co-branding efforts can be measured when the logo is a live Web link, simply by counting how many site visitors arrive through that link.

In Part II, "Audience Development," we'll explore how to raise awareness of a Web site through advertising, public relations, online communities, and other means. All manners of Web marketing contribute to a positive brand image, however. Many "legacy" companies, including Federal Express, Charles Schwab, The *New York Times*, Nike, Levi Strauss, and Ford Motor Company, have demonstrated that they are 21st-Century market leaders through their effective use of the Web.

Figure 1.2

Intel's sleek home page often changes to reflect its branding initiatives.

Branding is even more important if the product is new or the company not an established leader. Unlike other media, which expect little of the consumer beyond passive attention, the Web invites netizens to get involved with the brand, delve into details about the product, sign up for special services, return to the site regularly as a resource for a specific topic, and otherwise play an active role in the marketing experience, closely bonding with the brand along the way.

There's probably no better way to sell software than on the Web through product demos, downloads, and constantly updated tech support. Even products found on grocery shelves, using sites that are closer to show-biz than utilitarian, stand to impress the Web's demographically attractive consumers simply by having more user-interactive sites than their traditional competitors. (See Figure 1.3.)

Household names like Procter & Gamble have been late to figure out the Web, but now are aggressively pursuing rich media, interactive ads, e-coupons, incentive programs, and viral marketing. One way to measure how this will affect consumers is tracking the purchase behaviors of those now eagerly buying groceries online through "Webvan" type services and **Priceline.com**'s popular "name your own price" marketing of groceries.

Figure 1.3
How do you make kitty litter products exciting? How about an animated product demo? It's cu-u-u-ute.

Lead Generation

Although the Web makes it easy to keep a product name in front of the right audience, many advertisers seek more immediate results than brand awareness. For such direct marketers, the Web is hog heaven. Its capability to deliver highly qualified sales leads with ease means that online marketers can regularly outperform traditional direct mail, with none of the cost of paper, postage, and other associated expenses. For B2B marketing, lead generation through email lists can indeed be the least expensive way to introduce a specialized product to a specific, small, and geographically dispersed buyer group. (See Figure 1.4.)

www.nec.com

Figure 1.4
Okidata takes a playful approach to direct marketing through email. See more of the do-it-yourself comic strip in Chapter 6.

Even though the Internet has an increasingly broader base of users, more than 75 percent of Americans online have attended college, and more than two-thirds report a household income greater than $50,000, compared to the national median of $35,000. Nearly 10 percent of households online report an income of greater than $150,000 (Source: MRI Cyberstats).

Those kinds of statistics make the online audience a more profitable market segment than TV viewers, who represent 95 percent of the households in the U.S. On the Web, marketers can easily find audience groups that are keenly defined by every kind of special interest. Add to that a wealth of techniques for further pinpointing user groups—with jargonistic names like *collaborative filtering* and *neural networks*, discussed further in later chapters—and the potential for target marketing online is tremendous.

Smart marketers will exploit both direct and brand advertising possibilities online. For example, in most cases the banner ads should clearly state the product brand for the benefit of the 99.5 percent of surfers who won't click on them, even if driving site traffic with clickthroughs is the marketer's primary objective.

As discussed further in Chapter 9, measuring the value of online advertising in terms of customer acquisition is more complex than it might first appear. A company's ad agency can help to achieve a higher-than-average clickthrough rate, and a publisher might charge higher prices for this. But clickthroughs in and of themselves are meaningless if they can't be related to clear objectives. Who exactly clicked through? A potential customer, or a randy teenager confused by a cryptic, teasing message? How many levels into the site did the visitor explore after clicking on the banner? How directly does a visit to the home page translate into a sale or other marketing goal?

Boo! A Cautionary Tale

One of the most spectacular failures in the online economy was the speedy demise of **boo.com**, a global fashion retailer based in London. Backed by no less than J.P. Morgan and the Bennetton and Bernard Ardnault family fortunes, this startup managed to amass $125 million in financing, and then managed to spend nearly all of it in less than a year. According to published reports, sales for the first three months of live operation totaled only $680,000, while no expense was spared flying staff first class to five-star hotels as offices were launched in New York, Paris, Stockholm, Munich, and Amsterdam. While its launch date was delayed by technical difficulties for several months, millions were spent on an offline ad campaign to introduce the brand through street media and glossy fashion magazines. (See Figure 1.5.)

Six months after launch, down to its last $500,000, the Web site was sold to **Fashionmall.com**, a pure play site that had been established in 1994 to direct online shoppers to an assortment of apparel company home pages. **Fashionmall.com** was already a survivor, one of the few "cybermalls" that succeeded partly because it focused on a broad but deep niche, and partly because it relentlessly wooed audience and affiliate partners through low-cost methods, such as revenue-sharing, search engine ranking, and redirecting visitor data to prompt ever-more-targeted advertisements to its repeat users.

Ben Narasin, a former garment industry executive who is the founder, CEO, and President of **Fashionmall.com**, has said that **boo.com**'s crisis might have been avoided by spending some of its start-up money on market research. Later analysis by Forrester Research in Europe estimated that 98–99 percent of home modems in Europe and the U.S. were incapable of downloading the complex imaging used by **boo.com** to display product information; anyone who logged in from a Macintosh computer could not access anything beyond the home page. (See Figure 1.6.)

"Boo's biggest mistake was a lack of ability to think they could ever be wrong," Narasin said. "And yet there's nothing they did wrong that we didn't do wrong; the difference is we did it wrong five years before, and for less money." (See Figure 1.7.)

Figure 1.5

Going, going, gone. . .Global fashion retailer boo.com became a cautionary tale in the industry when it managed to spend through $125 million in marketing dollars and startup costs its first year.

Figure 1.6

. . .only to discover that an estimated 95–99 percent of its target user base could not download the site's complicated animation and 3D photography.

www.fashionmall.com

Online Sales (E-Commerce)

What do you want to buy? Whatever it is, you can get it online—cars, furniture, chocolate, computers, office supplies, hot sauce, houses, stereo equipment, books, maple syrup, plane tickets, CDs. And you might be able to get it wholesale, through a buyer's cooperative such as **Mobshop.com, Mercata.com, Priceline.com,** or any number of industry co-ops that let smaller companies bid together to get the best prices on commodities such as copper or corn syrup.

That's not to say every online vendor is making money—far from it. But some are. Many of the biggest names in retail, such as The Gap, Nordstrom's, and Barnes & Noble, have launched commerce sites offering vast arrays of products. Small companies with niche products have found Web marketing profitable when they combine unique offerings with promotion strategies that cultivate the growth of online communities. For these businesses, cutting down mailing costs, increasing visibility, and taking advantage of tax-free shipping across state lines increases ROI in ways that traditional marketing venues, limited by the geographic boundaries of TV signals or zip codes, cannot. (See Figures 1.8 and 1.9.)

According to e-Marketer, 18 percent of all Americans bought a product online during 1999. By 2003, that number is expected to grow to 45 percent, comparable to the number of consumers that shop by catalog today. Forrester Research estimates the value of consumer goods sold on the Web will top $14 billion in 2003, while business-related e-commerce is anticipated to reach at least a trillion dollars in global sales.

No one can predict which kinds of products and services can be the most profitable when sold directly through the Internet, but the following guidelines might help. If the product you offer doesn't meet at least one of the following criteria, proceed with caution.

1. The product/service is computer-related or appeals to a technologically sophisticated audience.

2. The product/service appeals to a broad segment of the Internet audience no matter what their geography.

3. The product/service is a specialty item otherwise difficult to obtain in the "real world."

4. The product/service can be purchased less expensively, or more conveniently, or more efficiently, through Internet channels than in the "real world."

www.nordstrom.com

Figure 1.8

There's more than one way to sell a shoe online, and competition is fierce. Legendary legacy retailer Nordstrom's has successfully married its catalog business and outlet operation to offer a wide selection of shoes, often deeply discounted.

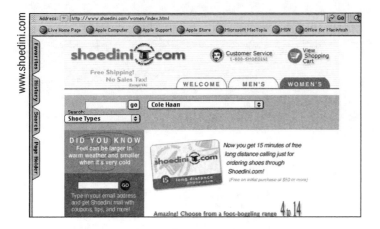

www.shoedini.com

Figure 1.9

Online upstart Shoedini, the inspiration of a third-generation shoe retailer in Georgia, sells at full price, offering free shipping and premiums instead of discounts.

Customer Support

Customer support is truly one of the Internet's killer apps. To date, few companies have realized the full potential of this opportunity. Some kind of visitor support online is becoming more of a must-have, as Netizens grow to expect higher levels of interactivity. This can range from simple frequently asked questions (FAQs) to "My Account" software programs that allow customers to privately view their shopping history on a site where they choose to be a registered user. Between those two ends of the spectrum, companies are aiding customers through staff replies to email inquiries, automated email responses, complex searchable FAQs databases, and live support chat.

Clearly it's an area for improvement: Some Web businesses let days go by before answering a customer email query. Others simply post a toll-free telephone number. Analysts predict, however, that in the coming years many companies will shift significant portions of their existing telephone customer support to the Web, or run joint "tele-Web" customer service centers.

The modern twist is online customer support supplied by real people. Applications available through solution providers such as LivePerson and eGain allow "voice over" interactions through the Internet screen, live-operator call back, or simultaneous-to-the-screen live Web chat. Retailers such as Nordstrom's, Land's End, the realtor Corcoran Group, and Internet companies Screaming Media and Harris Interactive were among the first in their categories to offer this old-fashioned level of customer service. (See Figure 1.10.)

Figure 1.10
Web sites of public companies invariably attract the hunting species known as the online investor. TIBCO Software's Web site devotes pages to the investor-relations side of "customer support."

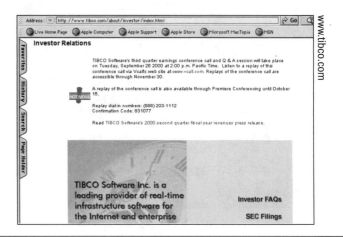

Whatever the business, using a Web site to improve its customer communications should never be disregarded. Sadly, this end of a business plan is often given less attention because, unlike a direct email marketing campaign, its results cannot be measured as quickly or so directly. It is possible, however, to measure customer satisfaction through surveys and, of course, results. Comparing the rise and fall of customer complaint levels with sales figures and repeat-sales data might provide all the proof you need of the ROI of any online customer service deployment. (See Figures 1.11 and 1.12.)

Figure 1.11
Buyers of luxury residential real estate expect the highest levels of hand-holding. At Corcorangroup.com, you can "chat with a broker" as you simultaneously sift through visual listings onscreen.

Figure 1.12
The Butterball Turkey Web site cruises most of the year, but its reason for existence is to augment the company's telephone hotline, which goes into high gear each November. In November of 1997, the first year of launch, the telephone hotline logged over two million phone calls, while five million visitors clicked on this home page.

Market Research

Increasingly, companies are recognizing the Net's awesome potential for market research. Market research consultants, of course, were quick to pick up on this. (See Figure 1.13.)

Market research in a variety of forms is an ROI available to most companies online. There is much information that users simply volunteer, if sites take the time to observe it.

Figure 1.13

Survey sites such as bolt.com collect data on teen trends.

www.bolt.com

Software by firms like Accrue, Art Technology, Macromedia, NetPerceptions, and Personify enables sites to study patterns in anonymous users' behavior and use that information to improve the site, surmise visitor demographics, and personalize content for users on-the-fly.

Online survey services such as **Survey.com** or TalkCity will also beat the bushes for a company, offering Net Surfers coupons or even cash for filling out forms. Or, as the company called ePrize once boasted in its ad campaign, "We get you information about your Web site visitors the old-fashioned way. We bribe them."

Of course, sites can conduct their own research simply by surveying visitors. If it's well planned, this can be effective. Unfortunately, many sites slap up user surveys or registration forms without a strategy for what data they need or what will motivate users to comply. As a result, many users lie on these forms or just ignore them, and the companies don't know how to interpret the results. (See Figure 1.14.)

We're Listening!

Win $500

Your Logo Here

We're listening! Will you answer a few questions about our site?

Powered by: e-satisfy

Sure!

Privacy Statement | About | Maybe Later | No Thanks

Figure 1.14
Online customer satisfaction surveys can be set up within hours if you outsource the work. E-satisfy.com is one vendor that offers pre-designed templates in "styles" from retro to high-tech.

Beyond the inconvenience of surveys and registration forms, user's fiercely guard their privacy online and fear their email addresses will be sold to reckless marketers. To overcome this, sites must earn users' trust and compensate them somehow for bothering to answer questions honestly for market research, ad targeting, or other purposes. (See more on privacy in Chapter 2.)

Gaining trust and motivation often pays for itself with desirable repeat business that can be triggered by a continuous loop of what's called "permissioned marketing." A common example is a site that offers a game or quiz, and then serves up a coupon that can be redeemed online. When redeeming the coupon, the customer is invited to sign up for future coupon offers, but the sign-up procedure involves selecting preferences, such as dog food or baby wipes. The more interactive value a site offers its users, the more information the users might reveal about themselves.

Retaining customers or upselling becomes easier the more a company knows about its customer; it might more easily sell an expensive doggie coat to a customer that has previously only ordered canned dog food if that customer has said his pet is a pedigreed Corgi, not a Pitbull mix. Measuring the cost of obtaining that information for a sampling of online customers, against resulting sales, is a simple test of ROI that might suggest the viability of a further foray into more expensive forms of data-mining.

Content Services

This last category is broad and includes many familiar online brands, such as Yahoo!, Excite, CNET, ESPN SportsZone, Microsoft Network, HotWired, Disney.com, and so on. All of these sites produce their own content and/or aggregate content, or provide content management services to Net users, such as search engines, localized entertainment guides, or real-time stock market feeds. The vast majority of these sites underwrite at least part of their costs by selling online advertising to sponsors. To offset declining banner ad revenues, many sites further subsidize their earnings with subscriptions, syndication agreements, transaction fees, paid sponsorships, affiliate partnership revenues, and a little e-commerce on the side.

To this category one can also add real Web "publishers" such as **iuniverse.com**, which sell downloadable electronic versions of entire fiction and nonfiction books. Ditto for sites that transmit or sell digitized music, spoken-word audio, interactive talk radio, or digitized video that has been either adapted or created especially for Web audiences.

Profitability in content publishing seems to lie in business models that adhere to a fee-for-service structure. It's no surprise that online versions of daily newspapers and magazines don't make a profit; they're giving away content for free that other, offline users pay for, and are perpetually forced to sell advertising space at firesale prices so as not to undercut their print ad rates.

Under a fee-for-service structure, the content publisher must take care that the expenses for producing and delivering a content product to a consumer, or the costs for delivering a consumer to an advertiser, are less, not more, than the revenues received for delivering the eyeballs. Results can be measured in direct sales, or in the case of ad delivery, can be measured by transaction-based performance ratios.

After years of being told that "information wants to be free" Netizens are now coaxed into paying for subscriptions, or paying for content. A few print-oriented sites have been successful all along in charging a flat subscription price to all users, *The Wall Street Journal* being a notable example.

Newspapers, which have historically yet to see significant profits from any of their online ventures, have recently begun selling off the old inventory by the piece and by the pound. An old news item, for example, from the Silicon Valley business pages of the *San Jose Mercury News* at **Mercurycenter.com,** is about $2 a hit. *The Economist,* one of Europe's most respected financial publications, sells the white papers and market reports it amasses for its own coverage through an e-commerce Web site, **economist.com,** with the prices of some reports $10 or more.

Innovative forms of content management on the Web include the many flavors of B2B "solution providers," the Business Service Providers (BSP) and Application Service Providers (ASP) catering to other Internet businesses. On the consumer side are providers such as **iharvest.com,** which enables users to bookmark not just Web pages, but also stored data, without filling up their own hard drives (see Figure 1.15). Most controversial of all are the so-called peer-to-peer (P2P) management sites such as **Napster.com,** which enable computer users to directly swap digital music files and other copyright-protected content.

Figure 1.15
The iharvest Web site stores downloaded files.

Pure Play Sites and Eyeball Aggregators

There are a handful of companies, such as Netscape, that aren't principally in the publishing business but do attract so much traffic to their sites that they can get into the ad and affiliate revenue game. For most marketers of real-world products, however, this version of the content ROI model initially looked like a fringe benefit.

Today, some Web businesses are launched for the sole purpose of attracting traffic and directing it to other Web sites. Such models are sometimes called "pure play" because they own no inventory and are merely intermediaries between marketers and customers. Think of them as "eyeball aggregators," because the core business is to attract users to a central Web site, and then send the users on their merry way to other sites through ever-more-clickable links.

Buried deep within the content category are the millions of Internet destinations maintained by nonprofit, governmental, organizational, and personal (fanatic or enthusiast) entities. These are visited in turn by millions of "eyeballs" seeking free but useful information. We call these "accidental aggregators" and believe they can be used effectively in viral marketing (see Chapter 6) or recruited as affinity or affiliate partners (see Chapter 7). (See Figure 1.16.)

Affiliate partnerships show some promise as modest revenue generators, and might be adapted into a Web business plan. Eyeball aggregating, however, accidental or by pure play design, seems to be maturing into a fee-for-services model. As discussed in Chapter 9, advertisers now expect to pay not for mere exposure, but by documentable performance. Results can be tracked, projections and service pricing can be adjusted, and the overall profitability of aggregating can theoretically be measured with the same ROI as direct sales.

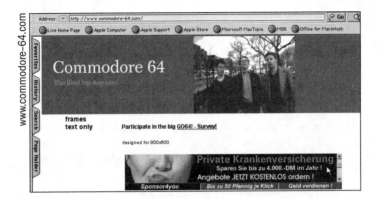

Figure 1.16

Accidental aggregators in action: The Web site for New York-based garage band Commodore64 sells CDs, runs video clips, and provides a live link to an insurance company in Germany.

Due Diligence and the Business Plan

Web start-ups and existing Internet businesses in search of new financing are increasingly being asked to provide proof of the viability of their marketing budgets. Along with the personnel and legal due diligence required prior to acquisitions, mergers, or venture capitalization, a Web business plan should prepare what has come to be called *marketing due diligence*. This is a document justifying the company's proposed or ongoing marketing strategy, infrastructure, and expenses.

It is hard to believe that companies now marketing on the Web will continue to spend aggregate billions on Web banner advertising—given the 0.3 to 0.5 percent response rate for Web banner ads—without measuring results, and then making swift adjustments to ad placements. New enterprises will not be given lavish budgets for either Web or offline advertising without showing some well-researched documentation on projected customer acquisition or customer conversion cost ratios.

A small handful of Web consulting companies now provide marketing due diligence (IMT Strategies and New Canoe among them) as the initial spadework can involve far more than just ad metrics. Research areas include review of a company's current marketing team, marketing technology infrastructure, marketing successes to date, and marketing strategy and plans (including current programs, spending levels, and target markets).

Industry analysis that venture capital partners look for, for example, include click and mortar category penetration (the extent that real-world customers can be converted to online buying) and wallet share (what percentage customers will spend online, versus offline).

continues

continued

If a business plan is a direct sales model, marketing due diligence prior might include *demand modeling*, a computer simulation of projected buying behaviors based on the information that's already been gleaned from focus groups, brainstorming sessions, and competitive intelligence.

Much industry information can already be found online. The projected size of e-commerce, broken down by category, is a standard offering by Jupiter Communications, and available either free or by subscription through its Web site at **www.jup.com**. Jupiter's site also provides statistics from Media Metrix, which measures traffic patterns and user behaviors on the Web; and AdRelevance, which serves up effectiveness studies of online advertising. Rival firms, like eMarkete, also supply industry reporting and trends forecasting. Online versions of trade publications are another source of projections and market share data.

 **Resources**

The Internet Advertising Bureau

http://www.iab.net

- The leading association for companies concerned with Web advertising, whose members include leading online publishers, advertisers, software makers, ad agencies, and others. The site offers a wealth of free resources and even more to paying members.

eMarketer

http://www.eMarketer.com

- Provides industry news, business forecasts, marketing statistics, and research. Offers a free email newsletter provides a wealth of information.

Forrester Research

http://www.forrester.com

- Sells analysis and trends forecasting, and often fills its Web pages with free and useful statistics.

Iconocast

http://www.iconocast

- Contains Web-at-a-glance demographics, research, and reports.

IMT Strategies

http://www.imtstrategies.com

- Provides market research and implementation of Web marketing.

Jupiter Communications/Media Metrix/AdRelevance

http://www.jup.com

- Another well-respected analysis firm whose reports and statistics are widely distributed throughout the media. Tantalizing tidbits appear on the pages devoted to its three research arms. Subscribers and other paying customers can get customized data and access to deeper levels of research.

continues

continued

Millward Brown

http://www.millwardbrown.com

- MB put itself on the map with a landmark study of banner ad recall back in 1997. A revised edition of the study is expected by the end of 2000.

Tenagra

http://www.tenagra.com

- Another research firm, which offers newsletters and data of interest to online marketers.

Recommended Reading

The Industry Standard

http://www.thestandard.com

imarketing news

http://www.imarketingnews.com

Red Herring

http://www.redherring.com

IN THIS CHAPTER

chapter 2

Web Value Propositions

THE WEB HAS BECOME one of the most compelling media for one-on-one communications on a
global scale. But sadly, most businesses treat their
Web sites not as the opportunity to develop a
uniquely individualized sales experience, but as
something more akin to a highly decorated trade
show booth. Streaming video, stereo sound, and eye-
popping, action-packed graphics are not what lead
people into the Internet. As Web ad agency designer
Sean Carton once pithily remarked, "People don't go
on the Web because they feel they're not getting
enough commercials on TV."

When a potential customer wanders into a bricks and mortar store, a good salesperson immediately greets that person, tries to identify what the customer is looking for, and begins to customize a buying experience.

But what happens when a customer enters the average business-to-business (B2B) or business-to-consumer (B2C) Web site? There's usually no greeting, and there are an array of menus to take a person here or there. Just like a trade show booth, there is some glitzy business (live video cartoons, pop-ups, banners, and flashing buttons). Maybe there's a demo to view, a contest to enter, or a T-shirt to win. Please put your email in the register field so we can send you our junk mail. For all the fuss, many Web sites are pretty passive for the user, who may wander from page to page, and perhaps find what she is looking for. Just like the average trade show booth, if the site keepers don't recognize the user as a familiar customer, no attention will be paid. So, the user will wander off to the next booth, or Web site, leaving no trace of a possible sales lead.

B2B Web sites have learned that their online communications must be quite different from B2C sites. However, a number of traits that characterize strong, successful sites, using the Web and Internet in a way no other medium has done before can be identified. A strong site is likely to exploit many, if not all, of these features. The best Web architecture possesses the following traits:

- Interactive
- Personal
- Infocentric
- Instantaneous
- Measurable
- Flexible
- Interlinked
- Economical

These are the features this chapter will explore.

Pundits often compare the development of the Web to the development of early television. If that's the case, the Web is no longer in any proclaimed "golden age" akin to the 1950s, or even in the exploratory mid- to late-'60s. Thanks to "Web years"—a measurement gauged by many as similar to "dog years," or 7/1—what seems like a year in the Web's maturation is really only about two months. By such measurement, the Web's current growth pattern as a medium can be seen as similar to that of television in the early to mid 1970's—a period marked by slavish imitation of successful patterns and catering to "the lowest common denominator."

It may not be accurate to compare the Web to television. According to data compiled by Morgan Stanley, it took radio 38 years to reach an audience of 50 million homes. Television took 13 years to reach the same number. Cable, from HBO's 1976 launch, took 10 years. The Web did it in four. Between 1993—when 23-year-old Marc Andreesen wrote the first graphical Web browser, Mosaic—and the end of 1997, conservative estimates say the Web reached 50 million users worldwide. By the middle of the year 2000, the estimate of Web users in the U.S. alone was 65 million, nearly half of a worldwide estimate of 131 million users.*

The Internet had already existed for 30 years before the World Wide Web, producing such earlier communication protocols as electronic mail, file transfers, discussion boards, and more arcane technologies like Telnet, Gopher, and IRC.

When the Web came along, and accompanied by a flourish of good graphical browsers—Netscape and Microsoft Explorer—for experiencing it, the Net's geekier features were left in the dust. As well-designed, compelling visual images began to replace text pages, communicating through the Web became something for the masses to do with a computer besides word processing.

What has made the Web such a breakthrough? That's a question the whole industry needs to keep asking itself for years to come. In the Web's go-go years of the late '90s, users turned to the medium to seek the forbidden (pornography and hate literature), to share thoughts (chatrooms and electronic mail), and to buy products more easily (through auctions, reverse auctions, buyer groups, and e-commerce). Most importantly, though, users turned to the Web to seek out specific and unique information to serve the user's business and personal needs. Through the power of search engines such as Lycos and such transparent logic systems as Ask Jeeves, the Web has increasingly become the place for users to find the answers to their questions, any questions—the place to find everything from life partners to the dope on Poland's latest banking crisis.

---

*Source: David Halprin, senior analyst, eMarketer

Interactivity

In the ceaselessly inventive lexicon of cyberslang, a *cobweb* is a site that never changes.

For the marketer, the Web's most important value is direct interaction with customers. Static brochure sites—product photos, lists of retail locations, recipe collections, and so on—miss a critical point. The Web offers more opportunities than most other media, in which a business can only talk *at* its customers. Online, it's about engaging *with* them, listening *to* them, and learning *from* them through feedback features such as online focus groups, preference polls, and customer service email reviews (see Figure 2.1).

Figure 2.1
Online demos can be effective for business-to-business Web sites if the demo can identify what the user most covets. In this case, it's local sales leads.

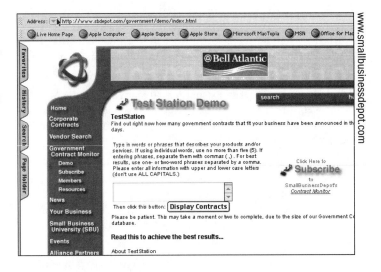

What Can I Do for You?

Small Business Depot's informational Web site, **smallbusinessdepot.com**, leads viewers immediately to an invitation to try the "Test Station," an easy-to-use database program that allows visitors who are small business owners to discover—free of charge—what contracts are currently out for bid within their area of market expertise. Microseconds later, the screen calls up a list of all biddable jobs sent out in the last 30 days. Although content offerings of **smallbusinessdepot.com**'s home page are refreshed daily, a user's initial visit encourages a deeper level of interactivity by engaging the small business owner with an offer that's hard to refuse—free sales leads.

Such an interactive invitation has two purposes: It both helps qualify the customer (you're either panting for hot sales leads or you're not), and it puts the customer in charge of what happens next. Letting the user lead and control at least part of the interaction on a Web site reaps many benefits in customer satisfaction and customer loyalty, as any used-car salesman will tell you. The more you can design your transactions around the customer's ability to respond to page offerings, the sooner you'll embrace the Net's interactivity, and you'll be halfway to realizing its awesome marketing potential. (See Figure 2.2.)

Figure 2.2

In the crowded field of sales premiums, Branders.com lets its Web site visitors take a "let me do it myself" approach.

Some of the Web's youngest business-to-business sites show a fine grasp of the value of "audience participation." One example is **Branders.com**, which sells promotional giveaway items such as T-shirts, coffee mugs, or tote bags with the customer's corporate logo on them. Using PhotoSample technology, the site allows customers to input their logo directly from their desktop computer and see how it will look on a red T-shirt, and then perhaps on a black T-shirt. Customers can also access a toll-free phone help line as they work in the "Design Studio," or peruse available products by price or speed of delivery, which is promised in as little as three days.

Participatory Marketing

One of the earliest strengths of the Internet in its pre-Web days was the discussion group. From useful Usenet in the beginning, to the bare-your-soul commentary encouraged on such consumer sites as **oxygen.com**, to the bitch-and-moan job site venting at **vault.com**'s Virtual WaterCooler™, Web designers have always known that Net users like to talk back. The trick has been to turn that preference into a marketing plus.

Amazon.com was quickly copied by other book publishing sites (not to mention video and music sites) when it allowed customers to "review" books they had bought on the site. Giving free rein to reader opinions made the entries in **amazon.com**'s catalog zing with crispy criticism and heartfelt pains to favorite authors. This certainly enlivened product entries that would otherwise have become static, particularly those that would not attract bestseller attention.

A more recent **amazon.com** innovation (also copied widely) now allows readers to judge the reviews as well, inviting people to note whether they found previous reviews "useful" or not. Book reviewing online has clearly become a blood sport to some, and in fairness, most book sites also allow publishers and even authors to comment or defend their books. For anyone involved in book publishing, online reader comments may be valuable grist for the mill of market research. (See Figure 2.3.)

Figure 2.3

Enthusiastic reviews, pro and con, shouldn't be left to bookseller sites. If you've got a brick and mortar base to your business, why not invite customers to vote or comment on their favorite store?

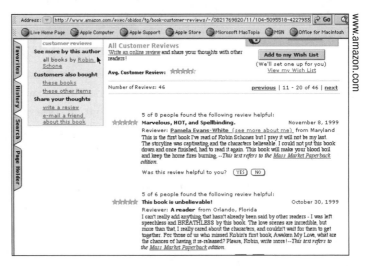

On **ebay.com** auction sellers may be rewarded with "gold stars" by satisfied buyers, or ousted as rogues by folks who feel they've been burnt in a bad deal. It is rare to find a buyer on this site who hasn't felt the urge to comment on his or her commerce foray.

The point is, people yearn to feel in charge and involved, and the Internet makes that easy. Simply providing a contact email address to the Webmaster isn't real interactivity, unless all the customer wants to do is complain. People want to know their opinions are being heard. They want to make a difference. They love to see their name and words in print, even if it is only in the glow of their monitors. They want to be part of the process.

Imagine two business-to-business sites, each offering a different commercial food product. One business takes the predictable route of listing a few recipes that incorporate its product. This requires no more than an afternoon's work by the in-house marketing team, which is exactly what it looks like to anyone from the restaurant business who is surfing the site. The second site invites visitors to submit their restaurant's own recipes using the site's product, with the best recipe to be posted the next week, along with a chance to win a free case of the product or the grand prize of a two-week cooking class in Florence.

Which site is a customer more likely to visit twice? Which product is she going to feel a closer loyalty to after seeing her restaurant's name and recipe posted on the site?

Free Focus Groups

Interacting with customers online is more than just a ploy to keep them coming back to the site. It's also a great way to learn how to better market a product, as discussed in the Market Research section of Chapter 1, "Return on Investment Goals."

That doesn't just mean having a link on the home page saying, "Survey: We want to hear what you think." And sure, there are sites that offer panels of users, paid for by research firms, to respond to frequent polls and questionnaires about products in their areas of interest. But a survey is a small fraction of the kind of customer research possible with two-way Web marketing.

Reading what customers say on discussion boards can teach marketers volumes about what their customers really believe, good and bad, about the product and the market. If a business is in a competitive consumer market, it can also be advantageous to drop in from time to time on the discussion boards on its competitors' sites. If customers are bellyaching about a certain product, or a service issue, it can tailor its own Web marketing approach to address those unmet needs.

Personalization

It's no coincidence that nearly every category leader in Web sales serves up a high level of personalized experience to its customers, and the best of the best customize that experience to every individual who logs on. Such pages are often described as visitor-centric or customer-centric.

Many of these sites tailor the experience based on simple, observable information about each visitor (browser type, operating system, time of day, and so on). Others watch how a user interacts with the site and then customize it accordingly, such as displaying sports up front for a reader who always hits those pages first.

Such control of screen displays, with split-second customization, can be automated at the Web site using software that runs the gamut from simple cookie recognition to collaborative filtering. Some Web marketers do not really understand personalization and, as a result, use the technology to create interactions that many users see as intrusive—for example, interrupting a reader's perusal of an online movie review with a pop-up, animated advertisement for a DVD movie product. This kind of interaction is not "personalized." The key to personalization is letting the user feel in control of the interaction. In this regard, some Web businesses even let their visitors customize the sites, or at least the arrangement of the page displays, by themselves.

Technographics

Every Web interaction leaves its own technical footprint. In addition to revealing the visitor's operating system, every Web browser automatically volunteers such technical data as the user's Internet domain (**aol.com**, **npr.org**, **bruner.net**, and so on), browser type (Navigator 3.0, Internet Explorer 4.0, WebTV, and so on), IP address (from which it is sometimes possible to deduce the user's geography), the time of the visit, and other data sometimes referred to as *technographics*.

A Web marketer can use this data to compensate for variants in the user's screen experience or, in the best case, exploit some of those variants to develop a more personalized experience for the user.

On CNET's site, for example, the Browsers Topic Center—which specializes in browser-related news and information—tailors the page view depending on whether the visitor is on a Mac or a PC (see Figure 2.4).

Business-related Web sites have but rarely tapped this information for sales purposes. For Web ventures specializing in non-technical content, technographic data may be irrelevant. But if, for example, a site is selling software to graphics designers or publishers, the preference for a Mac rather than a DOS platform in these and other creative fields might create the opportunity for the site to personalize its sales, or at the very least qualify sales leads faster.

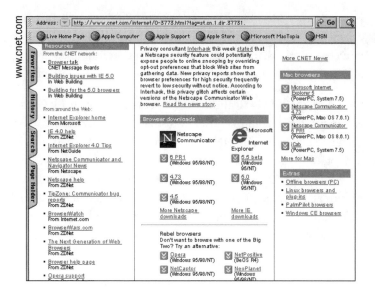

Figure 2.4

CNET understands that Mac diehards appreciate any favors they can get.

Knowing a user's platform will be much more critical in the future—particularly if the customer is likely to access the Internet from something other than a desktop monitor, portable PC, or notebook computer, but from a palm-sized, hand-held wireless Web remote. Those fancy, moving graphics on the Web site may not be readable if the customer is viewing them from a four-inch diameter screen.

Wireless Web downloads are already being used to access lifestyle information, such as up-to-the-minute sports scores and restaurant listings. Increasingly, the industry's field soldiers and road warriors are tapping into not just email but company Intranet databases while working away from the office. Taking advantage of the voluntary nature of technographic data is one way Internet companies can adapt their sites to compensate for the limitations of hand-held remotes and the possible proliferation of competing text and image formats.

User-Driven Environments

For more intimate personalization, many sites let their users do the customization themselves. For business-to-business applications, this can mean allowing customers to design their own online order forms so they will be in compliance with existing purchase order forms.

For consumer sites, the *TV Guide* site is a fine example of user-driven flexibility (see Figure 2.5). From the home page, users have numerous options, including links to current entertainment industry stories, sports and news highlights, movie listings, and more.

Of course, the site also features the TV listings for which *TV Guide* is famous. The detail of those TV listings is remarkable. A user need enter only his ZIP code to receive comprehensive local listings of all programming on broadcast, cable, and direct-satellite television. Furthermore, he can customize the listings in a number of formats, such as to include only his favorite channels and certain genres, such as mysteries or science-fiction, laid out by day or by week, with favorite shows highlighted and so on.

Within two or three links from the home page, the user can create a personalized version of the available information. After

Figure 2.5
At the *TV Guide* site, users can enter their zip codes and the massive database of TV listings returns their local daily listings. The site lets users further customize the data seven ways from Sunday.

customizing the listings to his particular preference, he can bookmark the page and return thereafter directly to his one-of-a-kind TV directory, something *TV Guide*'s print editions, though numerous, could never hope to achieve.

Personalization Software

A number of software companies specialize in personalization software by using different flavors of artificial intelligence, such as *neural networks* and *collaborative filtering*.

Aptex, Autonomy, and Nestor make neural networking software, which was first developed for use by the military, police, and banks to scan volumes of data (such as credit habits, fingerprints, or terrorist cases) for recognizable patterns. This same software can be applied to recognize users' behavior patterns on the Web.

There are many applications for pattern-recognition technology in Web marketing, including ad targeting, customer service, and market research. Most important to many sites, though, is the capability to customize content and other site features on-the-fly to match each individual surfer's preferences.

Makers of neural network systems say their software can "understand" the gist of text a user is reading online and can distinguish contextual differences. For example, the word "breast" might appear on a magazine site in the context of cancer, chicken recipes, or erotica. If a reader surfs from a chicken recipe to a story about nutrition to a restaurant review, the system understands that the visitor has food on her mind and may recommend other appropriate content or links.

Collaborative filtering, from software companies including FireFly and Net Perspectives, is a somewhat simpler technology with more limited applications than neural networks, but its results can still be compelling when applied properly. In a nutshell, collaborative filtering applications ask users to spend a few moments rating favorite examples within a well-defined category, such as movies, music, or books. As the collected sample grows, the system gets better and better at recommending items to new users based on the similar tastes of others.

The film buff's site **reel.com,** which both rents and sells movie cassettes, adopted collaborative filtering early on, scanning customer purchase records and combining them with data from other customers. Repeat visitors are greeted with recommendations to other films they might also enjoy. To a frequent user, the recommendations that pop up might seem eerily intuitive, because they go beyond merely matching movies by stars or by genre.

Privacy

A word of caution about the realm of personalized Web marketing: Online privacy is a bomb waiting to explode, so handle it with extreme care. Several studies show that the online public, fueled in part by alarmist press reports, feels strongly about privacy and security. (See Figure 2.6.)

At **reel.com,** clicking on the company's "privacy statement" gives the customer the assurance that only his preference and purchase data in the aggregate, combined with other customers, are being used to help "personalize his buying experience." The company states it does not distribute personal data, such as credit card numbers or email addresses, to outside companies unless they are required for service—to companies that ship the customer's purchases, for example. Surprisingly, if the customer reads all the way down to the bottom of the statement, he'll find the company will also give this data to law enforcement officials if it's forced to. . .but you have to admire them for being honest.

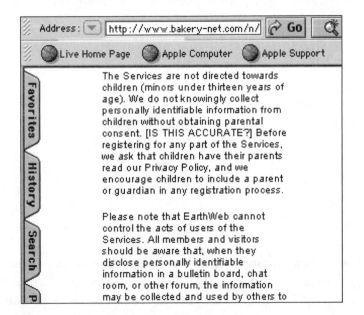

Figure 2.6

Earthweb.Com, a new portal for IT specialists, inadvertently left this draft of its privacy policy online. Many B2B and B2C sites are revisiting and revising their privacy promises. Web merchants have heeded and now take this into account. The first buffer against customer outrage is the "Privacy Statement," which should be included on every Web site.

Web privacy issues have caught the attention of lawmakers, and legislation to force e-marketers to police themselves and provide some consumer protections against spam is pending.

The organization TRUSTe (**www.truste.com**) provides precisely this service, auditing sites' privacy ethics with a recognizable set of labels (just like the Good Housekeeping Seal of Approval). Their approach is a compelling solution to a problem that concerns almost every commercial Web site. If nothing else, a TRUSTe seal can be a short cut to respectability, offering to a new Web business the aura of trustworthiness. (See Figure 2.7.) Businesses should investigate TRUSTe's model, or at least prominently publish their own privacy declaration on their sites.

Opt-In or Opt-Out?

The best practice for gaining customer trust may have further value to a business's bottom line. Specifically, you invite your visitors to register as customers or members, giving them the option to volunteer information only in their comfort zone. This process is called *opt-in*. Offering a benefit for providing personal data and making it clear that the user is in control of giving permission helps encourage cheerful opt-in.

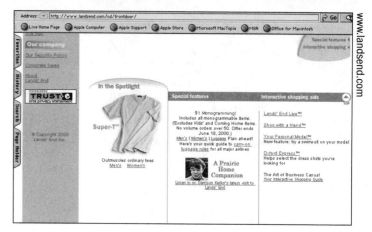

On many site registration pages, however, it's more common to see a question like "Would you like to receive email bulletins from our company?", accompanied by two submit choices, yes or no, with the yes button already marked. The user has to change the submission to refuse the newsletter mailings. That's called *opt-out*.

Web marketers who are pure in heart should take the high road to let visitors opt-in. Sneaky variations on opt-out, such as automatically defaulting to yes if submit fields are left blank, may backfire in the long run. ("Where did this email newsletter come from? Hey, how did they get my address?") But a customer who's opted-in feels more in control of the interaction, and is likely to be a customer who is open and willing to be enticed into deeper levels of permission marketing that make the Web site experience rewarding for all concerned. (For more about permission marketing, see Chapter 6, "Word of Web: Email, Permission, and Viral Marketing".)

Infocentric Design

People go to the Web for information; successful sites all seem to give their visitors 100 percent of what's requested, and then a little bit more. On the flip side, the hottest design and animation won't hold a user's attention for long without some informational substance to back it up.

For marketers whose products entail a lot of details that need to be explained, such as cars, financial services, or travel, infocentric design is a great opportunity. The more information-rich a site is, the better its chance is to present a complex product. For marketers of simpler products, such as soap, mayonnaise, and bubble gum, presenting the information may be more of a challenge. Value-added information, in the form of related text-based messages, is often used to bolster the sales pitch, but the real solution may be to design visual screen images that provide something deeper than immediate surface information, and are so emotionally arresting that they catch the customer's soul as well as his eye.

In the future, purely visual screen displays will be more emphasized, with icons used to direct screen visitors as they grow accustomed to gathering more of their Web information through graphic cues. But at the present time, the Web remains at heart a text-based medium, which is implicit in the names of its protocols—*hypertext transfer protocol (HTTP)* and *hypertext markup language (HTML)*. It's hyperized and otherwise jazzed up, but it's still good old text.

Text can never be ignored. The most colorful, complex, and compelling (and expensive) email marketing message created in HTML is first viewed by the customer as a short text "header" in her mail system inbox; in a microsecond she will choose to either open or delete that mail file. This is just one example of how a single, well-chosen word can be worth a thousand pictures on the Web.

Considered Purchases

Hypertext provides a great medium for offering detail; deepening levels present a golden opportunity for marketers to extol the virtues of many products whose complex features may not be done justice by a one-page magazine ad or 30-second TV commercial. These include big-ticket items and so-called considered purchases, such as cars, home computers, and vacations. Consumers are already using the Web to research such products, seeking out third-party write-ups, discount buying programs, and official product sites.

All of the major car companies were quick to exploit the info-centric character of the Web. Take Ford Motor Company, for example. For its industry, Ford's site produces few surprises, but it certainly does an effective job of conveying a wealth of information about the company and its products. The site has easily thousands of pages, covering corporate history, environmental commitment, career opportunities, a company magazine, financial and investment services, and more.

The star attraction of the site, however, is the virtual showroom (see Figure 2.8). With intuitive navigation and a simple design, Ford presents seemingly limitless details about dozens of models of cars from several brands, including Ford, Lincoln, Mercury, Jaguar, and Ford Heavy Trucks. For every model, the site offers exterior and interior photos, detailed technical and feature specifications, and even short video presentations. All of these pages also point to a dealer directory, pricing information, and a calculator for leasing and financing options (see Figure 2.9).

Figure 2.8

Ford Motor Company takes the direct route when touting the merits of its many products. Clicking on the visual image of any model takes the user on a tour with specs galore.

Car buyers who are intimidated by salesmen can effectively make their purchasing decisions in the comfort of their living rooms, print out the site-generated financing terms, and walk into their nearest dealer with the confidence of knowing exactly what they want.

Taking the guesswork out of cheaper products works, too. At **homedepot.com,** an online calculator model lets the user input wall and ceiling sizes to find out exactly how many cans of paint she should buy. The purpose of many brick and mortar informational sites is not to sell a product online, but to prepare the buyer for a pleasant experience in the real-world store.

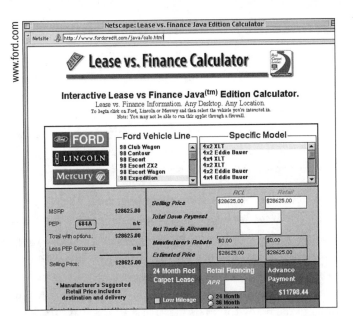

www.ford.com

Figure 2.9

The Lease vs. Finance Calculator is one of the many strong informational features on Ford's utilitarian site.

Staple Goods

For consumer products deemed information-poor (such as gum, root beer, or light bulbs), the challenge is to find some hook by which to engage the visitor with the brand. Strategies that have been tried include taking the jazzy, show-biz approach, with Shockwave games, contests and animated or video-run info-tainment, and heavy banner ad campaigns or sponsorships. Many successful sites, however, tend to find some aspect of their expertise they can offer in the form of additional information value. Others strive to create a user community around their products to foster brand loyalty. (See Figure 2.10.)

www.kotex.com

Figure 2.10

In the Girlspace section of the Kotex site, teens and preteens are encouraged to ask intimate questions among an online community of their peers.

Instantanity and Impulse Buying

The speed at which modern computers process and relay information makes the Web the most immediate mass communication medium. It's more timely than even live TV news because it's nonlinear. Viewers don't have to wait for a news anchor to finish his current boring story before getting to the topic they want. Users just load the home page and go straight to the headlines, weather, sports, or whatever else they're looking for.

How a news site benefits from this is obvious. The Web editions of *The New York Post* and other daily papers frequently scoop their print editions on breaking stories. They can post the stories on the Web long before the print editions, with their daylong production periods, can catch up. CNN goes into greater background detail on top stories, offering a multitude of links to the many topics its massive staff is always tracking. (See Figure 2.11.)

Figure 2.11

The Web site of the New York Post newspaper features up-to-the-moment weather information and news updates several times each day. A feature called "Keep Me Posted" allows readers to receive breaking news on certain topics directly through home or office email.

Real-Time Excitement

In computer jargon, there's a concept called *real-time*, meaning that data can bounce halfway around the world and back in a fraction of a second. The Web provides this. Its timeliness has been exploited by marketers in numerous creative ways, such as real-time audio concert broadcasts, celebrity chats, online customer service, time-sensitive promotional offers, and more.

The popularity of online auctions and stock-tracking Web sites has surged because they merge two valued constructs—time and money. For many users, the excitement of bidding, buying, and selling online in real-time creates a fever pitch comparable to a hot, high-stakes poker game or horse race—except, of course, surfing such sites is considered so much more socially acceptable that many do it on office time. (Real gambling sites are a business we won't get into here.)

Even in the more mundane aspects of Web life, such features as instantly updating inventory can create excitement. On **nordstrom.com**, the "special sales" pages warn a customer that only 10 hot pink cotton tank dresses are available at 50 percent off. . .then nine, then eight, and so on.

For the business-to-business crowd, providing current customer account information is another way to exploit the Web's immediacy, such as showing customers their records, business-to-business transactions, or retail shopping histories. Part of FedEx's famous online package-tracking service is its immediacy as it delivers up-to-the-minute package location information from its giant logistics communication system.

Certain industries, such as travel, have thrived online thanks to the Web's immediacy. Ever since American Airlines led the charge with its Net SAAver Fares program, most airlines have followed suit, providing short-notice email and Web alerts for heavily discounted tickets on flights that aren't sold out. Many entrepreneurs and established travel services are also doing booming business by selling up-to-the-minute fare discounts.

For online retailers, the Web's fast pace can mean quick response to inventory availability. **Barnesandnoble.com**, a constant rival to **amazon.com**, recently upped the ante for all mass-market retailers by promising same-day delivery of books in Manhattan. But in many major cities, service companies, such as **cosmo.com** and **urbanfetch.com**, have already elevated the concept of "home delivery" from pizza and videos to Palm Pilots and Ben & Jerry's ice cream in an hour or less.

A marketer who studies the patterns of user behavior while the user is online can immediately offer special promotions, modify the site's structure and content, or replace banner advertising that's performing poorly. Changes that could take weeks or longer to implement in magazine, billboard, and television advertising campaigns or national retail sales promotions can be programmed online to take effect on a user-by-user basis.

Measurability

The wonderful thing about computers is that they compute. This makes Web marketing a tremendously accountable medium. In the wake of the recent wave of dot.com failures, companies have discovered a new interest in measuring interactions in all sorts of ways, and they are exploring new ways to present this information to users or ways to sell well-mined data to other firms.

Stats for Consumers

Many sites take the Web's bounty of numbers and offer it back to Web surfers as an added value to the sites' basic services. For example, at a glance a visitor may be able to see the size of files available for downloading, the number of visitors present in various chat rooms, or how many replies various subjects have generated on a discussion board.

The popular Web dating service **matchmaker.com**, uses a more complex implementation of the Web's "numbers game." For a monthly fee, the service allows lonely singles to post information about themselves, browse the listings of other members, and trade messages with prospective mates.

When SurferBoy browses CyberGirl's introduction, the system reveals a variety of statistics about her. It tells him, for example, how many times she has logged on to check her account, how many others have browsed her listing, how many have written her messages, how many of those she's replied to, and whether she is online right now (see Figure 2.12).

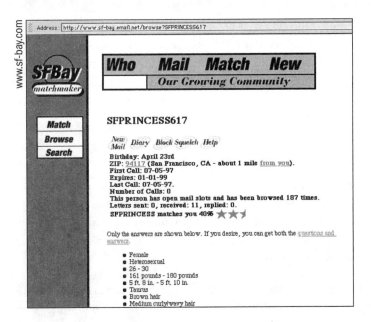

Figure 2.12

SFPrincess617 isn't kissing any frogs these days. Her Royal Highness hasn't checked her messages since she first signed onto this regional match-making site, although a few Prince Charmings have tried their luck.

Stats for Marketers

Philadelphia department store magnate John Wanamaker coined an axiom of marketing when he said, "I know half of my advertising is wasted. The trouble is, I don't know which half." On the Web, however, that no longer needs to be true.

If an advertiser uses clickthrough or conversion rates on ad banners as a measure of success for direct response objectives, it will be clear in a matter of hours which creative material generates the strongest response. The proverbial "other half" that isn't performing can be readily identified and replaced with more effective advertising.

But that's just the beginning. Software products, some off the shelf, some embedded in the business's host or server platform, can supply the business with exact numbers to determine which click responses actually resulted in sales. They also interpret extended user interactions, for example, how many internal pages were viewed and how long the visitor viewed each page.

As discussed in Chapter 1, time constraints are no excuse for Web marketers to not measure results from all of their online marketing efforts, either as a pre-test of a campaign or part of the post-mortem. Well-defined demographic response rates of a site's current customer base might later be "monetized"—lists of email addresses can be sold, rented, or exchanged for value with Web business partners, and well-segmented site traffic statistics quickly become an asset whenever mergers and acquisitions are discussed.

Room for Improvement

Measurement on the Web is not yet an exact science. Due to the decentralized nature of the Internet, originally designed by the U.S. military to withstand the disruption of a nuclear attack, data finds its way from sites to end users through circuitous and unpredictable routes.

The delivery of a banner ad, for example, is much more complex than one Web server displaying the ad onto one Web browser. That seemingly simple transaction may also involve a regional *mirror* server of the site, a *proxy* server behind a corporate firewall serving an untracked copy of the ad from a *cache* file, and any number of routing servers in between. Not to mention the chance that the Web surfer may click the Stop button before the ad and page have loaded.

For such reasons, there is generally more activity going on behind a site's content than is reflected in a standard Web server log. It doesn't help that the very terminology of Web measurements remains vague. Web publishers use terms such as *hits*, *clicks*, *unique visits*, *page views*, *page requests*, *impressions*, *sessions*, and others to mean various things. An advertiser may face difficulty comparing the performance of the same banner ad on different sites that use varying lingo in their reports.

Despite such imprecision, a business that's determined to make sense of the results of Web marketing has much better data at its disposal than the cloudy estimates about audience penetration that television, magazines, and other media can offer. (See Figure 2.13.)

The good news for Web marketers is that lots of companies are constantly pushing the envelope on improving online measurements, including Accrue, Macromedia, Met Rating, Match-Logic, Internet Profiles (I/PRO), Media Metrix, and others.

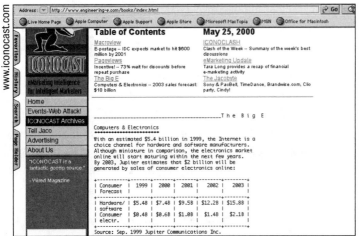

Figure 2.13

Marketing statistics and market projections can be found everywhere on the Web. Iconocast.com is a favorite source of free stats and purchasable market intelligence.

Flexible Design

At Alice's trial in *Adventures in Wonderland*, the King gives White Rabbit these instructions on how to present some evidence: "Begin at the beginning. . .and go on till you come to the end: then stop."

It's perfectly sensible advice for how to relate most stories, and indeed, it's how information is organized in most media. TV shows, books, magazines, letters, songs, radio traffic reports, and most other forms of communication have a beginning, a middle, and an end.

Web sites, however, break that mold. Online data is much more flexible and can be arranged and rearranged in a variety of non-linear ways, both by site designers and by surfers themselves.

Sure, a home page can be seen as the beginning of a site, but from there a surfer can normally continue deeper into the material from a number of different directions. Once the user has bookmarked a favorite "inner" page, he can navigate directly to that page, bypassing the site's home page entirely.

Consumer Convenience

Enhanced consumer loyalty is a strong marketing benefit of the Web's flexibility of data. In the aftermath of the disastrous Christmas season of 1999, when e-tailers found themselves unable to keep up with orders, the speed and ease of online ordering seems to have outplayed negative feelings. Consumers and business buyers now place more emphasis on a company's ability to deliver a product on schedule, if not within the hour.

The convenience for consumers is readily apparent at many online shopping services. Consider the real-life shopping experience of a six-figure-salary corporate vice president in a major city who discovered on Friday night that she needed a new battery for her cell phone. By luck she recalled there were two Staples office supply stores within walking distance of her location.

Once in the store, she must first consider where the batteries are located. On an aisle? In the phone section? Or behind the counter? Perhaps if she can buttonhole a busy clerk, she could find out. Having reached the right location, after zig-zagging through tall aisles crammed with office expendables, she discovered the store did not have her favorite brand or even the right model battery in stock. This process was repeated at the second store, which also had run out of batteries. There, the helpful clerk recommended a bigger store, a cab ride away. But it was closing soon.

Alternatively, the VP could have logged on to **Staples.com**, and then clicked on the words "Cellular/PCS Accessories" (see Figure 2.14). Here, that same day, the Web page showed a wide array of brand-name cell-phone batteries in stock. Ordering with a credit card, a next-day, Saturday delivery might have taken place, start to finish, in all of two minutes. If she chose to log onto **urbanfetch.com** instead, she might have been able to get the battery later that same evening, delivered to the restaurant by the time she was saying, "No dessert, thanks. Just coffee."

Figure 2.14

Two mouse-clicks from the home page, Staples.com shows all the cell phone batteries it carries, both in and out of stock.

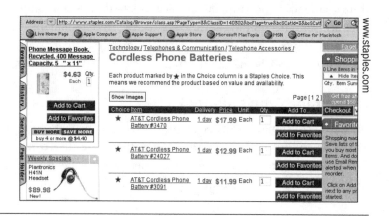

How much is a VP's free time worth these days? What do you think?

Interlinked Design

Obviously inherent in the Web experience are *hypertext links*, those words and images that the user clicks to go to a new page. These links give the Web its nonlinear structure, producing the effect of *browsing* pages in a seemingly random order.

Arguably, hypertext has its roots in centuries-old monastic texts and even experimental 18th-century literature. In the computer era, hypertext's roots go back to a visionary 1945 essay by Vannevar Bush, "As We May Think," published in *The Atlantic Monthly*. Mr. Bush's wide-ranging essay had a big impact on future technologies, providing not only a clear description of hypertext (which he referred to as "associative trails"), but also foretelling microfilm, digital photography, personal computers, and other modern technologies.

Ted Nelson coined the term "hypertext" as part of his ill-fated 1960s "docuverse" project called Xanadu. Later Apple, IBM, and others continued developing the hypertext concept through the '80s, but it wasn't until 1989 that a Brit named Tim Berners-Lee created the two protocols we know and love— HTTP and HTML. This laid the foundations for the grandest example yet of hypertext—today's World Wide Web.

Think Web, Not Strand

A Web site with few links is about as strong a promotional vehicle as a billboard in your basement. If the Internet is all about connectivity, it is not surprising to discover that strong sites tend to take the lions' share of links, while the majority of other sites get the crumbs.

A vast study by IBM's Almaden Research Center in San Jose recently looked at 200 million Web pages, and followed 500 billion links to and from each page, to discover that only 28 percent of the pages surveyed could be considered "strongly connected" to the rest of the Web, while many links simply petered out to dead ends.

The most connected pages turned out to be search engines such as Yahoo, portals such as AOL, large corporate sites, news organizations, and entertainment companies—about 56 million pages in all. Such pages often linked to each other, or linked forward to a second group of 44 million pages that did not link back to the center groups. Another 44 million pages, most of them from relatively young Web sites, linked to and from well-established center sites and search engines, but they were not connected in any way to the secondary sites.

The study also estimated that yet another 44 million Web pages, dubbed "tendrils," linked only to secondary sites and had no direct links to the popular central sites. Among these were fan sites, family Web pages, and similarly marginal interest zones. Most astonishing was that about five percent of the Web pages surveyed in the Almaden study were in total isolation, with no links to anybody else at all.

Since May 1999 the research group has run its experiment three times, using AltaVista's Scooter web crawler and Compaq computers equipped with as much as 12 gigabytes of random access memory. One change that has been noticed is a gradually increasing number of central sites that can be called well connected.

At play on the Web is the phenomenon of Metcalfe's Law:

The value of a network to its users is equal to the number of users squared.

That is, networks grow exponentially more valuable as they gain more users (and nodes, routers, and other communication points). As Bob Metcalfe, inventor of the Ethernet protocol, has analogized, "If you had the only telephone in the world, who would you call?"

According to this principle, every Web site is expected to play some role as a hub. It's the same way the intersections of strands in a spider's web lead in multiple directions, and how roads into a city generally exit in at least one other direction. (See Figure 2.15.) Sites without links are like loose strands on a web, leaving visitors stranded like dead flies. Or think of them as dead ends on the Infobahn.

Figure 2.15

Bakery-Net serves up enough links to be considered a hub or vertical portal (that is, "vortal") for businesses that retail freshly made cookies, cakes, and pies.

Surprisingly, many Web marketers missed this point in the early years. Most well-known consumer brand sites, such as Coca-Cola, Pampers, Saturn, Nike, and others, resisted outward links to other sites on the Web. Some companies even threatened legal action to amateur sites that dared to link *to* them. The most misguided sites would throw up technical impediments to the user's browser Back button or disable the browsers URL field, trapping the frustrated user into an inescapable loop that began or ended up at an unwanted home page.

Presumably, these marketers feared that by providing "exit" links they would lose visitors to other sites. That view today seems naive, and according to Web usability specialist Jakob Nielsen, "contradicts the basic nature of the Web."

Says Nielsen, "Users are in control of their own destiny. Get over it. You don't own them."

Today's savviest Web marketers take a different approach to outbound links entirely. They set up outbound links, but only to sites that offer an affiliate program. Under most Web affiliate structures, the Web site that's sending a user to another is compensated in cash (usually a few pennies) either per hit, per visit, or per transaction or sale, by the second site. In this way outbound links become not a lost opportunity for the first site, but a revenue stream. (To learn more about setting up affiliate partnerships, see Chapter 7, "Building Online Audiences: Affinity Sites and Affiliate Programs".)

Gateway Content

Almost without exception, sites increase their value to users by linking to recommended content elsewhere on the Web. It's just as Metcalfe's Law described earlier if we view one site as its own network. A site with no links is only as valuable as its original content, which, in the case of products such as carbonated beverages or soap, could get old quickly.

Links to other sites introduce the dimension of *gateway content*, opening up users to the vast resources of the Web without much extra effort on the referring site's part. Even after a user has seen everything there is to see at a marketing site, it may still be worth bookmarking if its links make it a gateway to a unique collection of new material.

However, sites need not take Metcalfe's Law literally by amassing as many links as possible. For most sites, the *quality* of links is more important than the sheer *quantity*. That said, it's no surprise that search engines and directories, the largest aggregators of links, are among the most valuable Web networks in terms of advertising revenue.

Look at the other sites that feature abundant links to external resources. Netscape, CNET, *The New York Times*, CNN, HotWired, and other Web titans litter their content with links to other sites, and none of them seem to be losing traffic as a result (see Figure 2.16).

Figure 2.16

CNN's Web site routinely provides links at the ends of stories to relevant information elsewhere on the Web. Most users, glad for such service, are likely to come back again. Setting the external information in a new browser window helps the news site distinguish its own reporting from others.

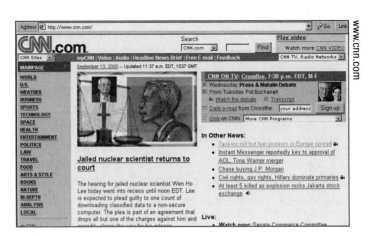

Link Partnerships and Affiliations

Not only can links serve as free, quality content, but for sites that generate substantial traffic, outbound links can earn money or other capital through partnerships with other Web ventures.

Amazon.com pays sites to link to it by offering sales commissions. Through its associate program, publishing companies, online retailers, and news sites that recommend and link to specific books for sale on **Amazon.com** can earn up to 15 percent of the transaction price if a surfer makes a purchase through the link (see Figure 2.17). Among other types of consumer product companies, the commission for an affiliate program is usually seven to ten percent of any resulting sale.

Other sites work out mutual back-scratching arrangements along the lines of reciprocal traffic-building or other alliances. **Giftcertificates.com** recently affiliated with **1-800-Flowers.com**, a union already blessed by a remarkably similar customer base of harried, last-minute gift-givers and corporate gift buyers. The vows exchanged included reciprocal presence on both sites, joint promotions outside of the Web, and a certain level of exclusivity within the online gift market.

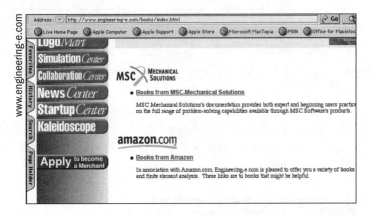

Figure 2.17
Enginering-e.com is one of thousands of business sites to join Amazon.com's associate program, collecting a sales commission of up to 15 percent for books sold through a link to Amazon.com. Similar revenue arrangements are welcomed through the Apply to become a Merchant tab.

Some sites employ a simple HTML trick in order to give their visitors the value of linking without losing them to other sites. When a user clicks on a link, the referred site opens in a new browser window while the referring site remains in the original window. When the user finishes looking at the new link, he can resume where he left off in the original site without having to use his "Back" button to get there.

This can be done by adding target="new" to a hypertext link's anchor (or "a") tag, like this:

```
<a href="http://www.usweb.com"
target="new">Visit MyCompany</a>
```

This command creates a new browser window with USWeb's home page when a user clicks the "Visit MyCompany" hotlink.

Most site developers don't use this technique, some because they probably don't know about it, but many because they think users will find it annoying. Our view is that linking the standard way—sending users from one business's site to another business's site within the same browser window—expresses more confidence in the quality of the business's site. (Visitors can come back when they're ready.) It also respects basic Web standards. Still, creating a new target browser for links is a legitimate tool for Web designers that may be useful in some cases.

Linking Netiquette

Usually, sites will welcome a pointer to them from another site. It is considered a general courtesy to notify the Webmaster when you do so, as some sites may insist that you link only to their home page, not an "inside" content Web page. Web etiquette also demands that you remove a link at the request of the owner of the other site.

Links go both ways, of course. If you're wondering how to encourage other sites to link to yours, see the material on affinity sites and affiliate partners in Chapter 7.

Economical Design

Another tremendous benefit of the Web is that it's still a comparatively inexpensive marketing medium.

At one end of the spectrum is the individual with a good idea. On the Web, he can sit at his kitchen table and run a publication, a mail-order business, a free information service, or whatever else with practically no startup costs or overhead. Self-publishing and micro-entrepreneurship were never so simple. Anyone with a computer and the determination to learn basic HTML coding can run a simple site for production costs of $50 per month in Web hosting fees.

At the other end of the spectrum is a large commercial site needing personalization, e-commerce, banner ad rotation, search facilities, dynamic page generation, good anti-hacker security, and a host of other special services common to sites of that size. After paying for specialized software, custom programming, design, and fast back-end bandwidth, you may be talking $1 million a year or more, not including staff salaries, TV marketing, and other expenses. (See Figure 2.18.)

www.disney.com

Figure 2.18

A site like Disney's, featuring animation, video clips, secure e-commerce, personalization, push technology, and more, doesn't come free, but it's surely less expensive than making a blockbuster movie.

Fortunately, there's lots of room in between for any business that has its ROI on straight. United Scientific Products, which sells disposable medical supplies to laboratories, launched **uspinc.com** for $1,400, paying "two college kids" to set up a simple online catalog with product pictures and drawings and to register its domain, according to the company president.

Promoted by direct-mail flyers to existing customers and prospects, the site drew less than a dozen hits a day in its first months, but 80 percent of the hits resulted in an order. Now the bulk of the business is re-orders as customers who had relied on a print catalog can now use a simple shopping program to check product specs, or re-stock lab supplies such as pipette tips, centrifuge tubes, and talc-free rubber gloves.

United Scientific's Web site isn't glamorous. The only shred of interactivity is the way it pushes the toll-free telephone number for its 24-hour customer service on every page. But it gets the job done, servicing clients between sales calls, reducing expenses for mailing and printing catalogs, and keeping the firm competitive with larger rivals in its niche market. (See Figure 2.19.)

Figure 2.19

At less than a penny per centrifuge tube, United Scientific Products knows how to work on low margins. This Web site launch cost less, only $1,400, and has paid for itself many times over.

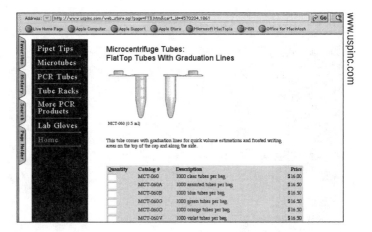

Resources

See the Resource sections of Chapter 1, Chapter 9, "Paid Media: Making Dollars and Sense with Web Advertising," and the Appendix for further online marketing references, as well as sources for demographic research, Internet history, and other related topics.

IN THIS CHAPTER

chapter 3

Design Optimization

NOW THAT YOU HAVE some ideas about what kind of strategic return on investment your company seeks from online marketing, and how you plan to leverage the Web's unique features to attract users with your compelling content, the next priority in getting your site right is the presentation of the material and "ease of use." In addition to the critical issues of the quality and type of content required to interest the user, you must be careful to optimize your network responsiveness and information architecture of your site to keep the user coming back.

Although most Web users accept that they must tolerate ad banners and similar distractions to finance free content, it is almost always their prerogative whether to interact with the marketer in any greater depth. A hint of slow response time, hokey graphics, or no obvious added value, and the site quickly loses any chance to interact with the users at all.

Design for the Lowest Common "Technical" Denominator

The flood of novice users to the Web means that Web marketers are no longer going to be exclusively addressing any technical or cultural elite. Recent studies by Activemedia and IDC have suggested that perhaps two-thirds of the most recent U.S. users have a household income of less than $35,000 per year. This is the group that helped fuel online auctions and discount buying sites, and the increasing number of blue-collar workers in this demographic hasn't been lost on companies such as Wal-Mart and Gillette, which have recently gotten more aggressive in their online initiatives. Just because they are inexperienced at using the Web, new users aren't any more patient than veteran users. In fact, they demand that sites have quick screen-page downloads and expect their navigational aids to be easy and self-explanatory.

Business users, who are often used to whizzing around the Web using corporate servers and high-speed DSL links in their office high-rises, also demand speed and simplicity. Another group to consider is international users. It's estimated that by 2003 the dominant language of Web users will not be English. According to a study by Global Reach in the year 2000, the next most frequently used languages on the Web after English are Japanese, Spanish, and German, with French and Chinese tied for fifth place. This becomes significant to U.S.-based Web markets in light of a concurring IDC study, which reveals that nearly three-quarters of U.S. firms involved in e-commerce draw less than 10 percent of their online revenue from foreign users.

Internet marketers in the U.S. should not ignore the possibilities of foreign English-speaking markets. One example is South Africa, where the population of English-speaking Web users passed the two million mark by the end of 1999. The IDC study also revealed that 28 percent of those responding to the study that surf in English would prefer to surf in their native language. However, translation poses less of a hurdle to Web page design than the less obvious fact that some of these rapidly developing international audiences may lag behind users in more developed countries when it comes to the latest computer gear.

Rich Media in Your Mix

What Web page designers call "rich media"—animation, real-time video, and audio—has further complicated the art of Web page graphic design. In many ways it introduces new opportunities and design possibilities (more on this in Chapter 9, "Paid Media: Making Dollars and Sense with Web Advertising"), but any artistic freedom is at the mercy of the way that users technically experience the Web.

Such curbs have always been with Web marketers. Modern computer screens, for example, can display at least 256 basic colors, if not thousands or millions of mixed hues. That's certainly an edge over traditional four-color printing, which restricts graphic artists to create all of their variations using a mix of black, cyan, magenta, and yellow. On the other hand, incompatible color standards among different operating systems and browser types means that designers more often will strip color palettes down to their lowest common denominator, rather than use complex color schemes. *De facto* standards, such as underlining a word and highlighting it in blue to indicate a hypertext link, quickly became shortcuts for harried Web page designers. As sites mature, their creators have once again begun to dare to experiment with color and with navigational aids.

HTML stands for *Hypertext Markup Language*. A "markup language" instructs the browser how certain elements should be displayed, but leaves the specific implementation up to the end user's own software. Text fonts, for example, remain a wild card on the Web. A designer can describe the type of font she wants, but, if a particular font isn't loaded on the user's system, the user's browser will automatically substitute whatever font is available. The user can also override these defaults and use whatever crazy font for the site he darn well pleases, and the designer has to like it or lump it. Of course, sites can fix stylized fonts into graphic images (like GIFs), but that is costly in terms of the time it takes a user to download the larger file. (See Figure 3.1.)

Figure 3.1
No, they're NOT. . .NOT. . . NOT, when you have to wait for this GIF from Hell to finish downloading.

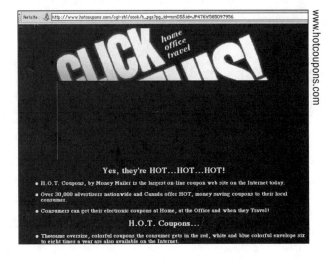

Live-action video, animations, and real-time audio can be compressed for transmission, but, in order to enjoy these delights, the end user's computer must be able to process the incoming information at high speeds, and that's not always the case. When it comes to rich media, designers can experiment as much as they want, but the extent to which this creativity will be seen depends a great deal on how big a user's monitor is, how fast his connection is, and so on. (See Figure 3.2.)

Figure 3.2
You need more than a color monitor to enjoy the animated installments of "Zombie College," which cannot be played unless the user's computer has the RAM and speed to process fast and large files.

Web design is a highly subjective area, of course. This book doesn't wish to crush your innovations, but rather offer some general, practical suggestions that may improve how users experience your site.

The Modem Factor

Just because a site's designers may be using 21″ monitors, fast processors, and a DSL or other high-speed connection, not all the visitors to the site may be so lucky. In 1998 more than two-thirds of all Internet users were connecting to the Web using their telephone lines and modems that ran at a speed of 28.5 kilobytes per second (KBps). Telephone service options and modem technology have been improved since then, and the "average" Web user now cruises at a speed of 56KBps.

In the year 2000, 56KBps is considered a standard modem speed for new computers, including the latest Intel-equipped laptops that process internally at 600MHz, and it's likely to stay this way for a while. Researchers at Jupiter, e-Marketer, and International Data Corp. (IDC) forecast that 56KBps is likely to remain the connecting speed for 70 to 90 percent of all Internet users at least until 2002 or 2003.

While faster connections (often referred to as "broadband" or "high bandwith") became a reality for some users in the new millennium, current statistics show that 90 percent of all U.S. users are still using dial-up connections through plain, old telephone service (POTS). According to Jupiter, 86 percent of all Americans are still accessing the Internet at speeds of 56KBps or less.

DSL, a broadband alternative that allows for higher speed processing, is available as a telephone service option in larger cities and suburban industrial parks populated by business users. Another option is the cable modem, which may gain a larger following among consumers. Cable modem installations in major cities are currently tripling each month, and are estimated to reach between 15 and 25 percent of the modem marketplace by 2003.

The merger of Time Warner, a cable giant, with America On Line (AOL) may be just the beginning. Unlike the telephone companies, which find themselves reinstalling wire to accommodate DSL and other high-speed transmissions, cable TV firms started rewiring for broadband nearly a decade ago, and they are actively looking to jumpstart their mature businesses with a product more attractive than sixty channels full of old movies. In less populated areas where DSL and fiber-optic cable are not practical, high-speed Internet connections may be done through home satellite units. (As with satellite television, direct-to-home satellite Internet is expected to be a hit only with rural consumers, and have a market share of less than one percent.)

What 56KBps Means to You

Most sites, unless their audience is exceptional, should optimize performance for users of 56KBps connections for the foreseeable future. If a business is courting a mainstream consumer audience, it might want to make sure that its Web pages would play decently on 28.8KBps dial-up modems as well.

For Web page designers, the best practice would be to keep most pages, and especially the home page, downloadable in their entirety as a modest-sized file, perhaps 50KBps per page or less. This can be a challenge to designers used to such graphics programs as Photoshop, which are notorious for creating large files that easily take up hundreds of kilobytes or even several megabytes. It's for files such as these that external storage devices, such as DAT and Zip drives, were invented. Designers are now expected to make powerful, exciting graphics, yet keep file sizes as small as possible. In the case of ad banners that are going to be shown on another site, the required image file size may be as small as 10KB or less.

Site performance—how quickly pages can load in viewers' browsers—should be a chief consideration in every aspect of Web design. Users are sick of the "World Wide Wait." Sites that are sloppy and don't carefully optimize performance for a variety of platforms will find that many users won't bother waiting around for them to load. (See Figure 3.3.)

Figure 3.3

Seventeen's Web site suffers from "magazineitis." Dense GIF artwork and long scrolling text that would work in a print medium simply make it slower to download, and slower to read.

The users' technology threshold for any particular site depends to some extent on the site's target audience. A business-to-business site aimed at corporate intranet administrators at Fortune 1000 companies, for example, may not care if they lose visitors from AOL who are using 28.8KBps modems. The majority of general consumer sites, however, should be cautious not to overestimate the technical standards of their visitors. (See Figure 3.4.)

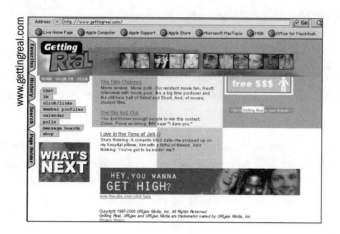

Figure 3.4

By comparison, URLjam's teen site, gettingreal.com, downloads fast and contains simple elements that can be viewed and quickly navigated by its young audience.

Even sites courting a business-to-business audience, which might assume that many of their users are on fast networks, shouldn't neglect traveling professionals connecting through notebook computers, small businesses with limited network resources, and corporate users checking in from home Internet accounts.

Why Size Matters

A general review of bits and bytes shows why size matters when it comes to a screen page. A *bit*—a contraction of the phrase *binary digit*—is the most elemental unit of computer information, and is either a 1 or a 0. Bit is used mostly when speaking of transfer units, such as the transfer of information by modems. Eight bits make one *byte*, which is a data storage unit equal to one ASCII character. Therefore, a 75,000-byte (75KB) file would take 20.8 seconds to transfer at 28,800 bits per second (28.8KBps), and 10.4 seconds to travel at 56,000 bits per second (56KBps).

This may seem fast enough, and it would be if all other things on the network were neutral, but they never are. Imagine that the site's server is busy. It's during peak traffic hours during a business day, and the end user's ISP is a bit flaky and won't allow connection at maximum modem speed. That 75KB image may take half a minute to download at 56KBps. That's the same time it takes two high-production-value television commercials to make their impact on viewers. That fat GIF sure better be worth the wait.

The Monitor Majority

Go into any computer electronics store and they'll try to sell you big monitors and flat screens, 17″ diagonals with "theatre-style" digital imaging. But, even though Web page designers may enjoy creating their work on bigger screens, not every home PC owner has shelled out for a bigger monitor.

For the millions of unlucky Web users using 14″ and 15″ monitors, many Web pages appear to be cropped at least two inches short on the right, and they scroll downward for ages. Just imagine how such sites look to the business traveler viewing it from a laptop, or something even smaller—say, palm-sized. (See Figure 3.5.)

If Web marketers haven't imagined their customers viewing their sites from Web-ready wireless telephones, or from handheld portable PCs, they should do so soon. The anticipated market may in fact be as overwhelming as the current product hype.

Figure 3.5

We've seen the future, and it's on a smaller screen. Hand-held, wireless Web remotes are the natural next step for the cell-phone crowd.

One early study of 1000 users in April of 2000 by Corechange/Cap Gemini Ernst & Young, boldly predicted that 80 percent of the U.S. population will be accessing some Web data from mobile phones—in their cars, on the beach, in the mall—by the time the real millennium rolls around in 2001.

It's likely that business Net users will be relying more on portable PCs with wireless Web connections, and the latest slim, executive laptops that all have 14″ screens or less. For designers, keeping smaller monitors in mind is a matter of pixel resolution. *Pixels*, a contraction of *picture elements*, are the little spots of light that make up a computer screen's image. The bigger the monitor, the more pixels you can fit into it. A 14″ monitor, for example, generally uses 640 × 480 pixels to make up its screen. A 17″ monitor can comfortably fit 800 × 600 pixels or more.

Palm-sized, wireless Web remotes use different formats entirely, and the problem is complicated in the U.S. as the three leading wireless service companies (Verizon, AT&T, and Voicestream) all have different formats that are not standardized. If a Web designer can visualize her customer using such a device to access her Web site, she should research these formats and plan accordingly.

Maximizing for Multiple Browser Platforms

Browser choice has remained such a compelling area of interest to the computer-using community that one research firm, Websidestory, devotes a portion of its **statmaster.com** Web site to a real-time pie chart showing browser market shares between the two main competitors, Microsoft's Internet Explorer and Netscape's Navigator, from daily samples of over 40 million sources.

There are dozens of "other" browser types still in use by a tiny minority, including IBM Web-Explorer, Lotus Notes, Lynx (a stubbornly popular text-only browser for UNIX), NetAttache, NetCruser, NetJet, OmniWeb, PageWatch, Prodigy-WB, SearchPad, Slurp, StepToWord, WebChat, WebCompass, WebMogul, WebShades, WebWalker, WebWhacker, and others.

Although these old browser systems might appear to be dinosaurs, the desire that many users have to tinker and control their screen views lives on in the new generation. The concept of a custom browser interface, also called a "skin," was first popularized by MP3 music devotees, who used them to enhance the onscreen appearance of MP3 player function buttons. (See Figure 3.6.)

Figure 3.6

Back to the Stone Age? Just when you thought browser choice was down to two flavors, Neoplanet introduces browsers that can be uniquely customized to bond users and Web marketers.

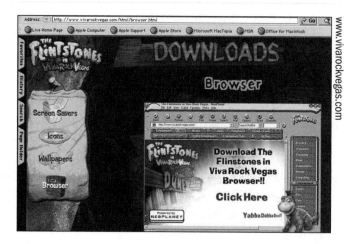

As with much of pop culture, the skin has been co-opted by Hollywood, or at least by Universal Pictures, which entered into an alliance in the year 2000 with NeoPlanet, a developer of customized browser software. The arrangement called for NeoPlanet to create a dozen browsers specific to the online promotion of a film, first for its theatrical release, and later for its DVD sales.

In order for a site to reach its biggest potential audience, its designers had better test it on as many different browser platforms as possible. They might ignore the "others," but they probably shouldn't forget about earlier versions of Explorer and Navigator that might not have been upgraded. What may appear dynamic on a Windows 2000 PC running Internet Explorer 5.0 might be illegible on the latest version of Netscape 4.1. Although Microsoft's Explorer dominates the world browser market, Netscape is still the platform of choice for America Online and its more than 30 million users. Recently, the government of the People's Republic of China announced it would use Linux to build its Internet infrastructure. Until you've looked at the site yourself through various browser platforms, you won't know if you're needlessly shutting out potential visitors.

Through experience, the most successful Web companies take this very seriously. Entire rooms have been set up with various hardware and software configurations, all for the sole purpose of testing new site features on multiple platforms, browsers, and machines. Even at mature sites several weeks may be spent making sure that new features on a redesign will work without a glitch when existing customers return.

"Gratuitous Digitalization" and Plug-Ins

This brings us to plug-ins. It is commonplace to receive software upgrades for all sorts of programs and utilities directly through Internet downloads, and that includes browser enhancements (often called plug-ins) for rich media. Web surfers quickly discover that if they don't own the software to run an animation program in Flash, or an MP3 music file in RealAudio, they can download and install a basic version of that program on the spot for free.

This only works if first, the user's computer has sufficient RAM speed to download and run the program, and if second, but perhaps more importantly, has the inclination to do so. It has been estimated that, when offered free downloads of Web-enhancing software, less than 30 percent of Web users opt to download. This means that more than two-thirds of current users are unable or unwilling to use such rich media features.

According to recent surveys, the lowest common denominator should continue to be a concern to anyone attempting to use rich media in a Web site's design. One such survey of browsers by **Statmarket.com** indicated that 65 percent of its user base could accommodate Java codes, and 85 percent could accommodate Macromedia's Flash. Simple HTML animations, however, were accessible to nearly all the browsers surveyed.

Tim Smith, CEO of Red Sky, a San Francisco-based Web design company whose clients include Land's End, Bank of America, and Sony, counsels companies to avoid what he calls "gratuitous digitalization."

"I tell all our clients to forget about the technology," he says. "It doesn't matter. When we sit down with clients, we clear the table of all the technical baggage—Java, CGI, back-end transactions—and ask them to concentrate on the experience they want for their users. Then we take it from there."

By no means is it recommended that Web designers not exploit the exciting multimedia features the Web offers. The point is, again, to know the audience and the site's objectives. If a Web designer believes his target audience, or at least a significant part of it, is *au courant* with the latest bells and whistles, and he believes such features strategically advance his marketing aims, he should push the envelope. If, however, his site blinks, wiggles, and sings Christmas carols just because he thinks that it's neat-o, he should probably think again.

As plug-ins have proliferated, they've become a means of qualifying customers. A game site, for example, isn't interested in Web users who don't have the computer firepower to download its Shockwave ad banners, and a business-to-business site may assume that if a Web user can't accommodate Flash, he's not worth adding to the site's traffic. But it may be a mistake in the long run to impose limitations on surfers, so that they cannot appreciate the site's fundamental experience without a particular plug-in, platform type, browser version, monitor size, modem speed, or any other technical constraint. For readers concerned about the "digital divide," which is still a gross inequity between individuals who can afford Web technology and those who can access it only at the public library, setting up hurdles like this may be a disservice to all. The Web was designed as an open-platform medium, and sites that fail to respect that simply don't get it. (See Figure 3.7.)

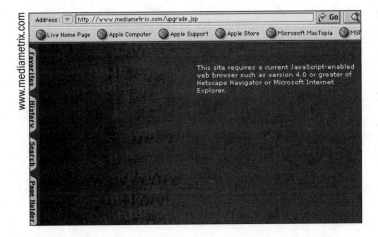

Figure 3.7

Media Metrix caters to business users, and is one of many B2B sites that has chosen to use a rather mild threshold of technology to help qualify potential customers. Restricting traffic to only those users who can handle Java scripts is a polite but effective barrier to some.

Variable Interfaces Options

One option that many sites embrace is to provide alternative ways for viewers to interact with the site that respect their different network bandwidths, user platforms, and technical savvy. **Enliven.com** and **Unicast.com** are two Web sites that showcase rich media platforms with "sniffing" technology, which is used to figure out automatically what format is appropriate for any given user's connection speed. (See Figure 3.8.)

Figure 3.8

Users without a Java-
enabled browser or platform
support for Java will automatically see a GIF version
of this banner ad created for
Fortune Magazine, but they
will still get the message.

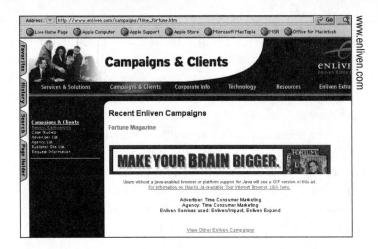

Fortunately, there's hope for everyone. New software prod-ucts—such as Macromedia's Fireworks and Generator graphics conversion programs—can help sites optimize their graphics for the Web's low-bandwidth restrictions. Macromedia's Generator is a program that automatically adjusts the site's graphics for different kinds of browsers, shaving days of repetitive tweaking from the busywork of page design.

Today, many Web software developers are building intelligence into their products that can determine which multimedia effects each user's browser can support, thereby giving each user exactly the level of experience their browsers can support, and serving up the appropriate format. For more information on the latest graphics management techniques, consult some of the design and coding resource sites listed in the "Resources" sec-tion at end of this chapter.

Consistent, Intuitive Navigation

In the behind-the-scenes battles of many sites for supremacy among artistic designers, programmers, and writers, the buck should ultimately stop with the business leaders who have defined the site's strategic objectives. In most cases, that means the site's design is secondary to its information.

Design in the online age, with the new Web dimension of hyperlink navigation, is fundamentally at the service of improving the user's interaction with the site's content. With some exceptions, most content boils down to text and occasional illustrations. A cool-looking site is nice, but not if it greatly slows the site's performance and doesn't somehow advance the site's sacred marketing objectives.

Whether a Web site contains frames, a table of contents in the left-hand column, JavaScript-enriched pop-up buttons, or some other popular navigation convention, every page should contain elements to orient the user as to where he is within the site's architecture.

Every surfer has gotten stuck at some site whose navigation is so confusing—frames that seem like a hall of mirrors so the user roams in circles, sloppy "redirect" commands in the HTML code that prevent backing up, forms that deposit surfers on pages with no outbound links—that the easiest way to regain their bearings is to visit another site altogether. (See Figure 3.9.) At the other extreme, some sites make navigation cues so painfully obvious, embracing every cliché in the book down to blue borders around every graphic link. Such sites lack personality and stifle some of the fun of exploring a site, like a new neighborhood for the first time.

Figure 3.9

A sloppy frames design, like this one, can make you feel like you're in the Hotel California, "You can check out any time you like, but you can never leave."

The important thing for a Web designer to remember is that she is not going to have a lot of time to overcome the users' learning curve for navigation cues. Idiot-proofing navigation is something that comes with time. Web designers of mature sites should always try to improve the navigation of their sites, and designers of new sites should make it one of their highest priorities.

A simple way to detect flaws in navigation is to give it the grandma test. That's right, have your Granny or your Auntie Sue or cousin Elroy sit down at the computer while you watch them click around. If they can't find a way around your Web pages, you've got some rethinking to do. The next level to this is hiring focus groups of users to road test the site's navigational aids for clarity.

Above all, navigation cues should be consistent, clear, and at best, appear transparently intuitive. Every Web site inevitably embodies a hierarchy in which its users progress by layers deeper into a logical tree of content. Designers must not only plot this structure carefully, but they should generally signal users as to where they are within the hierarchy on every page. Among other things, this means always establishing an "exit" that will allow cousin Elroy to backtrack if he gets lost.

Whether this is accomplished through buttons at the top or bottom, lists down the left side, or amorphous blobs in the middle of the page is up to the designers' creativity. What's important is that users can recognize the cues and quickly get where they want to go next, other than to new URLs.

Dead ends should be avoided. If the user has to rely on a Back button to exit a page, the site is losing the opportunity to engage that user further. Web designers should try to make sure every page clearly leads somewhere else. This can be important to help orient visitors who arrive at an interior page through some outside link, such as a search engine. Although the user may enjoy the content he finds on that page, if it's not clear how to get to the home page and other parts of the site, the new visitor will likely return to the search engine site. (See Figure 3.10.)

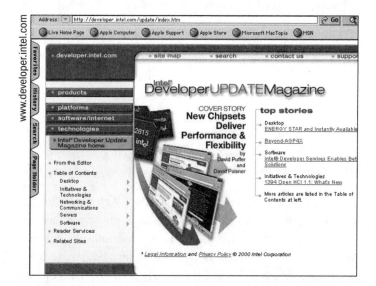

Figure 3.10

Intel places navigation elements on its developer pages in the same spot for easier random access to the featured material.

As we'll discuss in later chapters, designers can always correct their mistakes if they pay attention to how visitors interact with their sites. Careful analysis of traffic logs and more sophisticated customer intelligence tools can reveal weaknesses in navigation and design, such as pages where large numbers of users reverse their steps due to unclear navigation design, or those where users abandon the site altogether because of slow-loading graphics or other problems. Several specialty software tools, such as Accrue Insight, Net Genesis, Macromedia ARIA, Web Trends and other tools, allow designers to make the analysis of traffic patterns themselves, or they may wish to hire an outside agency to review the navigation loops on their sites.

Rich Media and ROI

Can a Web designer get along without rich media? Much depends upon the tone of his business, and the decision should be no more difficult than the way his top sales people decide each morning whether or not to put on high heels or suits and ties before embarking on a round of client sales calls. The timbre of the Web site should be in harmony with the business' offline and online branding efforts (discussed in more depth in Chapter 4, "Using Domain Names to Build Your Brand"), but he should always strive to make the site vibrant, and not dull.

Intel's developer pages, arguably targeted at a highly sophisticated technical audience, are noticeably bereft of flashy graphics, sound, and animation. Legacy retailer Tiffany's caters to both old and new customers by letting visitors choose pages that can be viewed simply in HTML or animated through Flash. A skip around the Web reveals what techniques are in vogue. In the past year, the Web has seen 3-D screen imaging and a plug-in that promises to generate smells triggered by clicking on certain page views.

Consumer e-commerce sites and pure-play Web sites often use the novelty *du jour* to generate the "you've got to see this Web site!" word-of-mouth that is critical to mass audience building. As novelty soon wears off, the cost of creating additional wowie-zowie pages needs be budgeted into first-year costs, and the rate of creative renewal anticipated and discussed well beforehand.

For many organizations, rich media elements are created by outside design teams, and it is not rare to see them used exclusively, and budgeted exclusively for special promotions, online advertisements, and email marketing, or created to jazz up temporary microsites rather than home pages. This allows their cost effectiveness to be measured by at least some business yardsticks. Resulting data might suggest that rich media be incorporated in a site redesign. (For more on microsites, see Chapter 9 "Paid Media: Making Dollars and Sense with Web Advertising.")

If a Web designer is going to use rich media on his Web site, what the site does is less important than where it occurs during a visitor's screen experience. Common errors include placing a home page animation so far down that a user with a smaller screen, say 14-inch, has to first scroll down to even see it. Bad strategies include using rich media pop-ups only for sponsored advertisements, without first exploring how surprise content-related interstitials might enhance an otherwise mundane inside content page.

Revamping a mature site to accommodate rich media can be a tricky business because there's only so much space on a home page to play with. **Salon.com,** which is to the Web what *Atlantic*

Monthly is to doctors' waiting rooms, launched a $50,000 home page redesign in late May 2000, and got an immediate response—hundreds of regular readers emailed their irate complaints. The old home page was re-established in a matter of days. The current page design, although admittedly a bit crowded, employs rich media features, but retains older capabilities that had been junked, such as the ability for a user to self-adjust the tiny text font size of the articles and headlines, rather than having to hunt for her bifocals. Adding features might be a technical challenge, but removing features is an audience issue, so do some research before doing so.

 # Resources

CNET Builder.com
http://www.home/cnet.com/webbuilding

- Part of the CNET family of sites, with a large editorial staff churning out high-quality technical information and the latest news for professional and aspiring designers.

Useit.com Hotlist
http://www.useit.com/hotlist

- This is legendary Web designer Jakob Nielsen's personal picks of useful design and navigation sites. You won't go wrong in looking at them.

WebMonkey
http://www.hotwired.lycos.com/webmonkey/

- Reviews, news, tutorials, a searchable index of techniques, and great tips and examples. An invaluable resource for designers.

Web Pages That Suck
http://Webpagesthatsuck.com

- Vince Flander's irreverent and cranky critiques of bad Web design provide useful insights for designers and marketers.

Yahoo! On Design Guides
http://www.dir.yahoo.com/Computers_and_Internet/Data_formats/HTML/Guides_and_Tutorials

- An index of design guides and related sources that are geared to beginners.

Recommended Reading

Designing Web Usability by Jakob Nielsen, 1999.
- A thorough and comprehensive guide to Web architecture, chock full of illustrated examples. Available through http://www.newriders.com and wherever serious Internet business books are sold.

GiftCertificates.com: Refining Usability

A WEB SITE is the most important public facade an Internet business can have. Unlike fleeting TV ad campaigns and remote head offices, a URL is an instantly accessible corporate representation that defines a company's vision to its customers, and is flexible enough to redefine that vision as the business climate changes.

GiftCertificates.com began as an idea and a name; its domain registered five years before opening for business in April 1999. The business was created as a service for harried last-minute gift-givers, offering gift certificates that can be purchased online by credit card, delivered by snail mail or email, and redeemed at participating businesses, either through e-commerce at those merchants' Web sites, or in person at their brick and mortar stores. Now in its third incarnation, this Web site has been repeatedly designed to improve usability and speed busy shoppers on their way.

The first version of the site was admittedly "brochureware," yet it attracted prestige merchants such as American Express, Brooks Brothers, Neiman-Marcus, and The Sharper Image. In two months these pages gave way to a robust shopping site, in time to assist more than 250,000 customers over the hectic 1999 holiday season. After the New Year, the decision was made to redesign the Web site to adapt to two strong new trends on the Internet: A surging interest in business-to-business transactions, and to take advantage of an ever-increasing focus on name brands and branding.

Some visual changes between the old Web pages and the new ones are subtle, and others are quite obvious. Business-to-business customers find their concerns addressed in the upper right hand corner of the screen—the prime placement in magazines and on Web sites. The left-hand column of merchants, at first listed only by categories (apparel, electronics, and so on), now brings the names of the best-branded merchants in each category (Macy's, The Gap, and so on) to the fore, where they lend their own brand status to the site's cachet.

Bertina Ceccarelli, Executive Vice President of Marketing for **GiftCertificates.com,** is quick to point out that all the design changes involved improving navigation by first-time visitors.

"We have the advantage of a good domain name," she explained. "This means we don't have to use space on our home page to explain what we do. People are either coming to the site to buy a gift certificate or to redeem one. And when the customers see the recognizable names of our merchants, instead of just categories, it's really clear what the customer's choices are."

The business-to-business focus is on the corporate gift buyer, who is quickly qualified with an on-screen prompt. "There's an interim page that asks the visitor if she's sure she wants to be learn more about the business part of the Web site," Ceccarelli said. If the user clicks "yes," she's transported to a set of different pages decorated in sharp, corporate greens and blues, a contrast to the softer pastels used on the consumer Web pages. Offline marketing collateral, from bus ads to the company's print brochures to the certificates themselves, is also divided this way, into brights or pastels that signal two product lines in a visually unified, well-branded presentation.

Focus group research showed that some first-time users were confused as to where to redeem the popular "SuperCertificates." On the new pages, a new visitor finds that information listed in four different ways on the home page, from click-on soft boxes to text in the upper and lower navigation bars. Important icons such as the "shopping bag" (in lieu of the "shopping cart") appear in the same spot on every screen page, up to the point of checkout and final sale.

Making Every Pixel Count

Clean design on **GiftCertificates.com** makes for fast downloads, even on older 28.5KBps connections. There's a lot of white space and the photographs, when used, are low-resolution GIFs. Not much moves, though the designers tried out some flashing animations in the earlier version.

"In our testing we found out that customers thought it was really annoying," admits Ceccarelli. "Redeeming a gift certificate is at its heart a shopping experience, so we've removed everything that might possibly get in the way."

Stripping the site down for maximum speed seems the perfect design strategy for a company that targets last-minute shoppers. But some of the improvements to speed and functionality are additions, not subtractions, and one actually has to do with shopping math. At every purchase point, visitors redeeming certificates online can now see exactly how much gift credit remains as they make their choices.

All improvements were tested on a variety of browser platforms, with an eye to PDA formats as well. When the next Christmas Eve finds exhausted mall shoppers grasping their Web-enabled cell phones in search of a last-ditch alternative, **GiftCertificates.com** expects to be ready for them.

chapter 4

Using Domain Names to Build Your Brand

IF THE THREE MOST important rules of retail are location, location, location, the online equivalent is *domain, domain, domain.* It's a fundamental principle that you get the site right—and if it's not right, you change it.

A site's *domain* is a cross between a name and an address. It serves as both an identifiable brand name and a pointer to the site's location. Technically, *domain names* are nothing more than mnemonic aids for the Web site's *uniform resource locator*, better known as the *URL*.

The URL is created from the Internet protocol (IP) numbers assigned to every host computer on the Web. IP numbers come in four sets of digits divided by periods, such as **205.134.233.1**. Because such number strings aren't particularly memorable to most humans, the architects of the Internet created a system of domain name servers (DNS) that cross-reference the IP numbers with alphanumeric domain names that are easier to recall.

Routinely, companies fail to recognize important nuances when choosing their domain names. Companies slow to get online have found that their trademarks are already claimed by shrewd Web startups, traditional competitors, or domain brokers. Indeed, disputes over domains have spawned a spate of legal actions and a new specialty among cyber-hip intellectual property lawyers.

Other companies choose long, clunky domains that invite users to make mistakes when typing in the URL, or choose cryptic abbreviations that surfers are unlikely to remember. One of the most common oversights of all is settling on one domain name and then neglecting possible variations of the name that surfers are liable to try by mistake or misspell.

Companies should choose a domain name that describes what they do. **GiftCertificates.com** is a good example that tells users exactly and immediately what that company does.

As the Internet becomes a more global phenomenon, a company's domain name, whether it's first glimpsed on a search engine or noticed in a list of URLs on another site, is likely to be the first impression the site makes on a Netizen—even before they see the home page. Companies have to invest the same intensity of branding power in their domain names as in their corporate trademark.

Companies with recognizable brand names in the offline world tend to jump quickly to the top of their categories once they enter the Internet fray. Among companies that derive most of their business from the Internet, a recent study by Greenfield Online, an Internet polling company, found that the most recognizable Internet "brand names" were also those that had, for years, dominated the Internet's consumer markets. In a ranking of 100 firms by 3,400 computer users, the top four were **Microsoft.com** (software), **Amazon.com** (books and general e-commerce), **Netscape.com** (networking), and **AOL.com** (Internet service provider).

But that's not the whole story. Ranked fifth in the same study was **ebay.com,** which rose from complete obscurity to become the leader in its market category (online auctions) in less than a year (see Figure 4.1).

The company **ebay.com** was not the first Internet business in the auction category, and it was launched with funding that was peanuts compared to other Web businesses that started up in the same rookie year. Offline category leaders the general public just might have heard of (such as Sotheby's) have since spent millions playing catch-up. But among Internet users, even those who do not visit auction Web sites, **ebay.com** remains the top "name brand" in the auction category.

Figure 4.1

ebay.com's URL domain and its corporate brand are synonymous, and have since become one of the best known brands on the Web. The name itself is a play on an auction term, "abey."

For some "dot.com" companies, the corporate name and the domain name are identical, like **Amazon.com**. The "dot.com" suffix, referred to as a top-level-domain (TLD) (along with .net, .org, .edu, .gov, and other TLDs) immediately tells the visitor that it refers to a Web site, just as "Inc." or "Corp." convey an official corporate identity. When you say, "Nike-dot-com," everybody knows that you're talking about the sports giant's Web site and not a new model of a basketball shoe. Like Nike's shoes, however, its site is a Nike product, recognizable by its unique brand. **Geocities.com/members/~hotsauce1/home.htm**, on the other hand, is a domain, but it is not a brand.

A weak domain name communicates to savvy surfers that a company isn't really hip to online culture. Ranking at the bottom of the Greenfield Online study, along with **Fatbrain.com** and **Wingspanbank.com**, is the Web site of Procter & Gamble: **PG.com**.

But why would an industrial giant have such a weak domain for its corporate home page? One reason is because typing "ProcterandGamble" into a search engine takes the user to the Web site of Dr. Peter H. Proctor, hair-regrowth specialist, whose cheery remarks on cybersquatting and the value of a good domain can be found at **proctorandgamble.com**.

Procter & Gamble is a slowly waking giant when it comes to being hip to the Web. Despite registering more than 200 product-related and generic domains, the company's Web pages have a static, rather obligatory feel, as if the company mounted them merely to satisfy expectations of shareholders. **PG.com** does have a B2B presence on its home page, reachable by clicking "Technology Submission and Licensing" in the corner of the page, but many product engineers probably wind up at the hair guy's site first.

By the time you read this, though, Procter & Gamble will probably have re-configured its entire Internet marketing presence. The reason? The popularity of buying discounted grocery products online through **priceline.com, webvan.com,** and others. This is inducing the makers of toothpaste, detergent, and other mundane products to strengthen their online brand awareness through email marketing, instant couponing, and pop-up screen advertising campaigns. As discussed in Chapter 9, "Paid

Media: Making Dollars and Sense with Web Advertising," such campaigns often link to a corporate home page.

There are, however, signs of life in **PG.com**. In the first few months of 2000, the sundry superconglomerate has been aggressively acquiring domain names it missed in the first pass, such as **crest.com.** As with many businesses new to the Web, Procter & Gamble has been challenged in its effort to secure good domain names, and not the least of its problems was that its own corporate name is easily misspelled.

Make It Memorable

The single most important point to remember when choosing a domain name is to make it memorable. It should be easy to type and, above all, easy to recall without referring to a business card or address book. Think of a 1-800 number. If it's a good one, like 1-800 FLOWERS, a customer hears it once and remembers it. It's not surprising that when this floral delivery company chose a domain name, it carried over this brand identity to the new medium and picked **1-800-flowers.com.**

A good URL should be memorable enough that someone driving in her car could catch a glimpse of it advertised on a billboard and not think twice about remembering it. Moreover, it should be clear when spoken, so a commuter could hear it announced on drive-time radio and could type it into her browser when she got to work without writing it down. This means avoiding homonyms, such as **writestuff.com** for a literary services company, or cute spellings like **nitestories.com** or **litefoods.com,** which beg for confusion for those who have only heard the domain name spoken.

Why is this is critical? In a 1999 survey of 360 Web users by IMT Strategies, 20 percent cited "word of mouth" as their primary way of discovering new Web sites. So, if a company's domain doesn't come trickling off the tongue of a satisfied customer, the site could be losing one in five potential new customers.

For established companies, the domain should ideally be a short, logical extension of the corporate name—**sun.com** for Sun Microsystems, **adage.com** for *Advertising Age* magazine, or **fedex.com** for Federal Express (see Figure 4.2). Network

Figure 4.2

What other domain would you expect for Federal Express? No search engine needed.

Solutions, Inc. (a company that plays a large part in the "Domain Name Game", as we'll see later in the chapter) uses the domain **netsol.com**, as well as **networksolutions.com** and **nsol.com**.

Companies attempting to secure their Internet domains for the first time might find that the most obvious versions of their corporate names are already taken. And for a new company, it is critical to search out what Web domain names are available before settling on a corporate name so the corporate brand is consistent.

If the company's name is not available, it might use the name of its top product in the domain name. But it's never a good strategy. Take, for example, the company Autonomy, which develops personalization software for Web sites. According to Autonomy's president, Mike Lynch, **autonomy.com** was already taken by a guy who used the domain as a personal vanity site and stubbornly would not sell it. So Autonomy used **agentware.com**, referring to Agentware, its main product. The confusion was a marketing headache, to say the least, for a Web-specialized company. When Autonomy went public in 1998, it bit the bullet and purchased the domain **autonomy.com** for an undisclosed sum that was likely quite high.

Investing heavily in a prime domain brand name is not rare. AltaVista, the search engine company, originally began as **altavistadigital.com**. It failed to register **altavista.com** when it began and later had to buy the name for $3 million. But relax —most "taken" names sell for $10,000 or less today. (See Figure 4.3.)

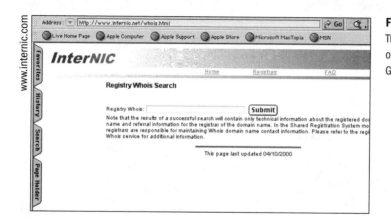

Figure 4.3
The InterNIC Whois, where
one plays the Domain Name
Game.

Picking Unique Domain Names

If the domain name you're seeking has already been taken, there are a few handy options available to you besides legal wrangling. (For more discussion on disputes, see the "Domain Disputes" section later in this chapter.)

One route is to alter the company name in some way, such as a contraction of two words, such as **Metlife.com**. Or something can be added. Public relations companies almost all tack -pr at the end of their names to get a unique domain, although many forget to register the hyphen. So, **somethingpr.com** and **something-pr.com** are likely to turn up two different PR companies.

Using InterNIC Whois to Research Domain Names

To search the main register of .com, .net, .edu, and .org domain names and see what's available or who is leasing registered domains, a suggestion is to navigate to the InterNIC Whois search page at **http://internic.net/cgi-bin/whois**. After typing in a domain, InterNIC gives you the name and address of the registering company.

Network Solutions (**netsol.com**) once held a monopoly on domain name registration, but there are many competitors these days, such as **Register.com**. ICANN (the quasi-governmental Internet Corporation for Assigned Names and Numbers) listed over 150 "certified" registries by the summer of 2000. After going to ICANN's site to identify the registry, log in to that registry's Web site, and look up the name again in their "whois" section. This

continues

continues

quickly gives not only the contact name and address of the name's proprietor, but often the last date that the name was renewed or changed hands.

Find out more in the "InterNIC, NetSol, ICAAN, and Friends" section, as well as in the "Resources" section at the end of this chapter.

Another popular method along similar lines is to add a cyber-oriented prefix or suffix to a name, such as **netorange.com**, **orangeweb.com**, or **orangeonline.com**. Notice that the popular suffix net, as in **orangenet.com**, might lead to some confusion because .net is a top-level alternative to .com. Some surfers might look for **orange.net** by mistake. The solution to that, of course, is to register both **orangenet.com** and **orange.net**.

Carl Oppedahl, a leading expert on Web law and a partner in the law firm Oppedahl & Larson, says that sites can best protect against domain disputes if they invent a "coined, unique name," like Xerox, and trademark it (see Figure 4.4).

Figure 4.4

The one and only Xerox.

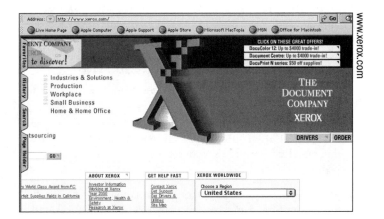

Another strategy is to pick a word or phrase different from but related to the company name. The Oppedahl & Larson law firm, for example, uses the domain **patents.com**. A company might pursue this strategy for one of several reasons. It might find that others have already claimed all basic forms of its name and there is no choice but to look for alternatives. Or the company might happen upon a word or phrase available as a domain that is more strategic than its own corporate name. Or it might opt to create a new online brand entirely.

An example of how a domain name choice can boost a business-to-business company can be found at **msc.software.com**. The parent company, which has been making computer software products for automotive and aviation engineers since 1963, was originally named for its founders, as the MacNeal and Schwendler Corporation. When the company created its first Web site 32 years later, it chose **msc.software.com** as its domain name. Using the initials was a no-brainer to prevent the inevitable spelling problems clients might have. The addition of the word "software" would help to distinguish the site from others with similar initials. (Not surprisingly, **msc.com** was already taken—and is still in use by the Molecular Structure Corporation, which makes industrial X-ray gear.)

Simple? Yes. Having become a leading developer of industrial simulation software, MacNeal and Schwendler Corporation actually changed its corporate name to MSC.Software Corporation in 1999. The name change enabled them to take better advantage of an online brand name that customers had grown to identify with the firm—to the tune of over $40 million in profits per year. A stockholder meeting had enthusiastically approved the new name and a new logo to match, decades be damned.

Part of the new Web strategy includes trolling for future customers worldwide who haven't yet heard of either name. In 1999, MSC.Software secured the domain **engineering-e.com** to help attract its target audience of engineers to a portal that serves up onscreen simulation demonstrations and business-to-business product sales (see Figure 4.5).

Figure 4.5

If you're an engineer, what are the odds that sooner or later you'd surf to engineering-e.com?

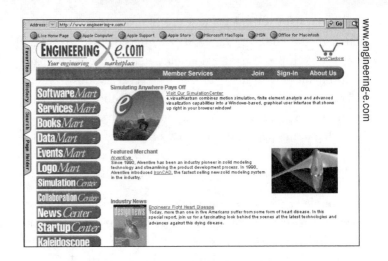

An example of a company creating a new online brand and really running with it is **ebay.com**. The name itself doesn't tell you too much about what the site is for—online auctions—but, thanks to an aggressive word of mouth and sustained promotion, it's still the most recognizable brand among the many auction-oriented sites.

(At least two of *Net Results*' three authors find this gratifying, if not slightly embarrassing, since **ebay.com** was an early client of authors Bob Heyman and Leland Harden when they started their first audience-development company, Cybernautics. "I have to admit that one of the first things we tried to do was get them to change the name," admits Leland. "They stuck with it because all the obvious names, like auction-dot-com, were already taken.")

noalphabetsoup.com

The simple advice to make a domain memorable might seem obvious, but countless sites don't follow it. One popular way to screw up a Web brand is with an "alphabet soup" domain. While companies are often known quite well in the real world by their initials, unless you already own the branding clout of a GM or IBM, a string of initials will be meaningless in the Internet's global environment, and cause for error ("Was that RLX.com? Or LRX? . . . ").

One of the world's largest catalog merchants and direct mailers with more than 50 years of experience in consumer marketing, launched a Web site that offered discounts on a range of products through online promotions. Shortly before the site launched, the company changed the Web brand from CoolOffers (**cooloffers.com**) to Direct Value to You. The new URL became **www.dv2u.com**. Get it? You probably do, but only after thinking about it for a moment.

Put this to the drive-time radio test, please. Imagine the company president being interviewed on a talk show, promoting the site. What percentage of drivers are going to remember that cute domain when they arrive at the office 45 minutes later? Was it **www.d2u.com? www.d2kv.com?** Something like that? . . .

Of course it didn't work. After a company merger, this domain survived as a pointer to **Mypoints.com**, which offers a variety of promotional opportunities for a business-to-consumer clientele.

www.slash-tilde.com/~goblDgook/index.htm

The absolute worst kind of URL for a company's home page is the extension of someone else's domain—the deadly "slash-tilde" approach. This might be fine for a teenager's personal home page, but a business won't be taken seriously with a domain beginning **aol.com/~**, **geocities.com/~**, or **tripod.com/~**.

Consider E-Net Web Design and Network Solutions, listed in Yahoo! as an Internet marketing experts' site. Their home page is at **www.bcpl.net/~dflax/**. The site is hosted by the Baltimore County Public Library (**bcpl.net**). Imagine their radio ad: "We are Maryland's premier Internet experts. Come see what we can do for your business online at double-u double-u double-u, dot, bee-cee-pee-el, dot, en-ee-tee, dot, slash, tilde-dee-eff-el-ay-ex."

Using a slash-tilde extension of someone else's domain, besides making for an impossible-to-remember URL, says to the customers that the business doesn't have enough faith in itself to invest the $70 it costs to register its own domain. (See Figure 4.6.)

Figure 4.6

You don't have to look beyond this Web agency's domain to size up their expertise. Frankly, we were surprised to see this company hasn't changed its URL since we last made fun of them in the first edition of this book.

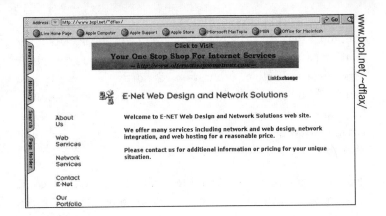

donttrytogetbywith.net

Another inadvisable route some businesses choose when the .com domain they want has already been taken is to register the same name as a .net domain. "Dot.net" domains are supposedly reserved for companies that play some networking role in the Internet infrastructure, such as Internet service providers. But some domain registrar services don't check too thoroughly, and will normally provide a .net domain to anyone who gives some technical mumbo-jumbo explanation of how they intend to use the domain.

The problem with using a .net domain when the .com version is already taken is that surfers are likely to search for your home page under the .com name and get someone else's site instead. Because .com is still by far the dominant suffix for commercial sites, the confusion is inevitable. Consider that the popular jargon for all types of Internet businesses is to call them "dot.coms." The wise marketer will register *both* extensions to avoid any confusion and prevent another service from accidentally or intentionally skimming off traffic intended for her site.

www.CGI/hiccup?boink*12345&aaahhh!!!!%etc.etc.html

Another pitfall to avoid is a long, unwieldy URL generated by CGI scripts and other dynamic page systems. Many dynamic page systems create such URLs, but a business should at least try to have a normal-looking URL for the home page. Some sophisticated systems, such as Documentum's RightSite, can generate pages dynamically (such as the results of database searches or personalized pages for individual visitors) with normal-looking URLs, so it's a standard that sites should push software developers to uphold.

Take the example of the Minolta Printers site. The URL has changed but still could be smarter. Although a user can reach the site by typing **www.minoltaprinters.com**, when the home page loads, the browser's URL field displays **http://www.minolta printers.com/mainframe.asp?productid=8&whichproduct section=1&whichsection=3** (see Figure 4.7).

There are a few problems with this. First, this URL is not exactly aesthetically pleasing as a component of the page design. Second, many surfers use the browser's URL field as a navigation aid, tracking what section of the site they are in through the traditional hierarchy of site sub-sections divided by levels of / marks. In this example, the string of alphanumeric symbols following the / is so long that a browser's URL field can't possibly display it all at once.

Third, as noted, the home page URL is a key component of the site's brand, and **http://www.minoltaprinters.com/ mainframe.asp?productid=8&whichproductsection=1&which section=3** doesn't present a very strong brand impression.

Finally, imagine the owner of a new small business is looking for printers and surfs to this home page through a link from another business page. He's impressed with the offerings and calls up his business manager to share it with her.

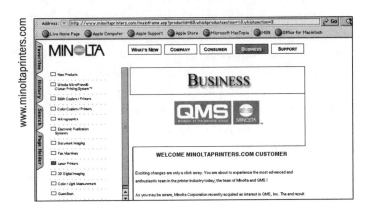

Figure 4.7
What's that URL again?

She says, "It sounds like I should check out that site myself. What's the URL?"

"What do you mean by URL?," he replies.

"The thing at the top of your browser that begins **http://www**. . .Just read it to me," she says.

"Okay, it's. . .Sheesh, it's really long. Maybe I should just email it to you."

If he knows how to cut-and-paste it into an email, she might get the information and view the Web page. Or, she might not. . .

Cover Your Assets

Having settled on a strategic domain name that is available at the InterNIC, many companies register the domain and leave it at that—another potentially big mistake.

Consider the browser's URL field (labeled "location" by Netscape and "address" by Microsoft) to be the ultimate Web search engine. If you were looking for the McDonald's home page, would you go to AltaVista and search for "mcdonalds," or would you simply type **www.mcdonalds.com** into your browser? Probably the latter, right?

Way back in 1994, when few people had heard of the Internet, Joshua Quittner, a journalist for *New York Newsday* and *Wired* magazine, typed **www.mcdonalds.com** into his browser. It came up blank. With a search of the InterNIC, he realized that McDonald's wasn't quite hip to the Web. So after a few weeks of vainly hounding Mickey D's PR department for comment on the matter, he registered the domain himself as a joke. He wrote some hilarious articles based on the stunt, and a few other publications picked up the story too. Finally, after convincing McDonald's to pay a paltry sum to buy Internet equipment for a grade school, Quittner gave the domain back to the fast-food giant.

McDonald's learned a lesson, but they still don't fully get it. What if a user was a bad speller, and typed **www.macdonalds.com**

into his browser? He would get a page hosted by a *domain broker*, one of the crafty devils who register and hoard promising domain names, selling them to the highest bidder (see Figure 4.8). The same thing would happen if a user typed **www.mcdonalds.net**.

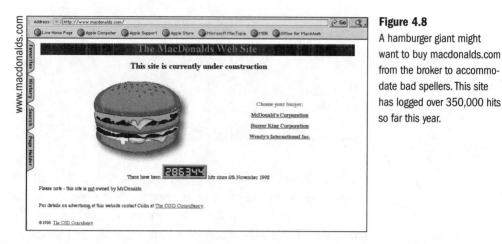

Figure 4.8
A hamburger giant might want to buy macdonalds.com from the broker to accommodate bad spellers. This site has logged over 350,000 hits so far this year.

The Domain Name Game

If you want to have some fun, play the Domain Name Game. It's easy. Just punch random phrases and well-known brand names into the URL field of your browser (or, for advanced play, the Whois directory of the InterNIC), or look up alternative versions of the product and company names of your competitors. The object of the game is to see who's asleep at which marketing departments.

Microsoft, the company everyone loves to hate, gets an especially low score in the Domain Name Game. **Microsof.com, micrsoft.com, microsft.com, microsot.com, micros0ft.com** (with a zero instead of the second "o"), **microsuft.com, microsoft.net, microsuck.com,** and almost every other variation of the name are registered variously or were registered previously to domain brokers, competitors, anti-Microsoft sites, porno sites, and other businesses besides the warm, fuzzy software giant itself. **Micro-soft.com** was recently registered by a small start-up company, Micro Dash Software, which is still looking for venture capital (see Figure 4.9). (Hint: Lose the piano music, guys.)

Figure 4.9

Micro-soft.com, treading lightly but bravely in the name game.

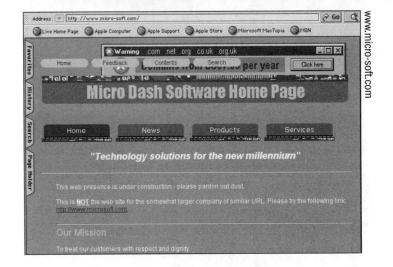

Several clever companies prey on careless typists by registering domains with the names of popular Web sites, but without the period between the www and the rest of the URL. In the case of **wwwmicrosoft.com**, for example, the resulting page politely informs viewers they've made a typo and serves up an ad banner.

No Dessert Till You've Registered Your Variables

The list goes on and on. **Amazon.com** took the trouble to register some 35 domains, including many variants of its name. But **amazon.net** is still owned by another company, currently registered to Nova, an Internet service provider.

CNET, which has aggressively accumulated some of the choicest domain names imaginable, secured **java.com** about a year after Sun Microsystems introduced the sensational Java technology to the world. Yet CNET neglected to register **cnet.net** before someone in Canada did in October 1997. It was also beaten to **c.net** in 1993 by some academic researchers. These and other companies have been playing catch-up ever since.

Figure 4.10

Webmethods raced to obtain this valuable URL, but many variations, including btob.com and btob.net, were assigned first to other sites vying for Web business eyeballs.

The lesson here is obvious for businesses. They should register every variation of their domain they can think of. This includes likely typos, plurals and singulars, both .com and .net domains, and, if they anticipate doing significant international business, specific country domains such as .jp (Japan), .uk, .ca (Canada), and so on. If a business's name could conceivably be hyphenated, it should register that as well. For a first-time registration fee of $70 per domain, registering anything short of every variation they can possibly think of is careless. (See Figures 4.11 and 4.12.)

Every online company should occasionally play the Domain Name Game as a matter of marketing strategy. Allocate a budget for leasing domains, a few thousand dollars a year if possible, to give marketers the liberty to secure all relevant variables of the company's name—a Web-marketing must—as well as to lay away promising available domains for possible future project development or resale.

Figure 4.11

Lipton's Ragu brand of Italian food products has logically claimed its product name...

Figure 4.12

...but shrewdly maintains a generic domain as well. Its strategy is presumably to pick up traffic among any surfers who will try *eat.com* out of blind curiosity.

Be First to Register Product Names

Why is this so important? Because most successful companies would rather control their trademarked brands in cyberspace themselves than leave the names open for someone else to claim. Take a lesson from the biggest conglomerate in the world, Procter & Gamble. It controls the domain for virtually every one of its brands, but was still beaten to the punch on one of its flagship products, **crest.com**, which it didn't get its hands on until 2000. Formerly registered to a small graphics company, this site now transports the user quickly to "brushing lessons" for kids.

It's amazing how many companies neglected to register their product names in the early days of Web-madness. Anheuser-Busch missed **bud.com**, for example. This site is still home to a cryptic, trippy page that seems to relate more to smoking a "bud" instead of drinking it. Anheuser-Busch got **budice.com** and **budlight.com** but not **buddry.com** or **budlite.com**, both of which are registered to "domain squatters" who are presumably holding several domains with names of familiar consumer brands for ransom. (See Figure 4.13.)

An anti-cybersquatting bill recently passed by Congress now makes it difficult for individuals to appropriate trademarked names, with penalties of up to $100,000. In the courts, resolved cases of domain name disputes have tended to favor the owners of trademarks that are literally household words.

With a small or brand-new business, however, owners might find it tough to win a disputed domain for even a trademarked product. After much haranguing and possible litigation, the company with the most money could likely win back a domain. But, negligent online marketing should not allow such disputes to occur in the first place.

Figure 4.13
Looking for a good domain name? Buy, sell, or lease a name, on several broker sites, including this one.

Don't Forget to Renew

Domain names for mature sites must be renewed, typically every two years. When not renewed, a URL is "deactivated" by the registrar, and the site goes down—pronto. If not renewed, ownership of the name expires, and someone else can get it. Kensington Publishing Corp., one of the first in its industry to launch a Web site, almost lost **www.kensingtonbooks.com** when its registration expired last spring. In the midst of the publisher's multi-million-dollar acquisition of another company, the site was down for an embarrassing two days, until the company president renewed, using his personal credit card.

A few weeks later, the Web site of J.P. Morgan & Company, a bank with assets exceeding $20 billion, also got its Web site "deactivated." According to the registrar, Network Solutions, the firm had failed to respond to three notices to pay the $35 renewal fee on **jpmorgan.com**. Not only the site but the company's email system was inoperable for at least one business day, a cautionary tale to all. Even though registries send reminders, a business should make sure someone at the organization is responsible for this task.

The Politics of Domains

As you've seen, the issue of domain names is not without controversy. In fact, it's increasingly one of the hottest topics of Internet disputes, along with privacy, security, child protection, and copyright.

The Players: InterNIC, NetSol, ICANN, and Friends

There are more than 100 top-level domains (TLD), although most of them designate countries, such as .hu (Hungary), .de (Germany), and .nl (The Netherlands). In most cases, country domains are registered with and administered by local authorities. Some countries, such as Tonga (.to), are eagerly selling their national TLDs to commercial entities, although the value of such a domain is questionable (when's the last time you visited a .to site?)

The most popular Internet TLDs—.com, .net, .org, and .edu—are registered with the InterNIC, a branch of the U.S. National Science Foundation. In 1993, the InterNIC subcontracted the behind-the-scenes administration of its huge TLD database, well more than a million .com domains alone, to a private company called Network Solutions, Inc. (NSI) (see Figure 4.14). In recent years, NSI has registered over ten million domain names, and has become a lightning rod for criticism from many quarters.

NSI's contract with the InterNIC was originally for five years, which means it expired in March 1998. That same year, the Internet Corporation for Assigned Names and Numbers (ICANN) was created, as a non-profit, private sector corporation formed by a broad coalition of the Internet's business, technical, academic, and user communities. ICANN is recognized by the U.S. Government and many other governments as a "global consensus entity," to coordinate the technical and legal aspects of domain turf issues. This has not protected ICANN from a barrage of criticism from nearly everyone who has a stake in the domain wars.

Not surprisingly, money is at the root of much of the controversy. NSI only began charging fees for domain name registration in 1995: $100 up front for the first two years per domain, and $50 annually after that. Although the fee was since reduced to $70 and $35, respectively, roughly equivalent to a business lunch, the fees do add up when a company covers its bases with multiple registrations, as recommended.

Figure 4.14
Network Solutions, now a for-profit company, is still the dominant registry, despite its new competitors.

Moreover, NSI's would-be competitors were outraged that the government would give one company an effective monopoly over the potentially profitable business of domain management. With more than a million .com domains alone paying annual fees of $35, it's easy to see their point. By 1999, through lobbying, lawsuits, and similar maneuvers, five competing registries existed, and the number of firms "certified" as registries by ICAAN has since grown exponentially. Many of these have joined the Internet Council of Registrars (CORENIC), a group often at odds with ICAAN.

Why would a business want to register its domain with anything but NSI, the leader? After all, ten million served, so far. Why register at a "brand x" registry?

Registering with another domain registry can be faster and cheaper (as cheap as $1 per name). Some long time Web users have switched because they do not want to see NSI become a defacto monopoly.

In addition, many parties are unhappy with NSI's policies regarding domain name disputes. Its original policy was to allot domains purely on a "first come, first served" basis and leave companies to settle disagreements about rightful claims to domain names among themselves or in the courts. More recently, however, both NSI and ICAAN have been accused of caving into pressure from powerful corporate interests, especially when the challenger has a trademark on the name.

While courts have already ruled that simply owning a trademark in a particular country or business category doesn't automatically entitle the trademark owner to a global domain name, more recent court cases seem to be favoring trademark owners. (See more discussion on these issues in the "Domain Disputes" section later in this chapter.)

The Impending Rush for New TLDs

NSI's critics, among both rival domain registrars and companies seeking to lease domains, would also like to see several new TLDs introduced, particularly to widen the choices for commercial Web sites beyond the predominant .com option.

In the late 1990s, a group of engineers from around the world formed the Policy Oversight Committee (originally known as the International Ad Hoc Committee) to propose new policies for the administration of TLDs. One plan calls for the creation of seven new Internet-wide TLDs—.web, .firm, .store, .arts, .rec, .info, and .nom. Other parties are pushing for even more TLDs, including .xxx and .tm.int (designating an international trademark).

In June 2000, ICAAN signaled it would most likely approve some additions to the mix, and called for proposals as well as public comment on TLDs, expressing the hope that some decisions could be made by the end of that year. (The "Resources" section at the end of this chapter will show you where to keep informed.)

We all saw what happened with domain registration the first time around. Organizations that didn't register their .com domains before other parties did so included McDonald's, *The New York Times*, MTV, Coca-Cola, ABC TV, Dianetics, Fry's Electronics, The Gap, the Better Business Bureau, and many others. With this much advance notice in the mainstream and Internet-industry press the second time around, companies would be foolish to make the same mistake twice by not registering under any new TLDs.

TLDs for Net TV

No discussion of the creative potential of new TLDs would be complete without mentioning DotTV. This U.S. firm made headlines by acquiring the geographical TLD ".tv" that had been assigned to Tuvalu, a small, independent Pacific island nation. Through an agreement with the government of Tuvalu, DotTV became the exclusive registry and registrar for second-level domain names in the .tv top-level domain. The negotiated price included an equity stake for the government and a minimum $4 million per year for ten years. The company hopes to register domain names to clients in the television industry; more information can be found at **www.tv.com**.

Domain Brokers

It's a popular misconception that all the good domains are gone. With a bit of perseverance and creativity, you can find plenty of unique names and combinations of words still unregistered at the InterNIC. And, if the name you *really* have your heart set on is already taken, it might be for sale.

So-called *domain brokers* are businesses and individuals that have amassed attractive domain names for heavily marked-up resale, like some kind of Third Wave intellectual-property commodity brokers. For an up-front $70 per name, it can be a lucrative investment for properties that can easily sell for a few thousand dollars or much more.

The Domain Name Game quickly reveals the abundance of domain brokers out there. **MSN2.com, onlinepricing.com, emerchandising.com, diamondforever.com, InternetLLC.com, ibusinesses.com,** and thousands of other decent to even great domain names are available for sale this way. (See Figure 4.15.)

Names are usually sold by auction. On any given day you can navigate to **ebay.com** and find several hundred domain names for sale to the highest bidder, with opening bids that range from a penny to millions of dollars.

Figure 4.15

You've bought it, now what will you do with it? This type of site is called a "placeholder."

Several kinds of players in the Domain Name Game collect good names for resale. There are the specialized kings of the industry, who've invested thousands of dollars in names, and whose own sites are located at domains like **domains.com** or **domainnames.com**. There are also the small-time hobbyists with credit cards, and all the other Web site owners who, for a variety of reasons, have invested in surplus domains.

If there is a domain name a business really wants that someone else has but isn't actively using, the business can safely assume the registrant will entertain an offer. Most starting prices, need-less to say, are negotiable.

Domain Disputes

A careful domain strategy underpins the successful Web branding of many leading Web ventures. Occasionally, how-ever, serious disputes over rightful claim to domains are bound to arise, which can pose a tremendous threat to a site's viability. (See Figure 4.16.)

If the horse isn't already out, shut the barn doors now by researching the trademark status of your domains. If they're not trademarked yet, try to trademark them. If they're already trademarked to someone else, think twice about using them for your Web brands, especially if you're up against a larger com-pany that could afford to bleed you dry with legal expenses.

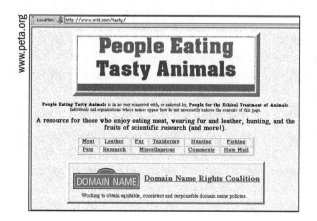

Figure 4.16
This site registered the domain peta.org before the well-known organization People for the Ethical Treatment of Animals (PETA) thought to do so. The peta.org domain is still in dispute.

One of Bob and Leland's earliest clients at Cybernautics was RockNet, the first online purveyor of music news and chat on CompuServe and America Online (where it was known as Rock-Line). The company was interested in bringing their Internet content to greater heights on the Web.

They planed to use their CompuServe name, RockNet, on the Web, but Bob discovered that a Phoenix-based car stereo company had already registered the domain **rocknet.com**. RockNet was undaunted because they had a trademark on the name. They had also launched on CompuServe in 1986, making them a true pioneer in cyberspace. With the trademark in hand, Bob contacted the stereo company on the client's behalf.

"At first the only person we could reach was the company Webmaster, who seemed oblivious to the issue," Bob recalls. "He said, in effect, 'You don't get it, man. The law doesn't apply to the Internet.' Eventually, I reached the corporate counsel and informed her that a cease-and-desist order claiming trademark infringement was forthcoming. That got the company's attention."

Rather than leaving the dispute in acrimony, however, they were able to negotiate a settlement that made both parties happy. The car stereo company agreed to give up the domain name, but in exchange received free advertising banners on RockNet to compensate for the expenses they incurred in changing the name, such as printing new corporate stationery.

Happily, geniality still surfaces at some hip Web companies, including the ones that don't harass their copycat "spoof sites" out of existence. Spoofs that live on include **mired.com** (which has no link, literal or figurative, to **wired.com**) and the online parody of **fastcompany.com** (whose URL is, alas, unprintable here).

In an attempt to regulate domain disputes, ICANN has recommended a Uniform Domain-Name Dispute Resolution Policy (UDRP) and offers an assortment of legal bodies for arbitration, including The National Arbitration Forum (NAF), which currently charges $750 per arbitrator, and the World Intellectual Property Organization (WIPO) which charges $1,000. The current rules of engagement, and a full list of arbitrators, can be found at ICANN's Web site, **www.icann.org**.

Arbitration certainly beats the old way NSI used to handle a name dispute—freezing the domain until somebody backed down. When the name in question involves a trademark, ICANN recommends that domain-name disputes be resolved by agreement, a legal case, or arbitration action before a registrar will cancel, suspend, or transfer an existing name.

In 1999, while libertarians slept, Congress passed the Anti-Cybersquatting Act, tacked inconspicuously onto a larger trade bill. This law clearly throws the advantage to trademark owners, and stipulates fines of as much as $100,000 to persons found to be holding domains for the purpose of harassment or personal gain.

The result has been a fast and hard bodyslam for cybersquatters and domain-name speculators. In one recent, well-publicized case, a WIPO arbitrator ruled that a Californian named Michael Bosman was not entitled to ownership of the URL **worldwrestlingfederation.com**, despite the fact that he had registered this domain name first and well before the World Wrestling Federation (WWF) had a chance to do the same. Bosman was alleged to have tried to sell the name back to WWF, although given the traffic in names that still exists today, there's no reason why he couldn't have offered this property to what no doubt seemed a likely customer.

The domain was given to the WWF, on grounds that it had previously trademarked the phrase "World Wrestling Federation" and used that trademark name on a variety of products, from television programming to souvenir warm-up jackets, for at least a decade before the dot.com version of the same phrase was acquired by Bosman. While things might change, it appears that trademark owners have the edge for now. (See Figure 4.17.)

If a business's existing Web site has a good domain, it should hold on to it. Million-dollar price tags for names will likely become a thing of the past, but as with the similarly intangible but priceable value of "good will," a good domain name can now be considered a solid corporate asset, if the company is ever sold or merged.

Figure 4.17

One for the history books: General Motors was asleep at the wheel when this guy registered generalmotors. com in June 1997, using it as a personal home page to rail against, among other things, greenhouse emissions. The auto giant now has control of this URL, but the previous owner managed to keep his site running for three long years. General, we salute you!

Stay Tuned . . .

Domain name policies are sure to change and get more complicated. New TLDs seem a certainty. So businesses should cover their bases, making sure they renew their URLs as needed, and remembering to add a line item for URL legal and trademark costs to their next business plans.

Figure 4.18

The future of Internet TLD policies may be spelled out at this historical policy site—please note the catchy domain name. Or was "get led, moo" an inside joke?

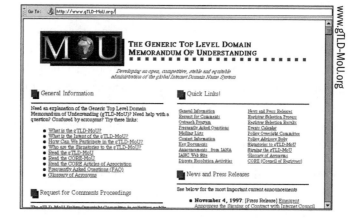

 **Resources**

InterNIC Whois

http://internic.net/cgi-bin/whois

- This is where you play the Domain Name Game. Simply type in any word or phrase, followed by .com, .net, .edu, or .org, and see if and where it's registered. If it's not and you want it, it's yours for $70.

The Internet Council of Registrars

http://www.corenic.org

- The non-profit Council maintains a whois database where you can also play the Domain Name Game, along with news, commentary, and links. This site is especially useful in providing the names and contacts for registrars in foreign countries.

The Internet Corporation of Assigned Names and Numbers (ICANN)

http://www.icann.org

- The top level of international Internet bureaucracy, at the moment, with pages on policy, history, news releases, and public comment opportunity. Check here for updates on new TLDs, registry politics, and related issues.

ICANN Watch

http://www.icannwatch.org

- A monitoring, often critical site that keeps tabs on Web politics. The latest pronouncements by Ester Dyson and other ICANN brass are often posted and dissected days earlier than they might appear on ICANN's official Web pages.

Oppedahl & Larson

http://www.patents.com

- Oppedahl & Larson law firm's Web site has useful links to further discussions of copyright, patents, trademarks, Web law, and other intellectual property issues. Some of the older domain dispute case histories can be found here.

continues

continued

John Marshall Law School Index of Cyber Legal Issues

http://www.jmls.edu/cyber/index/

- Researchers at this law school have put together an excellent free resource with case studies and links to vast amounts of material on Web and intellectual property law, including trademarks and a list of currently disputed domains.

Thomson & Thomson

http://www.thomson-thomson.com/

- A leading trademark search service. There is a fee for the searches. For other trademark search services, refer to links at the preceding sites of John Marshall, Georgetown, and Oppedahl & Larson.

The Generic Top-Level Domain Memorandum of Understanding

http://www.gtld-mou.org/

- For the historically curious, this hopeful plan by the Policy Oversight Committee, known by the hideous abbreviation gTLD-MoU, distills the contributions of hundreds of interested parties, preserved in Internet amber, circa August 1999. Among its recommendations is the introduction of seven new TLD extensions. Some of its recommendations seem likely to be adopted, changing the whole way the Domain Name Game is played.

Electronic Frontier Foundation (EFF)

http://www.eff.org

- The EFF lobby group keeps an up-to-date list of case studies and related news, though it deals less these days with domains than with privacy issues.

The Domain Name Rights Coalition

http://www.domain-name.org/cybersquatact.html

- This site contains commentary, links, and other resources, plus the full text of the Anti-Cybersquatter Act, as passed by Congress in 1999.

Part II

Audience Development

IN THIS CHAPTER

chapter 5

Find and Be Found: Strategies for Search Engines and Directories

IN THE EARLY DAYS of the Web, registering yourself with a few search engines and Web directories was 90 percent of the work for online promotion. Soon, your site would appear in a category next to three or four other similar sites, and you'd sit back while the traffic flowed in.

With the vast expansion of the Web since then, your site is now likely to show up alongside dozens or even hundreds of listings in a directory, and among thousands or even millions of results on a search engine query. A Web surfer might have better odds winning a million dollars at **Freelotto.com** than finding the ideal reference he's looking for on some Web search engines.

Nonetheless, many if not most surfers still begin their forays into cyberspace at search engines and directories. This is one reason why search engines generally rank among the top-trafficked sites and biggest ad revenue earners on the Web. They're growing ever more powerful and show no sign of going away anytime soon. So, a site promoter has little choice but to learn to love them—or at least understand them. (See Figure 5.1.)

It is important to distinguish between *search engines* and *directories*. Whatever the business, it needs to be listed on both. But the business' approach should be different because search engines and directories differ in how they interpret information.

Figure 5.1

A search on Infoseek for "Internet search engines" renders nearly 5 million results. Got plans for the weekend?

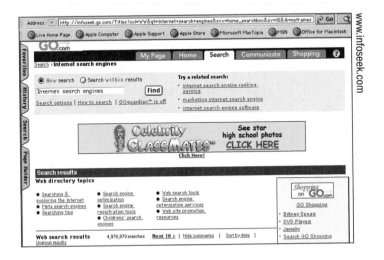

Search Engines

A search engine refers to an automated system, such as Hotbot, AltaVista, or InfoSeek. Such services rely on special software agents—called *spiders*, *robots*, *bots*, or *crawlers*—that explore and index every nook and cranny of the Web (and, in many cases, other aspects of the Net, such as newsgroups). The spiders extract relevant text from the pages they discover and create digests of them in the search engine's database. When a Web surfer does a search, the system looks at its database of pages the spider has imported, rather than performing a live search across the Web each time.

Directories

Directories, the largest of which by far is Yahoo!, do not depend principally on automated spiders. Rather, they index the Web the old-fashioned way, employing legions of recent college graduates to toil at terminals. To a limited extent, these "surf teams" discover uncharted territory on their own and use spiders to tip them off to new sites, but, to a much greater degree, they depend on Webmasters who register their own sites with the directory. The directory's staff visits these sites, qualifies them for inclusion, and edits the appropriate descriptions and keywords before putting up links to the sites.

Coherent Versus Comprehensive

The different approaches between search engines and directories produce different kinds of results, for both surfers and site promoters. For surfers, a human-edited directory is likely to organize pages in a more coherent manner than an automated program. Yahoo! doesn't group 50,000 Web pages together into a single category, but AltaVista will regularly return at least that many pages for a typical request.

It's no surprise, therefore, that Yahoo! is the most popular navigational guide among users. According to 1999 data from Media Metrix, Yahoo! was visited daily by more than 50 percent of U.S. households on the Web, as opposed to less than 30 percent using its nearest search engine competitor, Excite (see Figure 5.2).

Figure 5.2

Excite and other search engines pay big bucks to become the "default search" on browsers packaged with consumer computers. But their owners can easily customize the browser page to feature another search engine.

Several of the leading search services are a hybrid of directories and pure search engines, such as Lycos, which relies on both automated and human help to search and categorize Web pages. There are also specialty search engines such as the WAP search engines, **waply.com** and **wapaw.com**, which provide a less-cluttered entry point to only those pages that can be viewed intelligibly by wireless Web remotes. To keep up with the vast numbers of new Web pages generated daily, the services often "borrow" listings through partnership agreements, or share collected data on mega-databases such as Inktomi.

How Netizens Search

Next to email, conducting a search is the most popular activity on the Web, with an estimated one-half of all log ins involving some kind of search. If someone is searching for a known organization or Web resource by name, she generally starts with a popular directory such as Yahoo!. Data on searching behavior reveals that many new users often simply employ the first search engine that appears on their browser page, particularly if it appears to be part of their online service package.

When seasoned netizens are searching for a specific phrase or relatively obscure concept likely to be buried in the text of an unknown site, such as "number of emu ranches in America," they are likely to log in to a search engine such as HotBot or AltaVista for a more refined search. Search engines are more comprehensive than directories. However, as the Web continues to grow exponentially, they too have backed away from their claim to list everything.

Services that are a cross between directories and search engines, such as **google.com** and the Lycos service Ask Jeeves!, allow users to type in actual questions that result in a range of prompts to refine the search further. For example, the question, "What are the traditions of a Polish wedding?" on Ask Jeeves! leads the user to the Web site of The Kosciosko Foundation headquarters in New York, which offers a short pamphlet on Polish wedding customs.

Finally, if the user is curious about what people are searching for on any given day, say in Switzerland or on their Web remotes, Search Engine Watch supplies a good list of "voyeur" sites at the following URL:

http://www.searchenginewatch.com/facts/searches.html

Degrees of Site Owner Control

For site promoters, the automated approach of search engines provides a bit more control over how a listing is displayed. Through the use of techniques such as meta tags and the careful construction of other page elements (see the section "Optimize Your Ranking" later in this chapter), a site designer can influence the search terms and page descriptions that many search engines will use when displaying results. Directories, on the other hand, are edited by subjective human beings who are apt to write their own description of a site and categorize it as they feel most appropriate, ignoring programming techniques that have been designed to influence spiders.

Register Your Site

When a site is ready for prime time, it should be registered with all of the top directories and search engines. As with all types of online promotion, however, it is important for a developer not to jump the gun on this step before his site is ready for masses of visitors. Every site is perpetually "under construction," of course, but announcing the site to the world for feedback when the site is still in beta is generally a mistake. There are only a few seconds available to make that critical first impression on visitors while their twitching fingers yearn to click the Back button. Bad news travels faster on the Web than anywhere, and it might be months, if ever, before a surfer returns to a lousy site to see if it's improved.

Don't Wait to Be Found

In theory the spiders from search engines eventually track down the site whether it's registered or not, but there's no guarantee of this. Current research suggests that search engines catalog no more than 10 to 20 percent of all pages existing on the Web. Registering directly with the search engines gives the business greater control over how soon its site will show up (it can still take days or weeks, depending on the search engine). Manual registration gives the business more influence over which descriptions and keywords the engine associates with its site.

In the case of directories like Yahoo!, the chances of their surf teams finding the site among the millions of other sites on the Web are remote at best. There is no choice but to register manually with directories.

Registering a site with even 10 search services is time-consuming because each guide requires slightly different information (site descriptions of varying lengths, more or fewer keywords, and so on). The Web site designer should prepare a text document of basic information about his site, such as its name, contact persons, descriptions of it in 10 words, 20 words, 25 words, 50 words, and 100 words, sets of 5 keywords, 15 keywords, 30 keywords, and so on. For each search service, he should cut and paste the appropriate prepared texts into each field as necessary to save time.

Several services exist, both free and fee-based, both automated and personalized, that can administer this process. There are even off-the-shelf software programs for submissions. Purely automated services have fallen out of favor, however, and for a business-to-business Web site, they make no sense at all. The better strategy is to take the time to carefully craft a manual submission to the most important general search engines and directories, and then apply to the small number of specialty directories likely to be searched by the customer base.

A site designer might use an auto-registration tool (such as Submit-It) for the hundreds of other relevant search engines and directories once he's satisfied that the site's URL can be found at his early target sites. If it is the designer's job to jump-start a mature Web site that existed before 1996, an auto-registration tool helps to get the site listed on search sites that were missed in the first pass or have since been established.

Follow Your Browser to the Leaders

The search engine and directory market is changing faster than most other segments of the Web. Rather than naming today's top search sites, only to find them out of date shortly after this book's publication, the Web sites of **mediametrix.com, netratings.com,** and **netvalue.com,** post a ranking of the most visited search sites. They also post current leaders nestling comfortably on the navigational guides listed on Netscape's Navigator and Microsoft's Internet Explorer browser pages. Search services pay millions of dollars a year to appear onscreen as a browser's primary or default search option. In exchange for the fee, these links are the ones built into the "search" buttons or in a "search" menu on the browser page.

Explore all the search services listed on Netscape and Microsoft's search pages, including the smaller links to the side of and below the large graphic links. These are the industry's current search leaders with whom sites need to be listed.

Getting Starship on the Radar

The scene is the Heyman home, the summer of 1995, 3:00 a.m. on a Monday morning. The phone rings. Bob, then a senior vice president of audience development at Cybernautics, grabs the receiver and mumbles, "Hello?"

"Why the #$@* don't we come up before page 4 on this damn thing?! Page %#+@ing 4, you *@*%ing morons!!" the voice on the other end shouts.

Examining the alarm clock and smiling meekly at his wife, Bob asks, "Huh?"

continues

---

continues

The caller was the manager for the rock band Jefferson Starship, one of Bob's early Internet clients. He was throwing a tantrum befitting a rock industry executive in the middle of the night over the fact that the Web site recently built for the band appeared several screens down in a search of "Jefferson Starship" on a particular search engine.

As it turns out, the band was on the road and the manager had wanted to show a club promoter how hip Starship was to have its own Web site. Unfortunately, he couldn't remember the URL (**www.jstarship.com**, now defunct), so he resorted to a search engine lookup. To his considerable annoyance, the page didn't come up especially close to the top of the list.

The next morning, Bob dragged into the office a bit sleepier than usual, gathered the staff and explained that mastering the art of search engine ranking was a new company priority.

Optimize Your Ranking

Many Web developers, after lovingly crafting a wonderful site and then registering it with various search engines, have reacted with horror to discover that the site appears as item 74,592 in a search of relevant keywords on a typical search engine.

The good news is that a responsible site designer can move his site toward the top of search results through a better understanding of how search engines rank pages. The bad news is that these guidelines aren't standard across all search engines. Most search engines and some directories even penalize sites for employing especially aggressive techniques to bolster ranking.

Unfortunately, some site designers become obsessed with a never-ending battle to keep their sites near the top of search results, at the expense of more effective methods of online promotion and even the maintenance of their site's overall quality. After a certain point, it's okay for a designer to admit that his site doesn't have to be number one in its category, and then focus his energy on other strategies to keep its competitive edge.

Guides: Loyal to Surfers, Not Webmasters

All navigational guides, be they search engines or directories, owe their primary allegiance to surfers seeking information. Site developers who are trying to promote their pages are secondary. Of course, these search engines and directories wouldn't even be in business without sites to index, so they do recognize the promotional needs of Webmasters. They are on constant guard against attempts to abuse the system, however, and they will do their best to thwart all attempts at such manipulation.

Most search engines strive to provide a level playing field for all sites. They frequently change their strategies for rankings to prevent Webmasters from artificially weighting search results in favor of their own sites. Directories are often more upfront about what they expect from Webmasters who submit a URL. What follows is a short list of the key elements that affect rankings on both search engines and directories.

Keywords

When a search-engine spider finds a Web page, its main objective is to interpret various elements of the page to determine its dominant themes as they relate to future keyword searches. Each search engine uses a slightly different formula for weighing the importance of various page elements when calculating the page's relevance to given search terms. In general, however, the following elements all play a significant role in those formulas.

Page Title Tag

Along with the site's domain name itself, a Web page's title is possibly the single most significant factor that search engines use to determine a page's contextual relevance.

The title, indicated in HTML source code by the <title> tag, is the text that appears in the title bar at the top of the Web browser. The same text appears as the label if a user bookmarks the page.

From a search engine's point of view, the title "Sue's Cajun Flavors" would be much less effective in defining the context of a site selling hot sauce than "Sue's Cajun Flavors, for hot sauce, spicy sauce, pepper sauce, and other super-hot sauces and condiments." Although the latter title seems clunky and doesn't fit entirely within the average browser's title bar, a search-engine spider can read all that text and make it available for future keyword searches. (See Figure 5.3.)

Titles should ideally focus on one theme. The "density" of the theme in the title is generally important to ranking. That is, if the title consists of only one word, and that's the word a surfer searches, it's likely to be weighted more than a title containing that word along with several other words. In the previous example, the repetition of "sauce" and "hot" was an attempt to increase the density of that theme.

But long and repetitive titles won't aid a designer's efforts everywhere. Excite, for example, currently limits title tags to 41 characters, while Infoseek and AltaVista tend to penalize sites with repetitive title tags. On business-to-business Web sites, however, a page title that's too long can look awkward and unprofessional. Remember that users as well as search engines will see the page title: A short, concise, targeted title message—ideally, a domain name that contains the site's best keywords—provides polish to the page. In fact, a title that closely or exactly matches the domain name of the subject being searched can help push a site nearer to the top of a search ranking. A site with the domain **hotsauce.com,** for example, would likely rank high in someone's search of the keywords "hot sauce."

Figure 5.3
The Search Engine Watch site is the definitive source for search engine advice. Notice the long-winded title pertaining to all things, search engine.

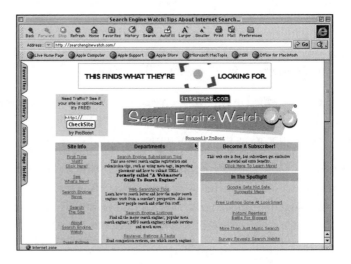

Headlines and Body Text

After a page's title, the headlines and first few sentences of the text are also heavily weighed by most search engines in determining the page's context. Unlike the page title, these elements are something readers will read carefully, so filling them with conspicuous lists of keywords is obviously impractical.

Nonetheless, those who live to keep their sites top-ranked in search results suggest emphasizing words that surfers are likely to chose as search terms when writing the text of Web pages, and to repeat key words frequently. It's at this point—when good writing style is sacrificed for the sake of a good ranking—that the shortcomings of search-engine technology become obvious.

Joe Kraus, cofounder of Excite, has advised that Webmasters stick to one theme per page. On a sports site, for example, write about golf on one page and about tennis on another. Writing about both subjects on the same page dilutes the weight a search engine gives to either category.

"It may seem like we're pigeonholing people," Mr. Kraus said. "Unlike a search engine, a directory edited by humans rather than software is a place where you can get listed in an appropriate category no matter how you present your content. But if you want a strategy for appearing at the top of a search engine's results page, it's an unfortunate fact that you're going to have to work within the bounds of how our technology tends to work."

Meta Tags

HTML *meta tags* are an important tool for prescribing how search engines should use descriptions and keywords for Web pages. They are not supported by all search engines, however. Some do not recognize meta tags on the grounds that site designers can too easily use them to "trick the engine" and mislead surfers.

Web browsers don't display the information in meta tags onscreen, but spiders can understand their instructions. There are several types of meta tags, but the two most common ones for the purposes of search engines are *description* and *keyword* tags.

Each meta tag, which is imbedded in the <head> section of the HTML code, is composed of two parts: a *name* field and a *content* field. The most popular use of meta tags in this context is to define the site description and keywords that a search engine should adopt. For example,

```
<HEAD>
<TITLE>Sue's Cajun Flavors</TITLE>
<META name="description" content="Buy hot sauces and other
condiments from Louisiana's Cajun cuisine">
<META name="keywords" content="hot sauce, cajun flavor, spicy
sauces, chili peppers, red hot, chilli, chile, Sue's Cajun flavors">
</HEAD>
```

Most engines that do recognize meta tags will use the description verbatim in their search results and take the suggested keywords into consideration. When determining page relevance, however, they might continue to place greater emphasis on the page title and other factors than on the keywords suggested in meta tags.

In the preceding example, notice the variations of individual keywords that form phrases. "Chili peppers" might be read by a search engine as a single term, but "chili" and "peppers" are also read separately. Ditto for "spicy sauces." Multiplying keywords in their variations, such as adding plurals, different verb forms (-ing, -es, -ed, and so on), or upper- and lowercase versions (chili and Chili), helps in a few search engines, but others, like AltaVista and InfoSeek, penalize sites for using this strategy. Do not forget, however, to consider common misspellings, alternate spellings, and possible typos, as previously shown.

More on Keywords

When the designer is submitting keywords into a search engine's registration and is limited to a certain number of them, she should opt for plurals or longer versions (for example, "skiing" instead of "ski"). The system is more likely to match a search for the shorter version when the longer one is listed than vice versa.

When a designer is deciding which keywords and keyword phrases are most appropriate for her site, she should invite friends and other outsiders to look at the site and give their suggestions. She might be so close to the project that she can't see the forest for the trees, and they might have a fresh perspective on which words come to mind to describe the site. She should also plug a few keywords she's sure about into a search engine and see which sites come up, and then look at the source code of those home pages to see which other keywords her competitors are using in their meta tags. There might be some words in there she hadn't considered.

A designer doesn't have to be a programming genius to do this kind of competitive intelligence, because the source code of just about every Web site can be viewed at will. Go into the "View" menu of your browser, and click on "Source." What you'll see is the bare bones HTML coding that describes the page.

One bad idea that some sites employ is including popular search terms such as "sex" in their list of meta tags, even though the site has nothing to do with that topic. The faulty reasoning behind this is that by picking such popular, although unrelated, search terms, they can misdirect some extra Web surfers to their site. The wise Web marketer should focus on results, not numbers. The site is unlikely to satisfy the prurient urges of someone looking for pictures of naked ladies with a $5 bottle of hot sauce.

Popularity

Several search engines adjust a site's ranking in their search results based on what the engines determine to be the site's "popularity." Engines such as **google.com** and **go.com** base popularity on the number of inbound links from other sites, though they will also weigh the "quality" of such links. A few hundred inbound links from amateur Web sites, in other words, might be balanced against whether or not a competitor is flush with inbound links from Yahoo! or Chase Manhattan. Of course, this isn't something a designer can influence when he's building his pages, but comes through gaining lots of inbound links to his site through all the methods of audience development and affiliate partnering discussed in the remainder of this book. Nearly all search engines allow the designer to check how many inbound links he has (see Chapter 6, "Word of Web: Email, Permission, and Viral Marketing").

DirectHit currently re-ranks sites on a daily basis according to how many users click through from its search pages. If an automotive site is #8 in the rankings of the automotive category, and enough people click through, the next day its ranking might rise to #7. Yes, the rankings are weighed to prevent "spiking" by automated programs and such. Which brings us to . . .

Spamdexing

As if the preceding strategies weren't enough to keep Webmasters busy, those who've become deeply obsessed by their ranking in search results often partake in a range of *keyword stacking* or *spamdexing* techniques. These include various ways to repeat phrases and keywords in such a manner that they're invisible to surfers but get noticed by spiders. Popular variations include the use of HTML comment tags or white text against a white background.

Search engines universally despise these techniques as a kind of cheating, and most attempt to punish sites they catch employing them by deliberately lowering their ranking in search results or excluding them from the search engine altogether.

The best advice is to avoid such techniques. If a designer can't resist, he should keep up with the cutting-edge spamdexing methods by viewing the source codes of porno sites, which can always be relied upon to pioneer the questionable innovations of Web promotion. (There, we justified the cover price of this book in one sentence. It's the perfect excuse if your boss catches you surfing the seamy underbelly of the Web: "I'm doing stealth market research!")

Follow the Leader . . . to the Source

If a designer prefers to take the high road, but she is still really stumped about why her site isn't appearing higher in search results, she should take a look at the source code of the sites that top the lists of her preferred keywords. What are they doing that she's not doing?

Figure 5.4

Business Web is one of several recently launched directories trying to gain a reputation in the B2B field.

Be careful, though. This is where good marketing strategies can turn into obsessive-compulsive behavior. First of all, if these competitors are topping the charts due to spamdexing techniques, bear in mind that copying such strategies might help you on one search engine but bar you entirely from others. Although the designer might achieve the position of top dog for a day, her competitors are likely to copy her code and unseat her with their own modifications, leading to a never-ending struggle to remain top-ranked when her efforts would be better spent on other site-promotion strategies.

In any event, she should not cut-and-paste copyrighted material from another site's source code, or she might find herself in real, legal trouble.

Pointer Pages

If achieving top-ranking in search results is indeed a burning priority for the site, the designer should consider contracting this task out to a service. **NewCanoe.com,** for example, like a handful of other consultants in the industry, can steer the designer to a full roster of rank-boosting boutique agencies, including firms that undertake the complicated and time-consuming creation of *pointer pages*.

Because the way engines weigh their rankings varies from one search service to the next, the best way for a site to remain at the top of all of them is for the designer to customize different home pages for each search engine. To the user, the content of such pointer home pages would appear identical, but the HTML code would vary according to what meta tags and other page elements best improve the search results for each engine.

Each pointer is assigned a unique URL, such as **www.hotsauces.com/a/index** for Excite, **www.hotsauces.com/b/index** for Lycos, and so on. The different pointer pages all link the same internal site content, except the home pages are customized.

Staying abreast of the minutely different and ever-changing strategies employed by each search engine is far more complicated and time-consuming for any site designer to bother with. Hence, outsourcing the whole headache of search ranking makes sense for many sites concerned with the issue.

Buy or Bid on Position

Another way to get a good ranking is to buy one. AOL will charge you megabucks to "buy" a keyword, so when its millions of subscribers search for "wingnuts," they'll end up at your site first, wingnutmania.com. On **GoTo.com**'s directory, a designer can bid the price he'll pay per click through to be listed among the top five or top 20 sites. The disadvantage to this free-market approach to ranking is that his competitor can outbid him (and hence outrank him) an hour later, by as little as a penny per click. **Kanoodle.com** seems to prefer a designer bid for placement when he submits a URL. Directories serving specific industry sectors might also rank Web sites higher if they purchase a position, or purchase banner ads.

Why Is Ranking So Important?

Search Engine rankings within the top ten listings of any category should be a priority goal for any company entering the consumer Internet marketplace without an already-established brand name. When surfers wind up with hundreds, if not thousands, of pages of search results—the whole lot grouped in pages of ten or so listings per page—it's obvious they are not going to stick around beyond the third, or even past the first page. This means that even though your site might be listed in a search engine, your customer might never bother to "drill down" deep enough to find it.

Avoid Dead-End Links

Search-engine spiders navigate their way around the Web by following the hyperlinks that join pages. But a great many spiders depend on clear text links in order to do this, because they only "read" text-based data. When text information is interrupted, the spider stops. So designers should try to keep spiders in mind when creating site navigation aids, especially the ones that appear on their home page.

Image Maps

If all the links on a given page are contained in image maps, a spider won't be able to follow them to the next level of the site. On pages with little or no text, the designer should use descriptive meta tags so search engines that support them can still index the content of the site. The best practice is to always include alternate text links in addition to graphic links so that spiders and visitors surfing with graphics turned off can continue to navigate the site.

Frames

Many search-engine spiders, like older versions of browsers, aren't frames-compliant and might not get past a site's first page if the designer hasn't allowed for a non-frames navigation route. Again, meta tags are useful on frames pages to allow spiders to index content topics, but designers should also provide an alternative navigation structure using the <noframes> tag. If months go by and search engines seem to be ignoring the site, the problem might be frames on its pages. (See the "Resources" section in Chapter 3, "Design Optimization," and the Appendix, "Internet Resources," for recommended HTML guides that further explain these issues.)

Password-Protected Pages

If some of the site's content is available only behind a password-protected page, the designer should make good use of meta tags on that page so search engines have some idea what lurks "behind closed doors." Some search engines can index password-protected sites if the designer makes special arrangements for them to have password access. That way, at least surfers will have an idea of what valuable content awaits within.

Dynamic Pages

If the site uses CGI scripts, database requests, or other methods to generate pages dynamically, the designer should be aware that most searching spiders and robots can't or won't index URLs with too many symbols, such as ?, /or the ever-popular =. The problem is purely technical: Some spiders can't see beyond a URL's first question mark. So the designer should consider creating some static parallel or pointer pages to register with search engines providing some context about her site, at least until this problem is solved. Search-engine companies are slowly moving toward establishing a standard method of indexing dynamic pages, and some new programming software exists that allows you to "rewrite" pesky symbols into language a spider can read. Look for updates on Search Engine Watch.

Robot Exclusion

There are some circumstances where a designer wants to prevent a spider from indexing her site or parts of it, such as during a beta-testing period.

The designer can accomplish this in more than one way. The quick and dirty way is by placing the *robots noindex* meta tag into the code of a given page, like this:

```
<meta name="robots" content="noindex">
```

But this doesn't work everywhere because not every search engine supports meta tags. Also, the tag needs to be included in the code of every page that the designer doesn't want indexed.

Better for this purpose is something called the Robots Exclusion Protocol, which allows site administrators to set up a robot.txt page with special instructions universally supported by search engine spiders (or *robots*). A robot.txt page can tell spiders to exclude an entire site or just specified sections of it.

This page must be created by the site's host administrator. If a designer uses an ISP or other service to host her pages, she'll need to coordinate with that administrator because she probably won't be able to upload a robot.txt page without special access.

The Robots Exclusion Protocol is a bit too technical to cover in this book, but you can find detailed instructions at the following URL:

http://info.webcrawler.com/mak/projects/robots/exclusion.html

If that URL is no longer valid, search **www.webcrawler.com** for "Robot Exclusion" and you should find the current pages.

General Submission Guidelines

As previously noted, a developer should wait until his site is fully ready before submitting it to search engines and directories. Likewise, he should resubmit the site's URL after a major redesign, with new descriptions and keywords as appropriate. Although the search-engine spiders should eventually track the site down regardless, some of them take months to revisit sites.

If the developer has several sections to his Web site that treat significantly different topics, he should submit each section URL to the same search engines and directories with unique descriptions and keywords so surfers can enter the site from various vantage points.

Whatever the developer does, however, he shouldn't resubmit the same page repeatedly to a search service in the span of a few weeks. Developers must be patient. Most of these services are receiving thousands of submissions a day, and it can take as long as three months to get posted. They should allow at least six weeks or so before deciding that the original submission didn't register. Most search services penalize sites that bombard them with duplicate submissions.

Yahoo!

All of the preceding advice about optimizing keywords in the site's title, meta tags, and so on, for the sake of search-engine spiders has no bearing at all on Yahoo! and other search directories. Yahoo!'s surf team doesn't look at meta tags and the like. They look at each site just as any normal visitor would. They take into account the suggestions for descriptions and keywords entered into their registration forms, but they might rewrite any or all of it in their database and stick the site into whatever category they see fit.

The most important thing for a site is to get listed at all. Yahoo! claims to have a liberal admissions policy, but it does reject many sites. In addition to making it easier for surfers to find good content, Yahoo! sees part of its job as keeping surfers from being distracted by bad content.

Many sites complain that trying to get listed in Yahoo! can be tremendously frustrating. The problem is one of scale. As the Web continues to grow at a phenomenal rate, Yahoo! is having trouble keeping up with the huge volume of submissions it receives. Search engines can generally throw more computers with faster processing speeds at the problem, but Yahoo!'s human staff has had much more difficulty scaling up to meet demand. It is in the developer's best interest to make their job as easy as possible.

Consider the Cool Factor

Although most of the sites in Yahoo!'s directories appear in alphabetical order in their respective categories, the surf team raises sites above the masses if they believe the sites deserve special attention. They also give a boost to sites deemed "cool" in staff or surfer's "Picks of the Week." Or they will put a "Review" icon next to those written about in *Yahoo! Internet Life* magazine. Refer to the "cool sites" sections with Yahoo! or a recent edition of the magazine to see what's currently interesting Yahoo! staffers.

Know Your Sub-Category

The first hurdle for developers to jump at Yahoo! is making a submission to the right subcategory, which saves the editors as much time in processing site submissions as possible. Yahoo! strives to keep its categories small and subdivides them when they grow too large. Topics such as flower delivery don't lend themselves to simple subcategorization, however, and do contain dozens—if not hundreds—of listings.

On the bright side, Yahoo! doesn't break up its listings of sites into 10 items per screen in an effort to sell more banner ads, unlike many of the search engines. It lists all the sites in a category on a single page, so even if the site appears low in the list, it's more likely that a surfer will take the time to scroll the whole list.

Forget About the ABCs

Once the site is in a Yahoo! category, it is listed in alphabetical order. So if the site's service begins with a "W," its designer can be pretty sure where it'll show up in the ranking.

A quick perusal of Yahoo! indicates that 372 sites think "A1" is a really clever name (see Figure 5.5).

Bearing in mind that Yahoo! itself begins with a "Y," where the site stands in the alphabet doesn't matter as much as what it has to offer. So, save A1 for hamburgers. Stick by a brand you can defend.

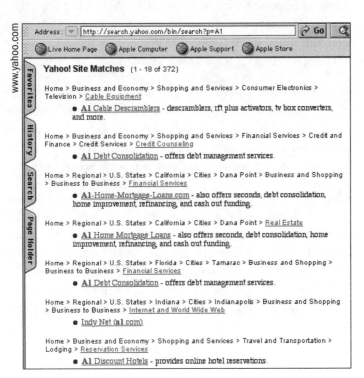

Figure 5.5
A1 apparently isn't just steak sauce anymore.

Use the Express Lane

The biggest problem with Yahoo! is that it can take as long as three months to get listed, so they added a new feature for business—the Business Express Submission Service. It is currently available only to Web sites submitting in Business and Economy subcategories—either under Companies or Products and Services. The invitation to partake appears on the screen after filling out the submission form.

The fee is about $200, which is an absolute bargain and the best investment a developer could make if getting his Web business launched is time-sensitive—and whose isn't? Rather than weeks, Business Express customers are often listed in a matter of days. The benefits to both businesses and directories that employ human searchers are obvious, and it is expected that by the end of 2000, both general directories and business-to-business directories will offer the chance for speedier service, at a price.

Specialty Directories

In addition to Yahoo! and the big search engines, there are thousands of specialty directories out there, covering everything from real estate to travel to gay services to science fiction. Whatever the topic, there's probably a specialty directory or five where it is beneficial for a site to be listed.

Where do you find such directories? Through directories of directories, of course. Yahoo! has a "Web directories" category. WebTaxi is also an interesting amalgamation of hundreds of search services, and Search Engine Watch keeps up as well. (See the "Resources" section at the end of this chapter for details.)

It's most effective for a developer to submit to the top directories individually so she can optimize each submission. Even with so many directories, only a few, perhaps, cater to the site's customer base and are worth the time and effort it takes to submit her pages—to each optimally. Should she feel the need to register her site with dozens of search guides or more, outsourcing the process to a consultant or automated service will save time. (See Figure 5.6.)

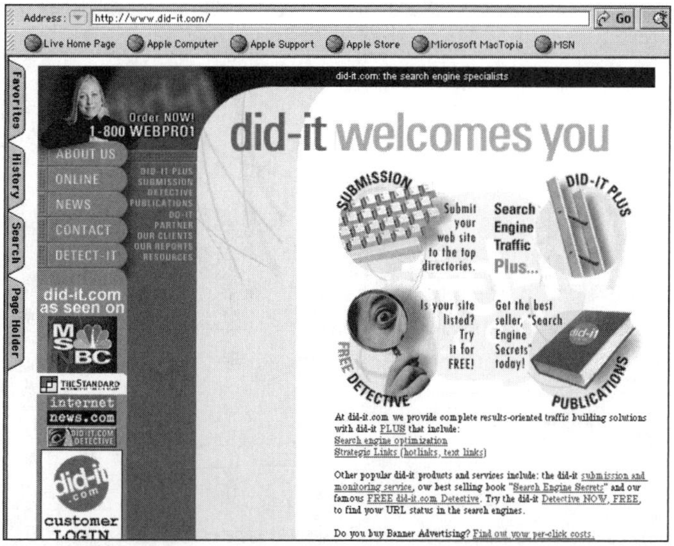

Figure 5.6
Did-it is one of several companies that provides submission services in a variety of packages, many with a free trial.

Quality Prevails

Registering a site with search engines and directories is a critical first step in promoting the site. It is by no means the lion's share of the promotion process, however. Developers should keep it in perspective, and not go overboard competing for top billing in search results. They'll only cost themselves ranking on other engines and waste energies better devoted elsewhere.

Along those lines, a final word from Jerry Yang, co-founder of Yahoo!:

"The good sites always turn up in the end. People somehow find them, not only through Yahoo! but by word of mouth. Those people who worry about superficial things, like whether their name starts with a triple-A, or who try to spoof search engines are generally running the sites without a lot of substance. Those who really devote themselves to good content or service always end up getting recognized in the end because the system is set up that way. People's patience level is very low for bad content, whereas they reward the best ones by telling other people. At that point, it's not anything that Yahoo! or AltaVista can do. Once you're good, *you're good*."

 **Resources**

Search Engine Watch
http://www.searchenginewatch.com

- Danny Sullivan created the definitive site about getting the most out of search engines, for both surfers and Web developers. The site offers a wealth of free advice, plus more detailed information for modest fees. Mr. Sullivan, based in England, also maintains a mailing list about the latest developments in the search engine field, to which you can subscribe from the site.

Planet Ocean
http//www.searchengine-news.com

- A subscription service that publishes *Search Engine News Update Newsletter*. New tips and techniques, plus frequently updated summaries of search engine requirements and must-to-avoids (such as, tricks that no longer work or are penalized) are also available to password-holders.

Submit-It
http://www.submit-it.com

- Founded in 1995 by Scott Bannister as a free service, Submit-It was acquired by Microsoft and has grown into a significant online promotion company, specializing in search engines and directories. Much information is still available for free, such as the section on "Search Engine Tips," but the more useful services are now fee-based.

Did-It
http://www.did-it.com

- A popular, scrappy site with a lot of good, free advice and a variety of fee-based services for submission and research.

New Canoe
http://www.newcanoe.com

- The professional team that practically invented the systematic practice of search engine optimization now offers strategic consulting and deployment of this and other forms of Web audience development.

Adability

http://adability.com

■ Vendor referral site with pointers to useful tools and services that process or verify submissions, check links, or help optimize your meta tags. Some, like Netmechanic's deadlink check and MSN's Site Inspector, are free.

Bruce Clay

http://www.bruceclay.com

■ Mr. Clay's site leans toward the ranking-obsessed, spamdexing school of thought, but the private consultant does provide some interesting advice, services, and links on the topic of search engines.

Position Agent

http://www.positionagent.com

■ Now a part of Microsoft's bCentral service. A free trial of a fee-based service enables you to check several search engines at once to see how your site ranks on each, according to certain keywords. Other services are also available. Worth a look.

WebTaxi

http://www.webtaxi.com

■ A funky conglomeration of hundreds of specialized and regional search services, but it's a valuable resource nonetheless.

Yahoo!'s Specialized Search Services Page

http://www.yahoo.com/Computers_and_Internet/Internet/World_Wide_Web/
Searching_the_Web/

■ Find links here to hundreds of specialized search engines and directories, including those in foreign countries.

Dynamic Page Workarounds

http://www.apache.org/docs/mod/mod_rewrite.html

■ This contains information about a module that rewrites dynamic page symbols for one flavor of server software.

Robot Exclusion

http://info.webcrawler.com/mak/projects/robots/exclusion.html

■ This page by Webcrawler explains how to prevent search-engine robots from searching pages you want to keep private with the Robot Exclusion Protocol, or robot.txt document.

IN THIS CHAPTER

chapter 6

Word of Web: Email, Permission, and Viral Marketing

FOR WEB MARKETERS WHO actively promote their sites to stand out against the masses, creativity and cost-efficiency demand they think beyond buying online banner and television advertising. While some industry reports predict that more than $50 billion a year will be spent on Web-related advertising by 2003, many additional routes to reach audiences are more cost-effective.

Numerous businesses already employ marketing techniques that take advantage of electronic mail, electronic paging, and real-time group messaging through the Internet. Many more recognize their strategic importance, but don't have the available staff or expertise to implement them. While it's true that many companies find it easier and quicker to outsource much of Web marketing, the most successful Web enterprises use in-house staff and resources to shape and direct these marketing strategies. And at a small site, a single individual might handle most of these activities alone.

To use the Internet effectively as a marketing medium, it is necessary to understand the evolving state of online interpersonal communications. This chapter deals with the delicate art of marketing through email messages, without ruining your reputation in the process.

Email Marketing without Tears

Sending unwanted, inappropriate or unsolicited messages to a user's email address is called *spamming*. More than simply the junk mail of the Internet, spam is reviled by all consumers and the Internet service providers (ISPs) that have to support a rising tide of messaging that slows down servers, crashes computers, spreads viruses, and irritates the heck out of anyone trying to download their business-related email on a Monday morning.

If you're hawking a get-rich-quick pyramid scheme through a P.O. box and a fortified anonymous remailer, then spamming might be reasonably effective online marketing. If you're trying to establish a legitimate online brand presence, however, don't even think about it. The damage it does destroys the reputation of your business online, not to mention your Web site's own email system, which is a sitting duck for the 100MB mailbomb files some angry recipient will arrange to send you 50 times in a row.

Some e-marketers keep insisting that people like to read spam. A survey released by FloNetwork, a firm that designs email campaigns, polled 1,000 users already actively buying products online, and found that most got an average of 10 unsolicited emails each week, but only a third of them considered it an invasion of privacy, and two percent actually liked it. But a whopping 65 percent reported it was no bother—they simply deleted the mail when it appeared.

All those surveyed were already volunteer members of a research panel of online users organized by National Family Opinion, a market research firm, and had agreed to be polled from time to time on Web marketing questions. Thus, in a group of 1,000 users already known to be marketing-receptive, approximately 650 were still deleting unsolicited email before it was read.

Netizens clearly distinguish between permissioned email and spam. Another phone survey by IMT strategies of some 400 adult email users found that more than half of all email users felt positively about permission (while most of the remaining are "neutral"). Nearly three-quarters of all email users report having responded to permission email with some frequency. By contrast, more than 80 percent feel negatively towards unsolicited messages and less than a third say they ever clicked on unsolicited messages more than once.

Cost Comparisons and ROI

What drives marketers to email in droves is that permissioned and well-targeted email campaigns can be inexpensive and highly effective. With regard to costs, if a typical print mail campaign costs 40 cents for printing and mailing, email delivery can be as low as 5 cents per unit. If purchased email lists are used, customer conversion costs might average $20 per customer; when existing, in-house email lists are used, conversion rates are typically higher, and conversion costs can drop to as low as $1 per customer.

If the goal is to create brand awareness and stimulate traffic to the site, consider a much cited Forrester Research study in April 1999. It found that email marketing was just as effective in stimulating clickthroughs as radio advertising and print direct mail, and slightly more effective than Web advertising using buttons or banners.

Clearly, then, one man's spam is another's meat and potatoes. When is an email message not spam?

- When it's expected.
- When it's targeted.
- When it provides useful information to the user.

Spam levels can theoretically be judged by the response rate. Perhaps that's why some email marketers shy away from measuring performance at all. A spring 2000 study by IMT Strategies queried 169 email marketers and found that only 59 percent were measuring email campaign performance by either click-through rates (CTR), conversion rates, or both, and 41 percent were not tracking performance by either measure.

Responsible email marketers should carefully track both click-throughs and conversion rates, to monitor not only costs but also "customer fatigue" caused by too-frequent mailings. A quick way to spam-test any past or current email campaign is to look at the "unsubscribe" rate. Because the act of unsubscribing indicates dissatisfaction by the recipient, any campaign with an unsubscribe rate higher than one percent should be red flagged, scrutinized, and altered if not dropped entirely.

Online Origins of "Spam"

There are a few theories about how the Hormel Foods Company's product Spam (a contraction of "spiced ham") came to mean "junk advertising on the Internet."

The most amusing idea is that it comes from a prank that some MIT students allegedly played. They froze a block of the luncheon meat with dry ice and then threw it into another student's dorm room. It supposedly exploded upon impact, coating the unfortunate student's living quarters with thousands of tiny Spam fragments. This story sounds too good to be true and is likely a cyber-legend.

Others suggest that it's an acronym for something along the lines of "Stupidly Posted Advertising Messages."

However, we subscribe to the most popular theory, that it derives from the classic Monty Python routine where a chorus of Vikings at a diner burst into song in praise of the stuff, repeating "Spam, Spam, Spam, Spam . . . " Online spammers, then, are likewise just repeating themselves ad nauseam. (A little pun there: "ad nauseam." Har, har. Pun intended.)

Meanwhile, some in the marketing community prefer the term "UCE," for "unsolicited commercial email," in deference to Hormel's trademark.

The Internet's obsession with Spam doesn't end with junk mail and Usenet abuse, however. In addition to dozens of fan sites devoted to the glory of the reconstituted meat product, a distinctly '90s pop art form has swept the Internet: Spam haiku. Search for those two words on any search engine and you'll find hundreds of these delectable ditties:

Pink tender morsel,
Glistening with salty gel
What the hell is it?

In the cool morning
I fry up a slab of Spam
A dog barks next door

Slicing your sweet self
Salivating in suspense
Sizzle, sizzle . . . Spam

Pink beefy temptress
I can no longer remain
Vegetarian

"Permission" Email Marketing

In the business environment of the Web, the fleeting benefits of attracting "eyeballs" pale in comparison to the joy of securing the email addresses of potential customers. Email addresses are now commodities, bought and sold on the open market. Paradoxically, in a medium where privacy is not just prized but legislatively fought for, addresses are solicited, swapped, and stolen with even more vigor.

Not just e-commerce sites but nearly all Web sites troll for addresses now. A fan site might invite the visitor to "sign a guest book" or a B2B might require the user to "register" in order to reach content hidden beyond password-protected pages. Even sites left wide open to user navigation might include the use of an address entry field, which must be filled out to enter a contest, qualify for a coupon, or test-drive an interactive sequence or online tool. (See Figure 6.1.)

The industry kids itself by calling this "permission marketing." In other words, you've provided the address; don't be surprised if you hear from us soon. Some polite businesses add a field or set of buttons that ask if the user would desire to receive news or data updates, or coupons and special offers, through email. That's the famous "opt-in, opt-out" sequence, guaranteed to protect the user against spam the way a piece of cheesecloth protects against a hard rain.

"We'll never share your email address with anyone!" the Web sites plead. "We promise! Never!"

The cynical might want to click on to the site's privacy statement, which further defines that promise as, "they won't share your information with anyone except related companies, affiliated companies, online partners, or parent companies." (See Figure 6.2.)

Figure 6.1

The New York Times now lets its registered users control the amount of "massmail" through this preference page.

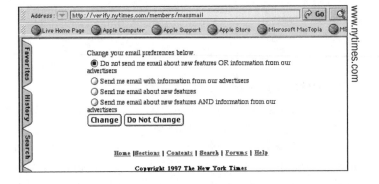

Figure 6.2

The New York Times Web site privacy statement notifies readers that it might give out their email addresses to its advertisers once they register an "opt in."

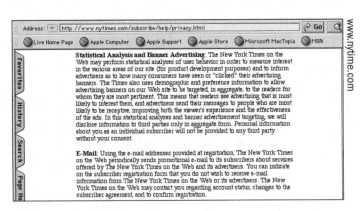

A great deal of address gathering is more subtle. A business Web site offering downloads of a market report takes down the user's address as it transmits the Adobe Acrobat file; a visitor with a question or comment must click to an email response page that records her address. News publishing Web sites typically give users the option to email an article to a friend or colleague. To do this, the user types in his email address and the friend's email address. Now the marketer has two names, not just one.

There is a big difference between all of this and the "best practice" email techniques that can gain clickthrough rates as high as 30 percent. The biggest difference, again, is making sure it's a truly permissioned list.

Some consumers will always click on unsolicited email, but that's no reason to hasten the arrival of that critical saturation point where customers close the door on further email solicitation.

Companies that attempt to operate in the gray areas of customer consent risk eroding customer relationships and destroying brand equity. Most importantly, marketers must appreciate that the window of opportunity permission email represents will close. Within three years, customers will become "email saturated." Only those organizations that establish customer email relationships, nurture permission list assets, and build a strong permission email knowledge and experience base will continue to reap maximum reward from permission marketing in the future. (See Figure 6.3.)

Purchased Lists

Some Web businesses exist solely to attract lists of permission-based email addresses to sell or rent to online marketers for controlled, targeted direct email offers. The larger players include NetCreations (the PostMaster Direct company) YesMail and MyPoints. Users opt-in to the programs, giving their permission to receive email offers for topics ranging from golf to investment news to C++ programming, along with demographic data about themselves. In the case of MyPoints, the service offers incentives for users to respond in the form of points that can be redeemed for merchandise and services.

Figure 6.3

Fingerhut's Web site takes the high road to active consent; if a user fails to choose opt-in or opt-out in the first pass, a second prompt screen asks again.

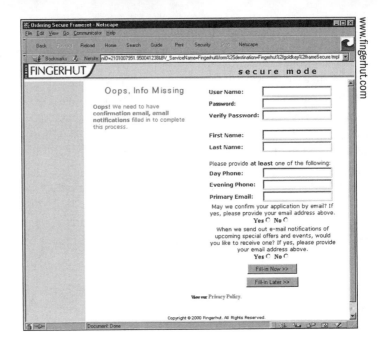

These services can represent reasonable acquisition vehicles for marketers, with campaign conversion rates typically along the order of direct mail response rates of 1 to 2 percent. Cost per thousand (CPM) rates for access to names are under market pressure to decline from present ratecard prices of $150-300 CPM. Critically, marketers must be careful to ensure that the highest standards in soliciting customer permission are used in the opt-in process when collecting email addresses. The previously named services adhere to the highest standard of permission—"double opt-in," which means users not only must actively check a box and say they want to receive mail from the service, but they must further reply to an email confirming they really intended to do so.

At the same time, there is no shortage of suppliers out there with thousands or millions of email addresses that should be scrupulously avoided by marketers looking to build long-term, customer-friendly, brand positive businesses.

Frequent ploys and scams to collect email with little or no permission include "opt-out" policies (when users must actively uncheck a box that is usually small and easy to overlook.) If they do not, they grant "permission" by default, or worse, without any mention of email marketing policies, and must opt-out after the fact by sending email to an "unsubscribe" address; sweepstakes and contests (bogus or otherwise) with no notification of email use policy; or the ever-popular search spider software robot scouring Web pages, discussion boards, Usenet, eBay and other public e-venues where email addresses are likely to be posted.

Make no mistake, these are worst-practices and should be avoided by marketers themselves and by all their e-marketing business partners. Marketers in search of the best return on investment in the short and long term would be wise to do business only with those permission list brokers who subscribe to the highest permission standard of double-opt-in.

In exchange for their addresses and demographic data, users are offered cash, free merchandise, sweepstakes opportunities, and other goodies. Participants are on the honor system to provide truthful data, take that as you will. On the other hand, if the audience is general and youthful, and the goal is to blanket the globe with brand awareness, the legions of casual surfers who keep themselves in pocket change by selling their multiple addresses might be just what is required.

As previously discussed, Net surfers often are induced to provide their individual addresses to lists that will be traded or sold. These users might prove unresponsive, if not outright hostile, to unsolicited messaging. A user that's traded his address in exchange for some freebie might be interested in the site's wares if he is part of a targeted list. As with print direct mail, purchased lists vary in quality by vendor, and are priced along the same lines, typically in the CPM range of $0.25 per address to $40 per thousand addresses. (See Figure 6.4.)

Higher-priced, well-targeted purchased lists are most useful if used by a start-up company with a clear customer market focus and no cache of existing customers. But bear in mind that netizens who have never heard of the company are likely to rate the unsolicited e-message pretty high on their spam-o-meters.

Customer-Generated Mailing Lists

The statistics of sales conversion argue that your best customer is the one who already buys from you. On the Web, the next best prospect is one that's already found your company Web site and knows that you exist. One of the reasons all Web sites now avidly collect address data is to do their own email marketing in-house. (See Figure 6.5.)

If a Web site hasn't been launched yet, a business-to-business firm can still have the start of a good list. Salespeople might already have the equivalent of an email Rolodex of clients, with whom they communicate through home or office computers. Business cards collected at trade shows and conferences, printed purchase orders, and snail mail stationery from prospects no doubt all include a general email contact, if not a personal email address of the target buyer.

A mature Web site running e-commerce software is sitting on a mother lode of address data. Tempting as it is to fire away an email advertisement to every address, Web marketers should try to restrain themselves, at least until they've seen how detailed their data can be.

Sales software that includes customized functions or cookie sales data can help separate customer addresses per product line. The most sophisticated products can not only detail who bought what, but will even deploy automatic email messaging that includes a customized coupon or offer.

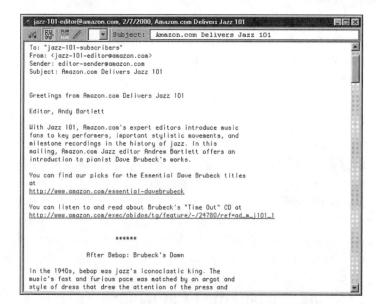

Figure 6.5

Amazon.com's jazz newsletter is sent only to customers who request it. The ratio of sales pitch to information is acceptably within range for customer Rick.

All cookie-generating software can be mined for useful data. Even a simple shopping-cart program can provide a print-out that shows which addresses have bought something within the last quarter or last year.

Names Versus Actively "Permissioned" Customers

Address lists gathered from other parts of a mature Web site can be useful, too. Folks who filled in a form to enter a contest might not buy anything, but an email message might prompt a recollection of the brand name. A coupon or special offer might tempt them back to the site. Ongoing, on-site promotions should always include an invitation to sign up for "permission" messages. Make the option friendly and stick to just an address field; asking for too much demographic data too soon is a turn-off.

Addresses culled from online chats or bulletin board discussion groups might be sent an invitation to join a market focus group. On a business-to-business site, complaints or comments received through customer service or online customer support can be scrutinized to see if anyone needs to be sent a conciliatory e-note (with a special offer enclosed).

Do not use these addresses for routine sales pitches, weekly newsletters, or anything impersonally targeted that it would be considered spam. The wishes of users who did not specifically "opt-in" to future messaging should be respected. Users who did not opt-in to receive messages should be left alone.

Many email marketers continue to insist that anyone who hasn't actively "opted-out" is fair game for a sales pitch, on the theory that a list of passive or possibly hostile recipients is better than no list at all. The inevitable result has been a dilution of the impact of email messaging. To cut through the clutter, the online marketer must be constantly on the lookout for creative packages to attract customers, while striving to retain and enhance loyal customers on their existing lists.

Creating Online Email Campaigns

While verifying and qualifying a list, begin to design what's called the "offer." As with print direct mail, good email marketing messages all have a call to action. The site will probably indicate that the recipient "click here"—either on a live text link or pop-up graphic image—to transport the recipient to hosted Web pages related to the offer.

The offer should provide an incentive to clickthrough, not just an invitation to view the site. Common incentives for business-to-business mailings include the promise of useful information (sign up for a newsletter, receive the latest business statistics on this or that) or a sales promotion (click for a 20 percent discount, special Web-only merchandise offer). Incentives for consumer mailings are a promotional giveaway, special sale or special item promotion, or the always-popular game of chance (sweepstakes, lottery, game with a prize). Let the bean-counters figure out how much you can afford to spend in customer acquisition and choose your incentive accordingly. Don't forget that for most of the Internet set, the offer of unique information might be a more compelling call to action than any sort of crackerjack prize. (See Figures 6.6 and 6.7.)

```
Hello Mia Amato!

By popular demand Oki Semiconductor has created a special multimedia
Comic Strip for you to customize and send to friends or associates.

In this episode "Marketing Attacks Engineering" you can help our hero
escape the mindless demands of product marketing by selecting a variety
of scenes, power suits, weapons and music to create your own comic.

View your comic at:
http://www.okisemi.com/card-redir.cgi?c=v0nrpJQiKiPJ&flag=new

Have fun -- courtesy of Oki Semiconductor.
```

Figure 6.6

This email invitation directs the user to a live link that promises a bit of humor during the business day.

Figure 6.7

Payoff for clicking is a do-it-yourself comic strip, with a selection of heroes, scenarios and hilarious musical soundtracks, which can be sent to colleagues. Passalong rate for this ad, which introduced a new product, was high in its target audience of MIS engineers.

I'm Gonna Sit Right Down and . . .

Writing the email message has two main elements: The *header* and the body text. The header is the text phrase that appears in the "subject" field of an email message. Like the headlines on a news story, the header telegraphs briefly what the message is about, and why it matters. "Lose Weight Now!" and "Make Money at Home!" are self-explanatory, and sadly, all too common headers. It's better to be specific—"Free DSL service from Globalcom" or "Congressional Telecom Update." Telegraph what the news is, and where it comes from. An individual's name is generally not advisable; use the space to brand the company. That's the name people are most likely to recognize.

Bodies of email marketing messages should generally be brief. Marketers debate whether short or long email messages work best, and there's evidence to support both sides; it appears to depend entirely on context. What's important is to be consistent. The messages should have the same look and feel each time and create for the customer a comfortable familiarity. Longer messages should be made easy to read and navigate; if it is a newsletter, consider using a table of contents at the top.

At the top of the message, include some introduction or greeting that reminds the reader why she is receiving this message, such as

> "Dear Joan,
>
> Here is your latest issue of Wingnuts News. You are receiving this because you signed up to subscribe at our Web site. If you believe this message reached you in error or you wish to unsubscribe, see the bottom of this message for details."

It is standard best practice to give users the opportunity to remove themselves from a mailing list with *every* message sent, in the form of an email address they can reply to for auto-removal and/or a URL where they can unsubscribe simply on a Web page. Messages should always provide the email and phone number of a contact person, should anyone have a question.

For more complete best practice standards, refer to the "AIMing for Best Practice" sidebar in this section with the guidelines for responsible email from the Association for Interactive Media (AIM), a subsidiary of the Direct Marketing Association (DMA).

AIMing for Best Practice

The Council for Responsible Email, part of the Association for Interactive Media (AIM) suggested the following six guidelines to protect consumers from the scourge of spam. We amend them as follows:

1. Never use a false domain name or non-responsive Internet protocol (IP) address.
2. Never falsify the subject line to mislead readers about message content.
3. Always include an option for the recipient to unsubscribe.
4. When collecting addresses, always inform the respondent for what marketing purpose the respondent's email address will be used.

5. Do not harvest or purchase email addresses with the intent to send bulk unsolicited commercial email. (Harvest is defined by AIM as compiling or stealing email addresses through collection procedures such as a Web spider, or from chat rooms, or other publicly displayed Internet areas that list personal or business email addresses.)

6. Be wary of sending bulk unsolicited commercial email to any email address unless you enjoy a prior business or personal relationship with the user. (Opt-in lists, online correspondence, and registrations do count as relationships; well-permissioned lists purchased from a third party also count, as they imply the expectation of future communications from unknown firms.)

Some technical parameters that can be tested include using text-only messages, messages with HTML coding, or rich media messages sent in larger files, either in body copy or as an attachment. Many recent studies seem to indicate that rich media messages elicit higher response rates than straight text or HTML messages. Messages to permissioned addresses should be short and contain one, if not two, calls to action.

Personalized greetings are a plus, if you're sure you've got a permissioned list. Identify the organization in the "from" field at the top of the message and in the signature at the bottom as well (see "Tips on Signatures").

Rich Media in Email

Want to double or even triple your email response rate? Some companies have experienced very high response levels using enriched media (animation, audio, interactive games) within the body of their email messages. Animated mail is now familiar to anyone who's received an interactive greeting card from their Aunt Anne in Abilene through AOL, and no one knows how long the novelty factor will last.

Creativity need not be expensive. Don't feel you have to run a 30–second TV commercial when a snappy, five–second animation might be just as effective as an attention-grabber, and fits nicely into a 4K mail file. Aside from cost, the only obstacle to enhanced mailings is that current technologies don't deploy if the user is reading her mail messages while offline; live connections are required. This problem is likely to be solved as vendors such as Bluestreak, MindArrow, and Radical Mail continue to push the envelope (see Resources).

Keep Your Mail from Becoming Spam

The key is *frequency management*. If your sister-in-law telephones you every few months with news and a chat, that's welcome information. If your sister-in-law calls you every day, or telephones you at the office every Monday morning at 9 a.m., that's an annoyance. And if your sister-in-law sent you an email every Monday morning, with a big GIF photo of the kids or her new list of knock-knock jokes, you'd probably be jamming the delete key with speed, because that's spam.

An example of frequency management that's targeted to the individual user are the email alerts available by subscription through the Wall Street Journal's online information service, **wsj.com**. Users can subscribe to alerts in different business sectors; the "Technology Alert" service sends a message whenever a news item about a high-tech, publicly-held company appears because any information in the business press is likely to affect stock price. Needless to say, such information is always welcomed by a certain segment of this email audience.

Consumer products can also use this technique. Claritin, the prescription allergy medicine brand, offers a service at its site where users can enter their zip codes and what types of pollens they're allergic to, and the site will send them an email update whenever the pollen count in their area changes substantially. For a person with severe allergies, that service would probably be welcome every day, if it means the difference between taking extra medication or not.

Weekly email newsletters to customers can be classic spam; even when requested, a great many are never read. Earthlink sends its ISP members a 10KB file full of promotional copy and sponsored links, for example, which is absolutely extraneous to its core business. **CDNow.com**, which sells music products, became notorious for sending online customers three or four emails each week, whenever new releases came in stock. Automated mailings like this often infuriate people.

B2B newsletters tend to fare better, for even those without paid subscriptions are perceived as having high information value. But it only works if you *send* high information value in the form of exclusive reports, top-level consultant opinion, or "first looks" at new gear.

In business-to-business applications, try to restrict messages to real news, or truly fabulous price breaks, no more than once a month. Do not clutter an executive's inbox with press releases, routine discounts, or large attached files that illustrate the latest color product brochure.

Do include a live link to the Web pages in postings whenever an email offer involves an action step. Most Web-based email programs, even those accessed by wireless remotes, allow a quick jump from mail to Web and back again.

Personalizing the Message

In the Internet realm, personalization means the sort of targeted messaging that is based on a customer's past behavior online, which can be a rather substantial customer file of past purchase data. Privacy advocates should note that keeping a computer file of purchase behavior on a Web site is, truly, no different than a restaurant maitre'd's index card file of customer preferences (no smoking section, hates scungilli, orders brandy with decaf at the end of a meal, and so on). In the case of the Internet, increasingly, a merchant can know virtually everything about a client but, due to privacy firewalls, not know his or her actual name or home address.

Marketers dream of the day when personalization software serves up a product offering, or a product recommendation, even before the customer knows he has a need. Armed with cookie data and "permissioned" addresses, it is already possible that a user who just purchased an airline ticket to Bali on Web site "A" could immediately get an email sales pitch for swimsuits sold on Web site "B", and a cheery hello from Web site "C", which would like to know, does he need any traveler's checks or currency?

Properly executed, an email campaign using personalization can be perceived as a value-added service. One such popular and successful email advertising ploy is to sign up the customer for a "reminder service." Gift-related sites such as **crateandbarrel.com** send customers an email alert for anniversaries, birthdays, and holidays. **Officedepot.com** will, on request, send a reminder to check stocks of printer paper or toner before supplies run out. **Pampers.com** sends a weekly newsletter with advice for new parents; the information changes along with the age of the child.

A lot of these strategies mimic direct-mail and catalog campaigns of yore, but the Internet twist is to give these offers the glamour of real-time interactivity. Many customers will eagerly sign up to be notified of "special members-only offers" by email. Put a time limit (offer expires 00-00-00) on the email offer, embed the URL in the message, and see how it does.

Privacy issues cloud the future of personalized advertising on the Web. The notion that an online vendor is keeping a running list of all the books each customer has purchased online makes many folks uncomfortable. Will it be worse when a Web site starts tracking a woman's hip girth from Size 12 to Size 16?

When that woman gets an email invitation to view a "big gals" online swimwear catalog, will she be offended? Or grateful? When is personal too personal?

Response Management

Put an "unsubscribe" message at the bottom of each marketing email and use that to monitor the spam levels. Replies to messages should be examined by someone, not just kicked back to an auto-responder. Auto-responders can be used to track "dead letters" with undeliverable email addresses.

Coolsavings, which regularly recruits users for mailing lists, uses this polite method for unsubscribing:

"If you feel you have received this message in error, or if you no longer wish to receive reminders, please forward this message to: remove@coolsavings.com

Thank you for reading this CoolSavings email."

Part of the email marketing material should include an apologetic personal response to anyone who replies and accuses you of spam. Have one ready in the file—and with care you won't have to use it.

Viral Marketing in Natural Web Communities

Viral marketing is a natural consequence of any well-presented Web site branding effort. If the site is a good one, visitors will pass on the news to their friends, and more often than not, they'll pass that news along through personal emails. The savvy Web marketer can use a variety of techniques to speed up this process, taking care to use these personal channels without ever appearing to spam.

Deliberate viral marketing often pays off handsomely in terms of adding addresses to existing email lists. Some surveys cited from Jupiter have suggested that as much as 81 percent of those who receive an appealing, pass-along message will re-mail the news to someone else; nearly 49 percent will pass it along to two or three others.

Audience "Advocates" and Private Email

There so are many variations on "tell-a-friend" email marketing they might make a book just by themselves. Users reading content off a Web site can be invited to send that page, with its information, to a colleague or family member. All they have to do is type in their email address and the other person's, and click "send." Or a user might receive an email informing them about a special offer, in a message format allowing them to forward that email to another person.

The advantages of spreading a message through "known" messengers in a spam-shy marketplace are quite clear. Even if the header in the subject field means nothing to customers, they are more likely to open an email if the "from" field indicates the sender was their mentor or mother. Much in the same way the destructive "I Love You" virus permeated the Internet community in a matter of hours, a pass-along marketing message can vibrate from one end of the electronic universe to the other, piggybacking from sender to sender and so on. (Yes, this is why it's called *viral* marketing.)

Tell-a-friend techniques succeed when both sender and receiver feel they've gained something out of the interaction. Both sender and receiver might get an extra chance to win a prize or get discount coupons. In a recent branding campaign for **Productopia.com**, senders were encouraged to provide the email addresses of five friends to gain up to five extra entries in an online contest. The sender could also choose to send the pass-along message in the form of a colorful email greeting card, which further personalized the transaction between both parties.

Sometimes viral campaigns just take off. The movie *Blair Witch Project* famously received huge advance publicity with a beautifully executed email and Web guerrilla marketing campaign. The Dancing Baby, the hilarious 3D animation promoting a now-forgotten 3D animation design tool, was such a pass-along sensation that it became a plot point on a TV show (*Ally McBeal*).

Usenet and Listservs

One of the oldest traditions of the Internet is that of the non-commercial forums called newsgroups. There are about 20,000 such discussion forums, many of them global in scope, on every technical or trivial subject you can imagine. Some of these discussions have gone on for decades or more still archived on Usenet, a system of computer networking protocols that pre-dates, interacts with, and exists entirely independently of the World Wide Web in cyberspace.

Usenet communities began to evolve in 1979, originally to share technical data among computer scientists, and later as a medium for everything from political manifestos to pornography. Communications in newsgroups are simply typed in as text messages, also called "postings," which can be viewed by anyone with access to the hosting server computer. On listservs, electronic mail is used to post single messages to groups of subscribers, who can respond round-robin style, using mail commands such as "reply to all" or "forward." (See Figure 6.8.)

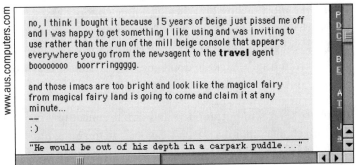

no, I think I bought it because 15 years of beige just pissed me off and I was happy to get something I like using and was inviting to use rather than the run of the mill beige console that appears everywhere you go from the newsagent to the **travel** agent booooooooo   boorrringgggg.

and those imacs are too bright and look like the magical fairy from magical fairy land is going to come and claim it at any minute...
--
:)

"He would be out of his depth in a carpark puddle..."

Figure 6.8

An Australian computer user reveals why he really bought a new HP Pavilion on the aus.computers newsgroup.

Threaded discussions have since been adopted into commercial Web sites, in the form of user bulletin boards, "forums" or discussion groups (more following). The heyday of Usenet might be waning, but it is perhaps only a matter of time before these "accidental aggregators" come to the realization that they are sitting on address lists and eyeball destinations that marketers crave. Some newsgroup moderators and listserv hosts have set up Web sites for the recompense of ad sales and affiliate program profit-sharing, but many more are less tempted by greed than afraid of "selling out" their loyal respondents. While these emotions are sorted out, it behooves the Web marketer to become familiar with newsgroup communities, for these include some sophisticated sets of audiences for specific information, audiences which are of value to both business-to-business and business-to-consumer Web marketing.

Because it's nearly impossible to quantify exactly how many users will find the site as a result of a newsgroup posting, many Web marketers ignore Usenet, which can be a mistake. As loyal followers of their particular topics, newsgroup members will frequently belong to other, commercial online forums related to the subject. As a result, they're likely to pass on news from the newsgroup to others through email and fan Web sites, helping build an audience by viral word of Web.

Thou Shalt Not Spam

The Internet purists reading this might already be outraged to see us advocating commercial promotions in newsgroups at all. Blatant advertising, especially across multiple newsgroups, is among the most deadly breaches of online conduct and can be met with serious consequences. Spamming a newsgroup is grounds for getting kicked off an ISP, if the mail bombs and viruses from angry hackers don't melt the systems, crash the servers, and shut the site down first.

There are several important do's and don'ts concerning promotion on Usenet, mainly, "Don't Spam," "Don't Spam," and "Don't Spam."

Find the Right Audience

The key to using Usenet effectively for promotion is to serve newsgroup participants' interests in a specific topic. The whole point of newsgroups is their extreme specificity. In alt.barney. dinosaur.die.die.die, participants want to discuss death fantasies about the purple-costumed children's television character and not much else. Craft the announcement to read more like a service to them than a service to a business. Instead of screaming "advertisement," murmur "helpful recommendation." Always aim for high information value in all newsgroup communications.

Some newsgroups, those that contain .biz or .marketplace in their names, often welcome text advertisements or press releases. Many .biz and .marketplace newsgroups, however, are little more than spam ghettos, less forums for active discussion than for free classified postings.

While nearly all ISPs provide Usenet access, the easiest way to find appropriate newsgroups is through the Deja News Web site, a popular Usenet search engine (see Figure 6.9). Deja News lets the user search for words appearing in the text of individual messages across Usenet. Try searching for your brand name and see if anyone is saying kind or negative things about it. Or search for terms related to its products to see which newsgroups might be interested in the site.

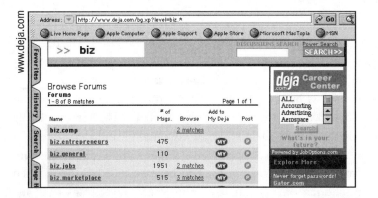

Figure 6.9

By far, the best Usenet search utility is Deja.com, formerly Deja News, a one-stop shop for all newsgroup activities.

How Not to Do It

An incident from the early days illustrates how the name of a newsgroup might not indicate its true character.

Coinciding with Microsoft's launch of Windows 95, Bob and Leland had a client, BPR Publications, which established an area of its site to track every press release issued about Windows 95, from both Microsoft and third parties.

They identified more than 60 newsgroups that were apparently devoted to the Windows family of operating systems. Next, they put together a short announcement calling attention to BPR's new service and posted it to those newsgroups.

The announcement was met with enthusiasm by all but one newsgroup. One of its members wrote us a civil note informing us that the newsgroup had nothing to do with the computer industry at all, but rather was dedicated to professional window washing!

```
Subject: Affiliate Tracking

John:

I just read your I-Sales posting. I don't know what is causing your
problem, but I think you're using the wrong technology. Why don't
you concentrate on doing what you do best and let an affiliate
management company concentrate on what it does best? They'll take
care of the fraud issues, serving the banners, online tracking and
reports 24 hours per day, mailing checks to your affiliates, etc.

We started in November with zero affiliates and now have about
```

Figure 6.10

Is this message making a pitch to this newsgroup, or is it offering brief, personal, and helpful peer advice?

Free Mailing Lists (Listservs)

Another type of community forum that evolved in the pre-Web era of Usenet were the "free" mailing lists, known as *listservs* (after the generic name for the software that administers them, spelled without the final "e" due to the eight-character limit on older IBM mainframe and UNIX systems). They are much like newsgroups in their sense of community and devotion to a single topic, but as their name implies, these discussions are email-based. Marketers need to be even more cautious when promoting on mailing lists, however, to avoid upsetting list members.

Today, companies such as eGroups and Topica have built their businesses on letting people create their own email discussion groups for free, from college cliques to industry influences, thousands of people have used the services to create large and small communities of their own.

Subscribers sign up to receive every message posted to the list directly in their email boxes. Because of this high level of commitment by users, mailing lists tend to have a strong "signal-to-noise" ratio—that is, they prefer quality information over pointless banter. The tolerance for shameless self-promotion, therefore, is especially low.

That doesn't mean members won't appreciate announcements of highly relevant information. Keep the hype to a minimum and be darn sure that submissions are keenly targeted to the list topic.

Finding Lists

Discovering which mailing lists serve a given topic isn't as simple as it is with newsgroups, which are listed together on every Usenet server. Mailing lists are maintained by thousands of separate servers across the Internet.

The best directory of listserv mailing lists is Liszt, founded in 1995 and still found at **liszt.com**, which was recently acquired by Topica (see Figure 6.11). At last check this site claimed to index more than 90,000 lists, Usenet forums, and Internet relay chats (IRCs). And, as a sign of the times, Liszt now sells its own "permissioned" lists.

Figure 6.11

The huge Liszt directory is the place to start researching listserv lists.

Guerrilla Marketing Through Online Groups

Some newsgroups, listservs, and bulletin boards remain uncompromisingly hostile to any contribution that smacks of commercial self-promotion in the slightest. But seeding discussions is a common tactic by Usenet-savvy marketers, and there are ways to cloak a ploy without inviting everlasting scorn by thousands of potential customers.

First, browse the discussions taking place and look for opportunities to answer questions that lend themselves towards a mention of the site. If replying as an individual to a legitimate question, few could fault you for slipping in a subtle plug. In providing straight answers to real questions, the company signature might be all that is needed to refer to the site. (See "Tips on Signatures" later in this chapter.)

Keep posts short (one or two paragraphs), write in a casual voice, and, as with all kinds of online messages, use a descriptive and compelling subject line.

A sneakier strategy is to initiate a discussion incognito, much like a magician using a shill in the audience who pretends to be an ordinary spectator but is actually in on the trick. Using an identity that masks your affiliation with the company you're promoting, ask a leading question such as whether anyone knows where to find such-and-such information. Then, using a second online identity, post an answer to your own question, recommending that your first identity visit the site.

Needless to say, this strategy doesn't come without risks. Make sure to use entirely separate domains in your return addresses. If discovered, you might well be met with outrage by newsgroup members who deem it cheating.

This is not endorsed as a regular practice, but in some cases it is the most appropriate way to share information about certain highly targeted products. Do so only when you believe your contributions would truly benefit members of a group that is otherwise unreceptive to more straightforward promotional posts. (See Figure 6.12.)

Figure 6.12

The Online Advertising Discussion List is a must-read for anyone involved with online ad sales. Many companies use the list to call attention to their own products and sites, but always within the context of an example that could benefit other readers.

Lurk and Learn

The need to lurk before you post is particularly important on mailing lists. A newsgroup might have dozens or hundreds of messages available for you to peruse in order to grasp the tone of the community. A busy mailing list, on the other hand, might generate only a dozen or so messages a day. For this reason, it is strongly recommended that you lurk for two weeks before posting. Frequently, lists archive discussions on a Web site, which can speed up a newcomer's introduction to the group.

Many lists allow, even encourage, well-targeted one-off announcements about new online services. Where possible, however, much more can be done for brand identity by fully joining the list community and establishing credibility through ongoing contributions in answering members' questions.

Marketers are encouraged to subscribe to the most important few mailing lists related to the topic of their Web sites. Think of mailing lists as perpetual industry seminars. Some of the participants on the industry's lists are likely to be the panelists at conferences that marketers will attend in the real world. Mailing lists give them instant peer access to these and other leaders in the field. It's networking, in many senses of the word.

Befriend Moderators

Most interactive lists and newsgroups have a moderator who reviews every submission before allowing it to be posted. In addition to leading discussions on occasion, the moderator controls the quality of the list, filtering out spam, offensive language, name-calling, and the like.

If a marketer wants to post an announcement to a list that he doesn't regularly read, a useful tactic is to send his announcement directly to the moderator. He should explain that he doesn't know the list's policy on announcements, but that he believes his post would be of interest to the readers. He should include the post and invite the moderator to decide whether or not it's appropriate, with thanks either way.

This tactic has two advantages. First, the marketer wins points with the moderator for being respectful, rather than just spamming the mailing list. Second, if the moderator does submit the brief announcement, it will bear her endorsement to the rest of the readership.

Tips on Signatures

An online *signature* (or *.sig file*) is more like a business card than its handwritten namesake. As anyone who's been online for a week has noticed, many netizens append their email and newsgroup messages with professional contact information.

Any good email software program lets users generate a canned signature automatically or on demand. The better email software programs enable the use of multiple signatures. Professional signatures are best kept short and to the point—name, title, company name, corporate slogan, telephone, fax, email, and URL. Snail-mail addresses rarely need to be included because anyone who really needs it can call.

Anything longer than four or five lines threatens the norms of good taste. Posting a message shorter than the signature is a classic *faux pas*. No matter how creative the message is, ASCII-art renditions of cartoon characters, or even a corporate logo in the signature, generally do not convey the most professional image. Likewise, forget about pithy quotes, jokes-of-the-day, and "Now on Special! 20 percent Off!" messages. Regular list members might resent such .sigs as a waste of email memory and screen space.

One way to use fewer lines in the signature is to create two columns of information, using the space bar to simulate tabs, even though it might not line up perfectly for readers not using the conventional mono-width fonts, such as Courier or Monaco. Or, string the fax and telephone numbers together with commas on the same line, do the same for the URL and email, and so on.

Viral Marketing on Commercial "Gateway" Communities

Online conversations are also popular among the subscribers to the big commercial online services, such as America Online, Microsoft Network, and "special interest" portal services such as **yupi.com** and **ivillage.com**, to name just two. It's estimated that nearly all of the 60 million American households with online capability belong to at least one of these services, and routinely start their Web search sessions from the home page of that service.

For sheer numbers, AOL is the most important commercial service for most marketers. While former market leader CompuServe peaked in the early '90s, AOL grew rapidly through aggressive marketing (the inescapable gazillions of free log-on disks it sent everywhere), surpassing 30 million members in 1999 and even gobbling up Time-Warner. While it still suffers a "churn rate" of up to 50 percent of its membership each year, AOL is a handy Internet-on-training-wheels for the newbie masses. And as such, it's a great place to find ordinary consumers and establish online brand loyalties when they start. (See Figure 6.13.)

Figure 6.13
Welcome to McCyberspace. Millions and millions served.

A contracted and paid link from AOL to a Web site can cost as much as $30 million dollars, but it is still possible to get a word in for a company for free. The most effective free venue for the online marketer are AOL's message boards. These are basic discussion bulletin boards, much like Usenet. AOL's captive audience, however, often generates considerably more dialogue on their message boards than most Usenet newsgroups ever see.

When using AOL's discussion forums to promote a Web site, bear in mind that some of AOL's users are likely to be new to computers, much less the Internet. Make sure the site design is friendly to AOL's browser, and don't assume much technical sophistication on the part of the audience.

MSN, CompuServe, and the Others

Warning

If you want to be taken seriously on the Net, don't give out an AOL address as your primary email account. It projects an image of semi-online-literacy to the broader Internet community. Owing no doubt to the Dilbert Principle, AOL addresses seem especially popular among top executives.

Microsoft Network, which ranked a close third behind CompuServe with just under 3 million subscribers in mid-1997, has gone through several metamorphoses since its 1995 launch to its present status as an entertainment network and access provider (see Figure 6.14). Besides offering email, search services, and a mix of news and entertainment to rival a newspaper or television channel, the network has served as the company vehicle to promote new technology such as the Microsoft Reader for electronic books. CompuServ, purchased in 1997 by AOL, still exists and remains popular among some professional groups, such as lawyers. The Well, an offshoot of Stewart Brand's Whole Earth empire, has changed hands a few times but retains much of its *digerati-artiste* membership.

Just about every ISP in every wired country, large and small, offers forums and chats as a community service. Unless the product or service is geographically limited, or if the marketer is already a member and is familiar with its forums, it might be more trouble than it's worth to do online viral marketing.

Figure 6.14

Microsoft's network now flaunts dating services, horoscopes, and Steven King.

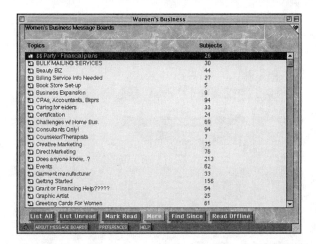

Figure 6.15
Women in business for themselves. Not a bad demographic. AOL's got them, as well as many more juicy slices of middle America.

Open Portals and Business Vortals

Other corporate entities were quick to notice the power of proprietary gateways when it came to channeling the late '90s mass surge of millions of Internet users into business-promotional Web sites. So instead of being just a "channel" on AOL, for example, the media conglomerates and Web companies that had supplied "content" for these proprietary gateways began to fashion their own sites into sub-gateways, or *portals*.

Yahoo! for example, quickly grew from a search directory to a full-service portal providing email service, live online discussion groups, headline news, and shopping opportunities at a glance. Many target audience segments, such as **ivillage.com**, which battles for womens' screen time with dozens of competitors, from **totalwoman.com** launched by a Web advertising agency, to **oxygen.com** that was godmothered by the mother of modern media synergy, TV talk-show mogul, Oprah Winfrey.

Other online examples include **Disney.com**, which targets families and children, and **efit.com**, which caters to folks obsessed with diet, exercise, and fitness. These are sometimes called "horizontal" portals, because the channel choices and available discussion groups cover a range of topics. An example of a "vertical" portal, or "vortal," is Global Supply's business-to-business Web site **JanCentral.com**, which supports janitors and entrepreneurial cleaning companies with bulletin boards, product reviews, and even an advice columnist (see Figure 6.16).

Figure 6.16

Buyers and sellers of cleaning services and janitorial supplies have their own vertical industry portal, JanCentral.com.

Most business-to-business vortals are subscription-based, with a "members"– only gateway to special services, such as reverse-auction and group purchase clubs. Consumer sites such as **Disney.com** and **totalwoman.com** are open to anyone, although they usually encourage "membership" or try to entice users to employ them as a "personal home page," with such goodies as free email, or special offers, either to gather a "permissioned" Web site address or to gain the traffic advantage of being that user's first gateway view whenever she turns on her browser. In both cases, the portals are collecting email addresses they will be happy to sell for email marketing (see the preceding section on Purchased Lists).

A pure-play vortal, for example, the business sites created by VerticalNet, Chemdex, or PaperExchange, might wind up being less useful to viral marketing than an information portal site maintained by a trade association or trade magazine. These types of organizations already have a targeted customer base, and they typically create sites that are content-rich, with job boards, information calendars, industry news, and commentary sections—all areas where a Web business might be able to post marketing messages with its URL, if not a free text link. And typically, any sort of free publicity a print trade magazine might offer, is attainable with its online counterpart. (See Chapter 8 for more about online publicity.)

To cost-conscious entrepreneurs, the value of business vortals and niche portals to marketing efforts rely on whether they can deliver the "right" customer to the home page by methods other than paid links. The inability of commercial niche portals to foster the kind of peer-to-peer information environment that blossoms into naturally-occurring Web communities seems to inhibit their viral reach. Consequently, stealth marketing through these avenues might soon be relegated to rainy-day activities for the marketing department. But, consider buying or renting a subscriber list for direct email marketing to test a niche portal's ability to draw customers before attempting banner ads or affiliate revenue-sharing programs.

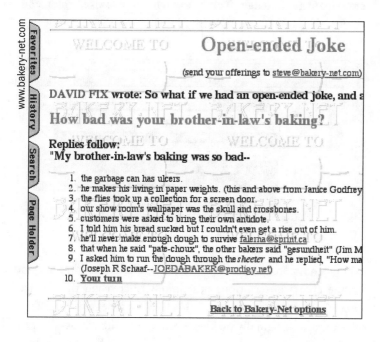

Figure 6.17
Peer-to-peer networking possibilities lurk on the back pages of business sites like Bakery-Net.

Web Discussion Boards, Web Site Forums, and Live Chats

A marketer can seed discussions on the forums, bulletin boards, discussion groups and real-time "live chats" that appear on gateway or portal Web sites using the same viral marketing strategies that work on Usenet and listserv communities. In the grand scheme of things, planting a question and an answer into a live online chat is no different from telephoning a live radio call-in show with a seeded comment or a leading question. Bear in mind that, just as in talk radio, real-time online discussions are both time-delayed and aggressively moderated, much more so than at nonprofit newsgroups. Comments that disparage the company sponsoring the chat, unrelated comments or even the mention of a sponsor's rival by name, are often deleted from the postings before anyone can see them.

If the product is global, don't neglect chats and discussion groups conducted in languages other than English. AOL learned this the hard way when it began deleting postings in Spanish on its discussion groups for the 1998 World Cup soccer matches. The backlash from bilingual users helped fuel the launch of several Spanish-language Web sites, whose forums attract consumers throughout the Western Hemisphere. (See Figure 6.18.)

Figure 6.18

Spanish-speaking sports fans have their own forums on the Web.

Many commercial sites archive their discussion threads and online chat transcriptions indefinitely, increasing the chances that a reference to the site's URL would be seen weeks or months after originally posting a message to the discussion, particularly if a surfer turned up the message in a keyword search. More effective still is securing permanent pointers and links to the site in a targeted area of a commercial site that attracts the customer base through the use of affinity sites and other strategic partnerships, as covered in Chapter 7.

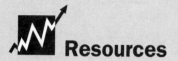 **Resources**

Tips on Netiquette

Netscape on Netiquette
http://home.netscape.com/menu/netet/

- Netscape maintains a reasonably good set of Net user guidelines, so-called "netiquette" and "forum decorum."

Tenagra's Links
http://www.tenagra.com/

- Tenagra has a collection of links to rules of the road. The resources focus especially on how to advertise appropriately on Usenet.

news.newusers.questions, news.announce.newusers, and news.answers

- These three newsgroups are good starting points for those new to Usenet, with lots of FAQs and advice for online promoters.

Anti-Spam

Junkbusters
http://www.junkbusters.com/

- One of many sites preaching the gospel against Usenet and email spam, this one has a particularly good set of resources.

Email Marketing Vendors

- The following is a (very) short list of some of the companies that compile and sell permissioned email lists and/or administer electronic mail campaigns. These individual Web sites often include case studies or product examples that illustrate current techniques, and all are worth a look.

Auraline
http://www.auraline.com

ClickAction Network
www.clickaction.com

Mail.com
http://www.mail.com

continues

continued

MyPoints
http://www.mypoints.com

YesMail
http://www.yesmail.com

Other Resources

Deja.com
http://www.deja.com

- This is a key resource for marketing on Usenet and by far the most powerful way to search topics being discussed in newsgroups. Engage in competitive analysis by searching for what your competition is saying, and see what users are already saying about your product.

Liszt
http://www.liszt.com

- This is a comprehensive directory of mailing lists, and lets you search them in a variety of ways.

VerticalNet
http://www.verticalnet.com

- Consider this an entry point into an assortment of pure-play vertical portals ("vortals") set up by industry, most geared to sales of hard goods, either by direct sales or auctions. Email registration is required for further exploration of each site.

Alkami BioSystems: Bootstrap Marketing for BioTech

ALKAMI BIOSYSTEMS FOUNDER Lisa Stewart created their Web site to promote and sell Alkami Expert, a package of software tools for DNA and related biology testing. A trimly-designed home page puts the product pitch up front, and offers a free download of one set of tools.

"Since our interest is in genetics, we're focusing on bringing the product to the attention of biologists," said Stewart. "First, we identified a protocol that biologists use frequently, the Polymerase Chain Reaction, or PCR. Then we built the Web site around PCR reference resources that biologists are familiar with and feel comfortable using."

To attract laboratory users to the site, Alkami purchased an email list from a bioscience Web site, and tested two different message offers. The goal of the campaign was to increase site traffic and further develop an in-house list through permissioned email follow-ups.

The campaign tested body copy, multiple price offers, and different headers ("Putting the word 'free' in your subject head really does boost response rate."), and further divided the email address lists by biotech specialty. To quantify the data, Stewart's team devised a version of its biology analysis software to perform a variant statistical analysis of the email response rates.

"For example, day of the week matters," she said. "Don't send your emails on Mondays—people are really grumpy! In our experience, there's a steep drop-off in responses after two or three days, for it's important to time your announcements well."

Respondants, some further qualified because they accepted the free software trial, are added to the in-house list and receive periodic announcements of new offers, to bolster brand recognition as well as traffic.

"Before people respond to a message, they need to see it many times," Stewart explained. "Every time we send a message, we are reminding our subscribers of the benefits and resources we offer.

"And every time we send out a new mailing, we see a spike in average site traffic of 200 to 300 percent over the first couple of days. After that it drops down to about 110 to 120 percent of the prepromotion traffic levels. During an eight month period of online marketing, we saw an 800 percent increase in average traffic rates."

Because the product line targets a specific scientific audience, related online strategies included posting information about Alkami to appropriate newsgroups. The announcements were restricted to notices about scientific review articles that could be found on the site, or free resource offerings. This also raised traffic and helped build the company's permissioned lists.

In the narrow but lucrative niche of biotech, this small company has created a loyal following among laboratory scientists, and has leveraged some relationships into e-commerce partnerships. The company has also been approached about licensing the statistical model it created that evaluates its email marketing.

"Every time we do an email announcement, either with our own subscriber list or one we've purchased, we collect and refine our marketing database," said Stewart. "Every time we run a new marketing effort based on previously collected data, our response rates are improved."

IN THIS CHAPTER

chapter 7

Building Online Audiences: Affinity Sites and Affiliate Programs

WHAT MAKES THE WEB a web, of course, are the hyperlinks connecting sites together. By its very definition, the Web encourages sites about related interests to point to each other. Indeed, most sites maintain a collection of recommended destinations and contextual outbound links.

Securing inbound links to your home page is an important part of online promotion. As thousands of businesses go online every month, the odds of a customer finding yours among the clutter get tougher. If you are trying to draw customers of a specific demographic, the best place to find them might be on someone else's site.

If you're planning to use your Web pages for direct sales, it might interest you to know that Forrester Research estimates that 13 percent of all online retail sales in 1999 were created as a result of affiliate-linking programs. By 2002, according to analysts at Jupiter, a full 25 percent of an expected $37.5 billion in Internet retail sales (not including cars and trucks) will have originated on affiliate sites, and that's a *conservative* estimate. Other research firms put the percentage as high as 50 percent by 2003.

Even if you're not selling anything, inbound links are a valuable part of branding efforts. If you're a new brand struggling for awareness, a link to your site from another site that is long-established and well-branded, will give your business an endorsement, providing credibility and a certain comfort level to the Net surfer tempted to click into your site.

Many established Web sites continually pursue new inbound links to help maintain their reputations and their traffic levels. CNET, for example, offers to pay other sites two cents per visitor clickthrough to promote and maintain its position as a news and information publisher for the Internet set, in the face of stiff competition from other online news media (see Figure 7.1).

Figure 7.1

At two cents per clickthrough, CNET offers an affiliate program to help drive traffic, with a goal of generating ad views and thereby increasing its ad revenues.

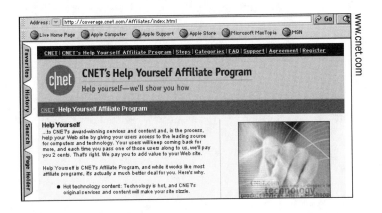

Affinity Sites: Partnering For Free Inbound Links

No matter how much you've heard about the glories of affiliate programs, paid links are not the best strategy for every Web site. You can't start up a revenue-sharing affiliate program if you have no revenue—if you're not doing e-commerce, ad sales, or direct selling. You must also consider that paying commissions on sales created through paid link partnerships hurts the ability to price products competitively.

If lowering customer acquisition costs is a goal, the marketing mix should include some free links.

Sadly, the days of carefree, reciprocal links are long over. This part of the business is changing rapidly, along with its terms and definitions, in the multi-million-dollar gold rush for traffic and "sticky eyeballs" to and from Web sites. For promotional and marketing purposes, a distinction exists between two types of strategic partnerships—*affinity sites*, providing inbound links without cash compensation, and *affiliate programs*, providing inbound links in exchange for a fee.

Along with news sites and niche directories, some nonprofit, educational, or amateur sites will still link to a company's site for free if they feel the site content is good enough and offers information value deemed to be of high interest to their visitors. Some might ask for a reciprocal link, which might or might not be in the site's best interest, but frequently they will link to it whether the site is compelling or if they view *it* as the more prestigious site.

A common example of this is the fan site. Many of the gushy, purple-paged fan sites dedicated to the popular Latino singer Ricky Martin link directly to Martin's "official" Web page hosted by Sony Records. If the product is popular with a teen audience, such links can be valuable word-of-Web if the company lacks the advertising budget of a media giant. (See Figure 7.2.)

Figure 7.2

This amateur's Ricky Martin fan site links to the official record label Web pages and to dozens of other amateur sites that help spread news of concert dates, new recordings, and press events.

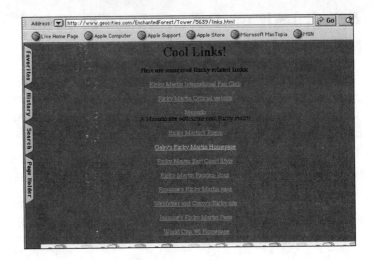

Complements, Not Competitors

Many similar sites run by small businesses catering to consumers find it to their advantage to band together. For example, hot sauce retailers online seem happy to link to others in their field, so much so that some of them have founded the Ring of Fire mutual appreciation network. Such cross-promoting *Web rings* are relatively common within certain fields. (See Figure 7.3.)

Obviously, some direct competitors see a conflict in linking to each other. That only leaves hundreds of thousands of other sites to choose from. Affinity sites complement, they don't compete. A romance fiction site and another one dedicated to selling handcrafted quill pens might both benefit from reciprocal links, for example.

A site should be designed to be information-rich. Publishing and news sites often provide a free inbound link to a site in exchange for the right to feature some of its content. They might want a weekly online commentary on the wingnut industry or a "Top Ten" list along the lines of the New York Times Bestseller List. In a content license agreement of this type, a site might waive a fee payment for the content in exchange for an ongoing, promotional link.

Figure 7.3

Firegirl's e-commerce site is a member of the Ring of Fire hot sauce network, with links to other e-tailers.

Some recent research shows that text links can actually have a higher clickthrough rate than banners, especially when seen on news or nonprofit sites. The assumption is that nonflashy text links are perceived as part of the originating site's content, and are viewed as an endorsement, not as an advertisement.

Uber-links

Not all links are created equal. Some might produce only one or two visitors a week. Others pass along thousands of unique visitors each day. These are the prized *uber-links*.

Uber-links (a term coined by Doug Moody) are sites that have become leading resources within their audience groups, whether that's lawyers or computer gamers or Trekkies. They're the sites that everyone else in the field invariably links to, and where every Web surfer searching the topic quickly ends up.

If a site gets listed on an uber-link site, other related sites can discover it and decide to add a link to it as well. Thus, linking gains its own momentum.

Real Value of Free Links

The incoming traffic generated by links can vary tremendously depending on the affinity site's quality and the character of its audience. But even 20 visitors a week from a free inbound link that the site has not paid for is a gift to its customer acquisition cost equation.

Compared to the cost of banner advertisements, it's easy to appreciate the real value of affinity site links simply in terms of what it costs to draw traffic. Let's assume a company has purchased a banner ad that is receiving a fabulously successful clickthrough rate of 1 percent (that is, one in 100 Web surfers who sees it clicks on it), and that it's paying only $20 per thousand impressions shown of the ad. That means the company would have to show the banner 2,000 times, at a cost of $40, to get 20 visitors a week.

Given that most links, however, stay up on their pages indefinitely, a site might secure 500 inbound links after six months of a diligent affinity link campaign. Then, assuming it only got 20 visitors a week from each one, it would have 10,000 visitors a week from those free links, for an equivalent banner ad value of an ongoing $20,000 a week.

Where to Find Affinity Sites

Finding 500 affinity sites willing to give free inbound links would certainly be a full time job. And instead of finding 500 links that might land 20 visitors a week, a Web marketer might prefer to winnow the list quickly to 50 sites that send 200 weekly visitors to the site.

Because linking is now deemed to have a real cash value in the Internet marketplace, don't be surprised if a site is asked to pay for an inbound link. In fact, if the site is well-regarded, smaller Web sites will soon pester it for links, eager to set up some sort of affiliate relation program (more following).

To locate possible free links, start with the obvious candidates. The first place to look is on a search engine or directory; type in the keywords for your own site and see what else comes up. You can also look on the Web pages of competitor's sites and see where their *outbound* links go. Or, do a UseNet search on **deja.com**, and then follow a few discussion groups to see which sites are referred to frequently enough to suggest they might be uber-links.

Currently, **linkpopularity.com** provides a free and very fast way to find out who's linking *into* competitor's Web pages. (See "Tracking Inbound Links.")

Less obvious places to search are the classified ads in the back of specialty magazines (which often include URLs), URLs on the invoice or business cards of friendly clients or suppliers, URLs of newly formed companies listed in an industry conference program, or the exhibitor's guide given out at a trade show.

To contact a possible link or a partner, identify and email the Webmaster, and then follow up with a letter or a phone call. If you can't find the correct contact information on the Web site, query **Register.com** or Network Solutions with a "Whois" search on the domain name, as described in Chapter 4, "Using Domain Names to Build Your Brand." (See Figure 7.4.)

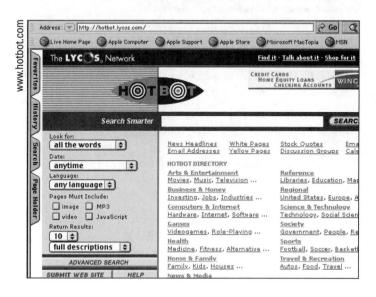

Figure 7.4

HotBot's business directories and global reach make it possible to conduct extremely detailed searches for companies that might link to yours.

Figure 7.5

Mark Holtz's Star Trek site might be nothing special to look at, but a link here can transport legions of Trekkies to your site.

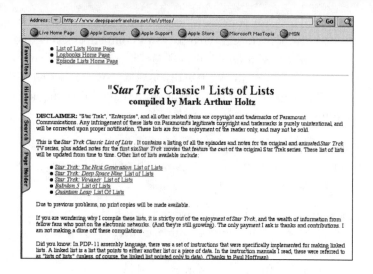

Although emailing Webmasters is the most direct way to solicit inbound links to a site, a large part of that process is also organic. Essentially, all audience development marketing—search engine registration, seeding online forums, contests, public relations, online advertising, and so on—has the residual effect of interested Webmasters discovering the site and volunteering links to it without further prompting.

Announcement Sites and "Cool Sites"

When a site is ready for public consumption, a good way to generate initial traffic and encourage links is to register with various *announcement sites*. The most famous of these is Net-Happenings, originally run by the computer department of the University of Wisconsin. Dozens of other similar services also exist.

Announcement sites are subscribed to by many Webmasters, Internet journalists, surf-junkies, and various other chroniclers of cyberspace. They're great for generating free links from interested Webmasters who often monitor announcement sites, and the site might also get responses from organizations wanting to create an affiliate partnership.

The Cool Site of the Day/Week award is a favorite of countless sites, both amateur and commercial. Being cited for excellence or coolness by a well-recognized award site might indeed benefit a site's online venture. Many print-media reviewers and Webmasters who follow such lists might check out the site and create temporary links to its URL. Certainly, it will experience a spike in traffic for the day or week the award is featured, and of course, it can forever display the award icon with pride (preferably somewhere tactful, not as the first image that loads on the home page).

As far as making an effort to seek out awards, it's worth a rainy afternoon's work at most. For that rainy afternoon you want to invest, however, check out Yahoo!'s Best of the Web sub-category (see the Resources section for the URL).

Tracking Inbound Links

Tracking sites that have linked to your site after contact is a bit complicated. Many Webmasters might never reply to requests for free links, but still go ahead and put up a link. Others might add the link to their pages unsolicited. Mature sites might already have active, free inbound links by the score.

Linkpopularity.com simplifies the process by identifying links on AltaVista, Hotbot, and Infoseek (see Figures 7.6 and 7.7). But most of the main search engines let you search for a URL to determine which pages are linking to your site. AltaVista, for example, allows you to omit all references of your own site's internal links from the search results, but you have to know the arcane search commands:

link:yourcompany.com/-host:yourcompany.com

Searching for a competitor's links on AltaVista is just as easy:

link:yourcompetitor.com

On HotBot, you need to change a pop-up menu on the home page from the default that tells the engine to search for "all the words" to "links to this URL". On other engines, you might go into the "advanced search" option and follow the link to "Search URL" or "Search Link."

For a thorough review of how to search for inbound links on the big search engines, the excellent site Search Engine Watch features a detailed description (see the "Resources" section at the end of the chapter for the URL).

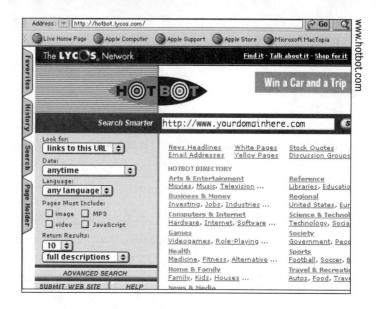

Paying for Links and Traffic: Affiliate Programs

Amazon.com helped pioneer the concept of the paid link in 1996, when it began to compensate other Web sites for driving traffic. When a book was sold, a percentage of the sale price was returned to the site that provided the link to occasion the sale. **Amazon.com** used its own proprietary software to tabulate the sales; after the sites that provided the inbound links started getting monthly checks, not surprisingly they began to discover more reasons to promote books and promote their link to the online bookseller. Amazon quickly expanded its affiliate program to include publishing house Web sites and e-commerce sites of every stripe, and in fact, to any site that woke up to the fact that, ye gods and little fishes, this was a *revenue stream.*

By the dawn of 2000 the affiliate program concept had exploded throughout the Web. Here was a strategy that seemed to work brilliantly on both sides. Small sites could move closer to profitability by gaining the revenues kicked back in customer referrals, and they quickly lost their fear of "losing eyeballs" to another site once the checks arrived in the mail.

Large sites, casting for ways to cut back customer acquisition costs, discovered that revenue-sharing made good ROI sense. Instead of paying thousands if not millions of dollars "up front" to another site to run banner ads, or paying large sums as per "impressions" or "clickthrough," a Web site only had to pay another Web site only if, and only *after, a customer sale had been made.*

The business models for affiliate programs are in constant flux, but here are some basics:

Unlike with banner advertising, a Web marker should think twice before paying another site for simply driving traffic to his site. Sensible affiliate programs are always based on measurable results—either actual sales if his site has e-commerce, or if his goal is branding and product promotion, counted by the number of "free trials" tried, coupons redeemed, or email sign-ups for a newsletter, contest, or sweepstakes.

Paying for clickthroughs only makes sense if a business model depends on high levels of incoming traffic. A new site looking for an audience might pay for clickthroughs to establish presence, particularly if the desired audience is very broad. If the site caters to a specialty audience or to the business marketplace, pay to gain introductory traffic through affiliates, but set up an introductory page on the site that makes the user jump through some kind of behavioral hoop, to further qualify the incoming customers. One way to do this is to create a microsite, a temporary set of Web pages (see Chapter 9, "Paid Media: Making Dollars and Sense with Web Advertising," to learn more about microsites).

Percentages paid for referrals vary by industry, and can range from the typical 1 to 2 percent (for computer hardware sales) to as much as 50 percent. A Web site selling t-shirts or paperback books with a $7.99 list price might offer an 8 to 10 percent fee, while a Web site pitching unsold $150 per-night hotel rooms might happily pay a referring site 50 percent on the sale of a room that would otherwise remain vacant.

Big, popular sites, such as search engines, directories, well-branded sites, and flavor-of-the-month top portals (auction sites and those catering to youth, news, sports, or shopping audiences) theoretically drive more traffic to a site, so expect to pay large sums up front to get these sites to set up an inbound link to your site. The other side of this coin is, if your site is well-branded, you can expect to be pestered constantly by Internet unknowns begging you to start an affiliate relationship with them, even if their own site couldn't possibly offer any sort of qualified customer base.

Welcome to the new Internet gold rush, Y2K edition. These sites don't care about your site; they just want a piece of its revenue. (See Figure 7.8.)

Figure 7.8
Who's the most popular? Webtrends provides yet another playing field (benchmarks) for Web competition.

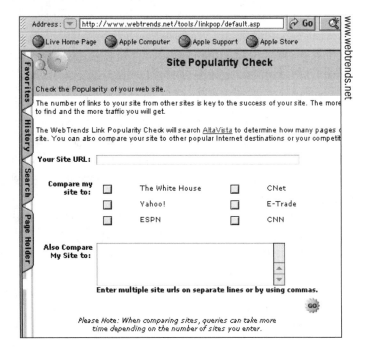

Hold on a Minute!

By mid 2000, it was not uncommon to see sites boasting "hundreds of thousands" of affiliates as if it was some measure of popularity, esteem, or validation. Big e-tailers strove for what was considered an "industry average" of 10,000 links, and **Amazon.com** remained king of the affiliate hill, claiming more than 450,000 affiliates.

Just as abruptly, the tide turned. Many Web businesses discovered that getting lots of inbound traffic wasn't as worthwhile as getting *quality* traffic, folks who would arrive to buy, not just browse. Having legions of affiliates proved unwieldy for many companies with small staffs, for they verified tracking, cut checks monthly, and dealt with dissatisfied affiliates clamoring for support and bigger percentage deals. Even firms that outsourced their affiliate programs soon realized that treating all affiliates alike, or even using the same percentage payment structure, was a wasted effort.

In marketing, the old 80/20 rule of thumb holds that 80 percent of the profit comes from 20 percent of the marketing efforts, and vice versa. In terms of Web affiliations, it now appears that the split is more like 10 percent of affiliates generating 90 percent of the business, or perhaps even 99 to 1.

Thus, at the end of 2000, the Net is no longer dragging in those who want to affiliate with bigger fish in the Internet sea. Instead, potential affiliates are "invited to apply" for affiliate programs. Prospects are considered for long-term value, and some small fries are rejected if they aren't a good catch.

Outsource or In-House?

Consultants often steer clients to "affiliate solution providers" if the decision has been made to outsource, speeding up the partner-hunting process. These agencies usually have a pool of potential affiliates to work with, and assist in creating cross-promotions.

On the plus side, using an affiliate solution provider, such as Be Free or Link Share, saves time and technical headaches. You don't have to buy the hardware for tracking and administering links. For a percentage of all transactions (anywhere from 2 percent to 30 percent) the agency not only finds but also monitors the links for you, provides performance reports, and even handles the affiliate payment process.

A minimum commitment for the first year averages $40,000-50,000. The agencies that administer the affiliate pool also take a percentage of all transactions, usually 2 percent. Taking into consideration that agency percentages and extra charges for such things as jobbed-out banner design, the actual cost can be as high as $200,000 in the first year.

On the downside, there's no guarantee that a provider firm will aggressively look beyond its own affiliate pool to find good partners, or ignore sterling potential partners simply because they belong to another firm's pool.

Do-it-yourself entrepreneurs also tabulate their affiliate fees and keep track of link performance using information provided by their ISPs or servers, and off-the-shelf software programs from such suppliers as Software Affiliate Shop, The Affiliate Program, and AffiliateZone, which cost $1,000 to $10,000. An e-commerce site that's already using a shopping cart program might find that program already includes some functions and built-ins for affiliate data tracking. (See Figure 7.9.)

Figure 7.9
The Affiliate Program is one of many do-it-yourself applications for the small business or entrepreneur.

Finding Affiliates; When Affiliates Find You

What uber-links are to free links, "superlinks" are to affiliate sites. Use the same strategies used to identify free links (see previous) to help identify which Web sites you might pitch for a link to your site.

A study done in March 2000 by Jupiter Communications supports the notion that the average netizen visits fewer than 20 sites regularly. At the top of the charts, not surprisingly, are major portals such as AOL, MSN, and Yahoo, each with an estimated reach of 50 percent of the online audience on any given day.

Yet in this survey of 1,500 respondents, 46 percent of users said they preferred specialized sites that focused on a single topic or genre of interest or catered to general needs of their identities, as families with young children, for example, or as single boomers. A full 39 percent of sites visited by the respondents were owned by familiar and well-known offline brands. Big sites, and those that deliver a more segmented market of users can exploit the difference by charging higher rates for Web advertising, and demand higher rates when feeding customers to less-known sites through affiliate fees.

The challenge for the marketer striving to create what Jupiter calls "invisible networks" of affiliations is to strive for affinities without paying dearly in affiliate fees. With regard to business-to-business traffic, the best sites might not be highly trafficked, but traffic will be targeted. One example is **pulpandpaper.net**, which serves the rag trade (see Figure 7.10).

Figure 7.10
Pulpandpaper.net is a daily news service for printing and recycling companies. Its required registration implies qualified users searching for links to suppliers and related business sites.

As with free links, agreements for affiliation are far more flexible than you might believe. Many merchant companies post information on their affiliate programs in full on their Web pages, including commission rates, rules, and regulations, and even full contracts. This allows affiliates to shop around, and many will use the posted information only as a baseline for negotiations. (See Figure 7.11.)

It's still a good idea to keep affiliate program information posted. And if the customer base is broad enough (all men 18-24; all women who buy shoes), register your affiliate program through an online affiliate directory (**refer-it.com, cashpile.com,** or **associate-it.com** to name a few). You can even announce you are hunting for affiliates on a submission service such as **affiliate-announce.com,** for less than $100.

If you expect to be inundated with applicants, decide ahead of time whether you want to do individual (manual) approval or use an auto-approve program customized to certain criteria.

You don't have to take all comers, certainly. After a potential affiliate applies to you, your criteria for accepting them should simply be, "Does their site relate to your core business? Does it offer you the right customer base?"

Visit the potential site. If co-branding is important to your strategy, visit the applying sites in view of both your short-term and long-term business objectives. Sometimes it takes two or three months for inbound clicks to start converting into customers. A site that looks "hot" for a seasonal product might prove cold ground for leads a few months hence.

Figure 7.11
Amazon.com has patented its affiliate program sourcecode, but makes its operating agreement available for review to all.

"Lifetime Customer Value"

Business-to-business sites expect to have a continuing sales relationship with a customer once he or she arrives through an inbound link and makes that initial purchase. Most business-to-consumer sites hope to reap years of what's called "lifetime customer value" from a referral. But once the customer stops logging in through the referral site, and begins to log in directly, referrals get harder to track.

In recognition of this, a merchant site might choose to compensate its affiliates at a higher percentage level, taking into consideration "lifetime value." The most often-cited example is again **Amazon.com**, which has publicly acknowledged that it expects to earn $120 per year in revenue for each new customer referred, and pays up to 15 percent commission. By comparison, Amazon's most direct competitor, **Barnesandnoble.com**, pays a commission of only seven percent.

An alternative is to pay a lump sum "bounty" for each new customer. This approach certainly simplifies accounting, and not surprisingly it is popular with financial institutions, such as banks and credit card companies. Capital One, for example, pays $25 for each new customer acquired online.

Some tracking software makes it possible to keep accurate records of each purchase from each sales lead from here to eternity, but few merchants choose this path. One that does is **Kiss.com**, which competes in the cutthroat world of online dating services. It promises affiliates a whopping 40 percent of each customer transaction, "over the lifetime of the customer." Perhaps it's cynical to suggest that this romance site is betting on its own success—theoretically, customers would find their soul mates in a month or two, and never have to visit the site again.

Calculating Customer Lifetime Value	
Average Annual Customer Revenue	$100.00
Average Number of Loyal Years	x 3.00
Profit	x 0.10
Customer Lifetime Value	$30.00

Bagging the Big Ones

Even when a marketer is prepared to pay good money for inbound links, not every site is going to be thrilled to link to his site. Some Web sites still fear "losing eyeballs."

Another reason for resistance is clutter. Many home pages are broken up and dotted with boxes, squares, buttons, and channel panels they look like a patchwork quilt. Web sites that put a high priority on Web page design are fighting a losing battle with elegance; the current compromise is usually one nicely sized bit of artwork and a gathering of tiny little buttons off to one side. Some sites relegate their affiliate merchants to an inside page devoted to e-commerce or news; others corral their affiliates into an "affiliates page" or a "resources" section. Any site that doesn't have a lot of ad banners floating on it already is going to be a challenge.

It helps to be the first or only vendor in a product/service category. On the other hand, if there are not any competitors or closely related sites to yours appearing on the target site, there might be a reason they wouldn't want a relationship. And don't waste a lot of time beating your head against bigger-name brands: If you're selling flower arrangements, it might not be worthwhile to pitch a site that's already got **1800flowers.com** prominently positioned on its home page.

A more level playing field can be found, however, at directory sites that encourage comparison-shopping. Users intending to make a high-end or complicated purchase, such as an automobile or long-distance phone service, might view the site among a number of competitors, and then click on it while viewing all sites in turn. Recent research done by New Canoe, for example, on behalf of a credit-card company, found that 75 percent of its referrals came from sites that displayed a variety of credit card company choices. This study also indicated that text links drove more referrals than banner ads, by nearly three to one.

Figure 7.12

Small Business Depot benefits by referrals from a giant-sized partner, American Express; this outbound link is located on the pages of the Amex site that provide value-added content of interest to small companies.

If wooing affiliates, have a few options in mind regarding page position and commission ranges, and be prepared in some cases to offer up-front fees. If money is not the main issue, consider offering a reciprocal link back to the affiliate. That's one perk you can offer an affiliate that a larger, better-branded competitor might not even consider.

"My Brand Is Bigger Than Your Brand . . . "

The biggest reason for resistance is a perceived dilution of brand. A well-branded site doesn't want to hand off its glamour to another, smaller player, and money is not always the answer. The site must be irresistibly attractive to the bigger site, or it must feed some hidden corporate agenda that can be discovered.

Community relations is an example. A large corporation in need of a little local PR might be swayed to link to a site in the hometown where it is building its new, multi-acre corporate campus. In other communities, a big firm might feel pressure to connect with more minority-owned businesses, so a minority-owned Web site might find it can swing a link. And yes, if your brother-in-law plays golf with the CEO's brother-in-law, bring up that connection. Alumni associations, Rotary clubs, and other time-honored entry points should never be ignored.

Figure 7.13

Forrester Research supplies a weekly roundup of the most trafficked Web sites in different market categories. Here are the big fish.

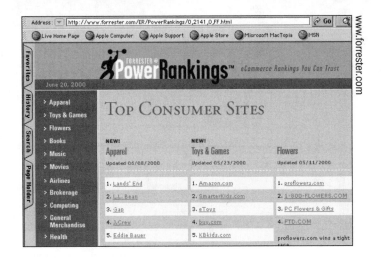

Web sites that have affiliate management teams now devote some staff time to travel and make live presentations to catch those bigger fish. But remember, the surest way for a site to be irresistibly attractive is to have a quality service or quality content that complements the bigger site and is unique or exclusive. The only reason a large corporation is going to feed its online customers to it, even temporarily, is because it thinks it will profit by doing so.

Care and Feeding

Managing affiliates over time should always be considered. It takes less than 10 minutes to disable a link, and you want to keep your most valuable partners from dropping your site in favor of a rival. This might mean re-negotiating a higher percentage for sites that perform well, or lavishing attention in the old-fashioned way—with sports box tickets, fancy dinners, or just touching base when you're in town.

The most successful affiliate programs on the Web today are run by companies that have dedicated staff for affiliate relations, usually a small department of two or three negotiators. **Amazon. com** employs up to several dozen people just for this purpose. Internet businesses already experienced with vendor and client intranets might find the politics of affiliate program partnerships are quite similar.

Trust

Trust is a key part of any business partnership. Given the speed at which Internet companies rise and fall, it is common that affiliate program contracts include a mutual termination clause that lets either party back out at any time. Mutual assignment clauses that permit neither party to transfer the partnership without permission are also common.

Not surprisingly, the biggest beef among affiliates involves tardy payments or fee payment disputes arising from conflicting reports that track transactions. Companies joining an affiliate pool administered by a third-party affiliate solutions provider might get faster collection and a built-in referee. As long as the third party remains neutral, affiliate CFOs can sleep well at night without worrying that their revenue percentage, from a million-dollar wingnut sale referral, somehow didn't get reported or mysteriously "fell through the cracks" on the server logs.

Scams and fraud are rare where affiliate programs are linked directly to sales performance. They have, however, cropped up in programs that pay for clickthroughs. If you're paying affiliates to drive traffic, checking logs twice weekly is recommended, especially if you've been saddled with a few hundred tiny, oddball affiliates that signed on before you took command. Irregular traffic patterns and performance spikes originating from a small site with fairly static content is one clue; a rush of Web addresses from a single server is another.

Figure 7.14

Commission Junction is one of many affiliate solution providers that administers revenue-sharing links among smaller firms.

Evaluations and Expectations

If you are working on a mature site and have been charged with the task of weeding out good affiliates from bad ones, pulling out the top performers is easily accomplished by glancing through tracking numbers. If you are lucky, there might be room in the business plan to reward these high performers with a higher percentage commission.

Affiliates that are less than stellar should be contacted by email or by telephone to share data and discuss any issues. Most would be happy to get larger commission checks and might simply need some guidance. Changing the position of a link on the home page, or moving the link to a different page might be suggested. A coupon test or other promotion can help.

Support to affiliates should always include prompt response to queries about tracking and payment, as well as regularly updated options in the form of banners and buttons. It might turn out that it is not the Web site that's underperforming; it might simply have the wrong banner or button message for the audience of that particular site.

Figure 7.15
Kiss.com offers its affiliates a choice of banner styles and updates the selection regularly.

 **Resources**

Useful Tools

Search Engine Watch on Inbound Links

http://www.searchenginewatch.com/popularity.htm

This page of Search Engine Watch, the excellent resource discussed in Chapter 5, "Find and be Found: Strategies for Search Engines and Directories," describes in detail how to use each of the leading search engines to discover which sites have links to yours.

Visibility Index

http://www.visibilityindex.com

This site, run by Word of Net, has a neat utility that sees which of two sites has a higher online visibility by counting in-bound links to each, as well as counting mentions in newsgroups and online news stories, among other measures. For a fee, the service provides much more detailed data.

Webtrends

http://www.webtrends

This site contains another tool that lets you count and compare inbound links to your site and to your competitors.

Power Rankings

http://www.forrester.com/ER/PowerRankings

This consultancy keeps a running list of top-trafficked sites in various business categories.

Services

Associate-It

http://www.associate-it.com/

This online affiliate directory is targeted to small e-commerce companies, and is a good source of free information, product news, and related links.

continues

continued

Affiliate Shop

http://www.affiliateshop.com/

Soup-to-nuts affiliate solutions for small businesses. Worth checking out.

Affiliate Zone

http://www.affiliatezone.com

This site sells affiliate-tracking software for do-it-yourselfers, and provides useful free advice on its own pages and through links.

Be Free

http://www.befree.com/

This service offers personalization technology to enhance the affiliate experience; the site also promotes conferences and technology of interest to the affiliate marketing executive.

Commission Junction

http://www.commissionjunction.com

This is a popular affiliate solution provider.

LinkExchange

http://www.linkexchange.com/

The granddaddy of banner-swapping services, now owned and operated by Microsoft's **bCentral.com**. Greatly expanded and a good source of news and happenings in the affiliate marketplace.

Link Share

http://www.linkshare.com

Another affiliate solution provider.

Announcement Sites

Net-Happenings

http://scout.cs.wisc.edu/index.html

The Internet Scout Project keeps tabs on Web debuts on behalf of library scientists, though thousands of Internet hardcores check in regularly, or subscribe to the Net-Happenings mailing list (now on a separate educational site) to find out what's going on online. A posting here can provide a critical jump-start for a new site, especially if it's of interest to educators.

Yahoo on Announcement Services

http://www.yahoo.com/Computers_and_Internet/Internet/World_Wide_Web/Announcement_Services/

Pointers to a variety of announcement sites and promotional services.

SmallBusinessDepot, Inc.: The Value of Good Company

SMALLBUSINESSDEPOT provides service to a range of small, entrepreneurial companies (from asbestos removal to software consultants) by generating job leads and bidding opportunities in their communities. Many of these businesses are women- and/or minority-owned, and most are interested in tapping into the more than $100 + million billion dollars in corporate, and state, local, and federal government contracts set aside yearly specifically for small businesses and minority- and women-owned vendor companies called "MWBE" enterprises.

The job leads and bidding notices are delivered as a subscription service through SmallBusinessDepot's Web site, **smallbusinessdepot.com**. The site also provides business news and online classes that teach the fine art of filling out governmental request for proposal (RFP) forms and contract fulfillment.

Business-to-business networking is a key component of generating client leads. It was obvious from the start that the site would have affiliate partners. Company principals JoAnn Mills Laing and Don Mazzella decided prior to launch to seek only well-targeted traffic, both to and from the Web site.

Early partners included Bell Atlantic (Verizon), IBM, American Express, First Data Corporation, and ADP. All these corporate giants maintain specific portions of their own Web site for attracting small-business startups. But as you might imagine, getting these sites to link to **smallbusinessdepot.com** took more than merely an email request for a link. In fact, securing such high-end affiliates entailed numerous face-to-face meetings with site administrators, with Laing and Mazzella arriving armed with PowerPoint presentations, market research documents, privacy assurances, and proof of technical capabilities between sites.

Mazzella says the experience sharpened their own approach as the site was launched and the company was inundated by hundreds of requests from Web sites asking to affiliate with them.

"It's true you can have thousands of affiliates, but then you've got to manage them," says Mazzella. "We realized that in any affiliate partnership there had to be a reason for us to be with them. When we'd been asking to affiliate with larger entities, we had to supply some good reasons and show why the link would benefit both parties. So we got picky, too."

Visitors to the SmallBusinessDepot Web site can try out the subscription service by plugging their location and business specialty into a "Test Station," which generates an immediate list of jobs open for bid. Half of the visitors who try the Test Station sign up for membership, so driving traffic to the site is the most important method of acquiring new subscribers.

Frank Colonno, Senior Vice President of Marketing & Sales at SmallBusinessDepot, vividly recalls the 14-inch high stack of email requests from would-be affiliates on his first day. At first, applications were processed manually.

"We still look at every request and check the site because we're looking for partners who provide added content value for our clients," said Colonno.

"We rejected a lot more than you might think. It had to be quality, and the companies had to understand what our product was, because it would be their responsibility to continue to drive the relationship."

Some affiliates receive a cash bounty for each membership acquired through an affiliate link. Most receive commissions ranging from 8 to 50 percent of completed transactions.

"In our business model, a payment is made per transaction, never just for delivering eyeballs," said Laing. Other negotiating points included page placement and assurance of logo consistency.

Because the company already has a complex and proprietary "back end" to process and contract data to deliver to its subscribers, the decision was made to manage affiliate tracking and affiliate payments in house. According to Mazzella, this job is done by one of the company's systems staff.

The company has been successful in getting well-branded sites to waive what might have been hefty up-front fees to display a link. Reeling in bigger affiliate fish isn't easy, says Laing. "We've been in talks with one company for over eight months," she said.

In their experience, cultivating a smaller, but more selected and more targeted base of smaller affiliates can be an asset when pitching a partnership with a much larger firm.

Persistence doesn't hurt either, says Mazzella. "There was a guy who kept calling us and calling us, he wanted to be our affiliate in the worst way," he recalled. "He finally gets me on my car phone as I'm driving over the Tappan Zee Bridge on Christmas Eve. So he got us. I surrendered."

 **IN THIS CHAPTER**

chapter 8

Media Savoir-Faire: Public Relations for a Digital Age

A PROPERLY EXECUTED PR campaign can be among the most valuable means of building an audience for a Web site. Publicity might not exactly be "free" advertising, but the price of a good campaign can be peanuts compared to advertising on the net or through traditional media such as TV. Furthermore, positive press coverage is often more credible to potential customers than any amount of advertising, and having a site's URL printed in *USA Today* will drive more traffic to it than any banner campaign.

The Internet is not so much a mass medium as a massing of media and communities. When you want to reach people en masse, turn to PR. But only if you're going to do it right. Think of it as media savoir-faire.

Even if you're jobbing out the PR work, you should read through the basics in this chapter, so you will know exactly how the publicity process works. The relationship between the media and the company publicist is a delicate one, and some top journalists in business media are haughty or prickly at best. Most reporters and editors accept that publicists play a significant role in the information food chain, however, and will tolerate them and even occasionally befriend them.

PR is an inherently good idea. Whether you are targeting print journalists, local TV and radio, or the new breed specializing in online daily news, all journalists are driven by the same need to generate stories on deadline. Your PR helps them meet that need.

Journalists in all media have been quick to adopt the Internet for research and communication, which only benefits the PR specialists who are trying to reach them. The problem lies in the fact that most PR attempts are so poorly executed that journalists despair, setting trash cans under their fax machines and filtering their email to delete all messages from certain company addresses.

The favorite technique of clueless publicists is to send long, badly written press releases, bereft of news value, to every journalist they can find in a database that's probably six months out of date. Then, for good measure, they top it off with a follow-up phone call just when the reporter is on deadline to ask if she's going to write about the announcement. You can guess the answer. (See Figure 8.1.)

More than anything, good media relations requires time and planning. Marketing managers who decide on a Wednesday that "we have to get this release out by Friday" should just throw their press releases out the window for all the good it does them. Well-executed PR is among the most cost-effective marketing strategies available to any business. Bad PR, however, all too commonly accounts for a tremendous waste of marketing resources.

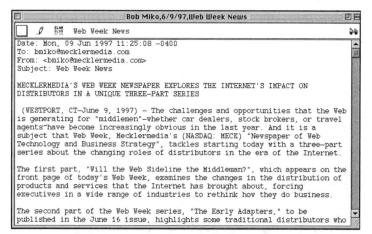

```
┌──────────────────────────────────────────────────────────┐
│ ▦      Bob Miko,6/9/97,Web Week News           回 🔲        │
│ ┌──────────────────────────────────────────────────────┐  │
│ □  🖉  ▦▦  Web Week News                            ▶▶  │  │
│ ├──────────────────────────────────────────────────────┤  │
│ Date: Mon, 09 Jun 1997 11:25:08 -0400                 ▲  │
│ To: bmiko@mecklermedia.com                            ▓  │
│ From: <bmiko@mecklermedia.com>                        ░  │
│ Subject: Web Week News                                ░  │
│                                                       ░  │
│ MECKLERMEDIA'S WEB WEEK NEWSPAPER EXPLORES THE INTERNET'S IMPACT ON │
│ DISTRIBUTORS IN A UNIQUE THREE-PART SERIES            ░  │
│                                                       ░  │
│   (WESTPORT, CT-June 9, 1997) - The challenges and opportunities that the Web │
│ is generating for "middlemen"-whether car dealers, stock brokers, or travel │
│ agents~have become increasingly obvious in the last year. And it is a │
│ subject that Web Week, Mecklermedia's (NASDAQ: MECK) "Newspaper of Web │
│ Technology and Business Strategy", tackles starting today with a three-part │
│ series about the changing roles of distributors in the era of the Internet. │
│                                                       ░  │
│ The first part, "Will the Web Sideline the Middleman?", which appears on the │
│ front page of today's Web Week, examines the changes in the distribution of │
│ products and services that the Internet has brought about, forcing │
│ executives in a wide range of industries to rethink how they do business. │
│                                                       ░  │
│ The second part of the Web Week series, "The Early Adapters," to be │
│ published in the June 16 issue, highlights some traditional distributors who ▼ │
└──────────────────────────────────────────────────────────┘
```

Figure 8.1

This hapless publicist has Rick on his bulk email list even though this release has nothing to do with what he covers for *Advertising Age*. Notice that he's addressed the message to himself, while Rick's address is hidden in the blind copy field along with probably hundreds of other journalists.

Understanding the Press

A company publicist must empathize with the press. Press rooms are bustling, noisy, and chaotic places; freelancers who work at home have to field domestic distractions constantly. The typical journalist has a phone receiver pinched in his neck while he types frantically on a keyboard as people shout across a crowded room above the sound of several ringing phones, between piles and piles of releases, industry white papers, and trade magazines.

That's not to say that most publicists, or for that matter almost all workers in the U.S., don't also work under tremendous stress. But in the special symbiotic relationship between journalism and PR, publicists get the short end of the stick. When a journalist calls wanting something, she wants it now. If the publicist succeeds in dropping everything and turning the information around immediately, he probably won't get extra points, but he'll definitely lose points if he doesn't.

And this is a key point: When a journalist calls a publicist, the publicist who responds promptly with information becomes known as a problem-solver. This builds trust and makes the reporter more likely to call the publicist again. Even better, when the publicist calls with a story idea, the reporter can lend a far friendlier ear.

As you can see, the dynamic between reporters and their sources is essentially one of mutual and friendly manipulation. The source wants publicity and is willing to massage the facts and leave out the ugly parts to get coverage. The journalist wants a compelling story and won't regret upsetting some people to get one. When these two objectives overlap, everyone wins. The journalist always has the upper hand in this game, however. Don't think that just because a publicist and a journalist were chummy yesterday that the publicist's latest misfortune won't look great tomorrow in 36-point type.

With Friends Like These. . .

Becoming a journalist's trusted source can be a publicist's most powerful marketing advantage. Journalists rely far more on their Rolodexes than on press releases to generate stories. But publicists should never forget that "off the record" is entirely subjective. They must never *assume* they're speaking off the record. Even if a publicist explicitly heard his reporter "buddy" agree to those terms, he should think three times before letting his words slip out if seeing them in print could cost his job or sink the company's stock price.

Nor does the publicist have a lot of recourse if he's unhappy about how his company has been treated in print. Haranguing the reporter's boss, threatening lawsuits, citing advertiser privilege, or vowing allegiance to the publication's competition certainly only makes matters worse. At best, his company will be ignored forever; at worst, it'll be subjected to vendetta journalism. As the old saying goes, don't pick a fight with someone who buys ink by the barrel. If absolutely necessary, the publicist could politely seek a correction. Otherwise, it's probably better not to call further attention to a damaging story with any follow-up.

For many companies, it can be more efficient to hire an outside PR firm to handle the ongoing work of cultivating press contacts. Professional publicists write press releases in their sleep, and already have a good "press list." The best have long relationships with journalists and editors, and are adept at handling damage control in the event of corporate bad news.

A company should choose its publicist as it would any vendor. If it's a small business, it might be more comfortable choosing a small PR firm in its local area, where it can deal face to face with a principal of the company. At a larger firm, it's common to dish off smaller clients to junior associates with less experience. If the company is planning an IPO soon, it should choose a firm or consultant with proven Wall Street media connections and some background in investor relations. It is quite all right to ask business editors at the local newspaper, or trade media journalists, to recommend local firms or individuals they work with regularly and respect.

The company should ask for client references and follow them up. After an initial meeting, a good PR firm will present a plan, with a budget and project time line. Most work only on a monthly retainer fee, plus expenses. A publicist on retainer will ask for a six month or year-long contract, but will be "on call" 24/7. Usually, the first one or two months are payable in advance.

Like lots of folks in the Internet food chain, some publicists ask for or accept equity in the company in exchange for a smaller fee. Some publicity consultants accept short term contracts for special projects, such as a Web site launch, or a trade show product launch, and they'll work with the staff to coordinate a press kit, write press releases, and secure at least some press coverage. Working with a consultant on a short-term project, with a firm budget, is a good way to try out a working relationship, but it should not take the place of a sustained PR effort that complements all the rest of the company's marketing plan. And, since media often "save" stories to fit their editorial schedules, it can take about six months to really evaluate good or bad results from any PR campaign.

Personalize, Don't Commoditize

The starting point for any successful PR strategy, as in all aspects of marketing, is to know the audience.

First, the publicist should identify who will be using the company's site, which, if she hasn't done by this stage in her marketing development, means she's in big trouble. Second, she should determine which media those customers pay attention to. Just because the company is promoting a Web site doesn't necessarily mean that technology and Internet-oriented publications, both print and online, are the place to start (unless its core customers are technologists). Although a site developer and Internet devotee might live by *Wired*, **News.com**, and *The Industry Standard*, are those the first media his readers turn to? If he runs an animal services site, it's possible to get it covered in *Web Review* if he works hard enough. But he'd get better results by devoting the same energy to placing a story with *Dog Fancier* magazine.

Third, and most importantly, she should find the right journalist at the right publication who is interested in the story the company wants to tell. Nothing screams amateur night more than a publicist who sends press kits to every editor listed, because news organizations are as internally specialized as any other. Careful reading of the targeted publication or news Web site reveals the byline of the writer who is most often covering issues that a company's news relates to.

Journalists' most common complaint about publicists, particularly since the advent of email, is being sent press releases that have nothing to do with the topics they cover. Spamming is bad enough when a company's trying to sell a product, but it's a hopeless strategy for gaining media exposure. Although recipients of sales spam have little real recourse, journalists who get annoyed by enough spam PR from the same company can always do a less-than-flattering write-up about that company.

Go to bookstores, libraries, and the Web, and find out which journalists are actually covering what the customers read. Peruse their publications regularly, tune into their broadcasts, and bookmark their Web sites.

In most cases, all the contact information a publicist needs—phone numbers and email addresses—can be found in the publication's masthead or hotlinked to the author's byline on the Web site. Beginning an email message with, "I really enjoyed your recent story about. . ." dramatically improves the chance that the writer will read the entire message and then decide to write about the company.

Become a Source

In truth, press releases are among the least-effective ways to get a story written about a company. It is far more effective for a publicist to get friendly with journalists or news organizations that might help him, and cultivate them carefully before he has something he needs to see in print.

So how does a publicist go about becoming a "source"? First of all, she targets a reasonable number of publications. She develops an "A" list of no more than 10 publications and a "B" list of another 10 or so. Journalists get their leads from sources they know by name. Unless the publicist is full-time, she probably won't get to know more than 10 to 20 journalists personally. She might develop a "C" list as well, for those to whom she simply sends announcements, after she's finished working her A and B list people on the telephone. But she should anticipate poorer results from reporters who recognize her name primarily as a bulk-emailer of press releases.

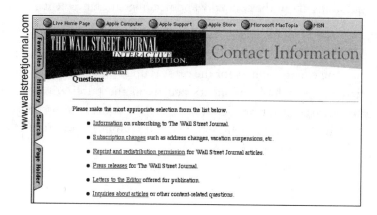

Figure 8.2

Popular business journals get hundreds of inquiries each day, so your search for press contacts online might only lead to an autoresponder.

Figure 8.3

Younger, more aggressive media sites keep their doors wide open for news. A hotlinked byline for SmartMoney.com's IPO reporter leads the way to her direct email address.

The Personal Touch

The best way to find out whether a journalist is interested in covering the company is asking.

Plan well ahead of an announcement and simply drop a brief email to the journalist, explaining that the company is going to be making some announcements in the future. Say that you believe, based on your familiarity with the journalist's work, that she is the appropriate contact for your type of company, but you want to confirm that before sending her any unwanted press releases. Keep it to a couple of paragraphs in a friendly, professional tone. Almost without exception, the journalist will be grateful for your direct approach. If she isn't the appropriate contact, she'll likely refer you to whoever is. If she is the right one, chances are she'll take the opportunity to ask you a few questions about the company and pending announcements.

How to Find Contact Addresses

Finding email contacts for the press is no great challenge. The first place to look, as mentioned, is in the publication. In many cases, print publications list email addresses for their principal editorial contacts. Online publications almost always do. (See Figure 8.4.)

Figure 8.4

Publishers Weekly, like many trade publications online, lists extensive editorial contact information.

Sometimes there is only one main editorial email address. Such a generic address is likely to be read only by a junior staffer. In that case, it is best for a publicist to request that his email be forwarded to the journalist he's trying to reach. If he simply emails a full press release to such a generic address, the chance of it reaching the appropriate person are slim.

If all else fails, here's a novel idea: Call the journalist on the telephone. Use a phone book if necessary, and simply ask to speak with the journalist. After getting her on the line, use the same frank approach, explaining that you want to verify that she's the right reporter to follow your company. And could she please tell you her email address for future reference?

If the front switchboard can't connect you because the writer is a freelancer, or for some other reason, ask to be transferred to the managing editor. Explain briefly why you're trying to contact the writer. If the editor won't give out the writer's personal email address, ask if you can have him forward a message to the writer. The editor will almost certainly oblige.

It's not in journalists' best interests to make themselves hard to reach. They depend on information, and if a publicist is offering useful information, they and their editors will open the channels to receive it.

Media Directories

Media directories are also sold. One is Bacon's, a big thick book (or if you prefer, a CD-ROM) providing contact data for thousands of newspapers and magazines. Online directories such as **MediaMap.com** are updated more frequently and are accessible by subscription; many Internet publicists use these services to stay up-to-date with Web business journalists, whose email addresses and loyalties often change (see Figures 8.5 and 8.6).

Figure 8.5

Media directories are a business in themselves; MediaMap is one online vendor with a good reputation for updated lists. Here's a free A-Z listing of current "Web" media. . .

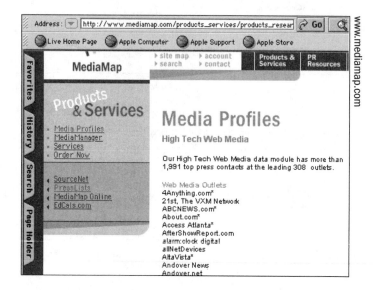

Figure 8.6

. . .But who has time to research them all? If you'd rather not comb through all these news sites to discover the right journalist names, MediaMap will rent you a mailing list specifically targeted to your industry.

Telephone Etiquette

Although email is the best way to make initial contact with journalists, especially those writing for Web publications, judicious use of the telephone is still an important tool for a publicist even in the digital age.

Here's the golden rule for calling journalists: Begin every call by saying, "Hi, [whoever], am I catching you at a bad time?"

You immediately make it clear to the journalist that you respect her time. If she answers "Yes," follow through on that respect and say, "Can I call back tomorrow?" Quickly agree on a time and hang up. Don't try to squeeze in a fast pitch, unless she explicitly invites, or you will blow that trust. Save it for the agreed-upon time. If the journalist really is on deadline, it's too late to pitch to her for the next edition anyway.

If you get a journalist's voice mail, leave a message only once. If it's really urgent, leave that one message and then play "Dialing for Dollars." Call and call and call until you actually catch her, and then act casually like it's the first time you picked up the phone since leaving your message. (Pretend you're back in college, trying to get a date.)

Quality Time

Once a publicist's A-list journalists know his name, and aren't cursing it, it's important for him not to be a stranger if he wants to be a good source. Don't wait until you have a press release to check in. Touch base once a month or so.

Whoever said, "There's no such thing as a free lunch," definitely wasn't a journalist. Forget about sending trinkets along with press releases. No reporter ever wrote a story because of a refrigerator magnet. If the publicist really wants to bond, he needs to get some face time.

If the journalist is in a different city, the publicist should find out when (if ever) his A-list reporters are likely to be in town and recommend a get-together. Likewise, he should take time to see them while in their neighborhood. When he goes to a trade conference, he should check in at the press room to see if they are also attending. Although the top reporters at *Business Week* and *The New York Times* might be above the flattery of a dinner invitation, most trade press reporters and freelancers are not.

Another way for a publicist to ingratiate himself to his A-list press is to feed them hot industry tips. Dirt on a competitor is always a favorite. He must not cry wolf with any old grime. But when he knows, without a doubt, that the CEO of a rival company is on the way out, that's something his best reporter contact would like to have a scoop on. A scoop means an exclusive, of course, so he must not mitigate the impact by shopping the same hot tip around to every reporter on his list.

Editorial Calendars

Whenever a publicist has a chance to speak with a journalist, he should ask what else the reporter's working on to see if she can fit something into a story underway for next week or next month.

Although hearing from a reporter firsthand what stories she's working on is the best way to keep abreast of her activities, many publications also maintain "editorial calendars," which are available publicly. By perusing the feature stories the publication has committed to covering, a publicist can find some topics fit well with his company. Some publications post their editorial calendars on their Web pages, while others will fax them upon request (ask the editorial assistant to do so, not your key reporter). (See Figure 8.7.)

Although such calendars are often useful, they're not 100 percent reliable. They're usually designed months ahead of time to give advertisers notice of special editions. Often, the editors are only dimly aware of the calendar commitments, and it might be challenging to figure out who's in charge of preparing a special feature. Such articles are usually prepared well in advance of the publication's normal deadlines, so concentrate on the opportunities several weeks or months in the future.

Figure 8.7

Publishers Weekly posts its editorial calendar on its Web page.

Planning News Announcements

Having sufficiently emphasized some avenues for getting recognized in the press, the next part of the discussion is effectively using that old PR staple, the news announcement (press release). The point is to avoid overly relying on press releases to get company exposure in the media. Nonetheless, a well-written, properly disseminated release announcing significant industry news can certainly build awareness.

Timing

The most important factor in a successful news announcement is to allow enough time to prepare properly. Calling a journalist *after* a press release has been issued to make sure she got it is not only the number one pet peeve of most reporters, but it's also too late to have much effect. If the publication has a strong news agenda, the chances of a reporter caring about a press release after it has been publicly issued are slim at best. This is especially true of weekly publications.

Consider it from their point of view. A publicist releases an announcement on PR Newswire or Businesswire (see the section "Disseminating Your Press Release" later in the chapter for more on these services), to which thousands of news organizations across the country subscribe. Then he sends it by email specifically to the publication he'd most like to see print it. Reuters, Associated Press, and various news Web sites might pick up the release off the wire, if it has genuine news value, and rewrite a story that same day. That means if a daily print newspaper picks up on it, they're already a day behind Reuters, AP, and the news sites. By the time a weekly publication has a chance to print it, the news is already a week old. Don't think that a weekly magazine doesn't view a daily newspaper as competition. They certainly do. And a daily feels the same way about a news Web site that can turn a story around in hours.

By definition, it's only news while it's new.

The point is, everyone must know to expect the release ahead of time. For weekly publications, this means the publicist has to *pre-brief* the journalists around a week in advance. For dailies (including Web news sites), it's a day in advance. For monthlies, the publicist might as well forget about briefing them on news. Few monthlies even attempt to cover news because they typically finish their editorial production of an issue anywhere from two to five months in advance of publication. Unless he's extremely well-organized and can brief them that far in advance, he should just send them the release when it's public and concentrate on getting feature and profile coverage from them, instead. (See Figure 8.8.)

Non-Disclosure Agreements (NDAs) and Embargoes

"But if I brief them in advance," a publicist might ask, "couldn't they go ahead and publish the news before we've put out our press release?" If what a publicist is really interested in is publicity, that's the least of his worries. The straight answer, though, is this: Yes they could, but they probably won't.

Figure 8.8
No weekly publication wants to cover next week what *News.com* just ran online today.

Every journalist is familiar with the concept of a *NDA*, or *embargo*. This essentially means that the journalist promises not to release the information until an agreed-upon date, namely when the publicist's press release officially goes out on Businesswire or PR Newswire. Although it was mentioned that speaking off the record is subjective, most journalists are pretty clear about whether or not they'll honor an NDA. Generally, it's not necessary to have them sign an agreement to that effect, but most would be willing to sign one if the publicist was really paranoid about it.

There are some publications and journalists who refuse to agree to NDAs as a matter of principle, but they're the minority. As long as the publicist doesn't start giving them the news before they've agreed on an NDA, this shouldn't be a problem. They'll tell him up-front that they don't agree to NDAs, and he can decide at that point to pre-brief them or not accordingly.

He should be prepared to share a draft copy of his press release with his A-level journalists when he pre-briefs them. Even if the release hasn't completed its rounds of official approvals yet, the journalists will expect to use it as a reference. The release should be clearly labeled as a draft that's subject to non-disclosure. The whole point of a non-disclosure agreement, however, is that it's an *agreement*. Simply writing "NDA" at the top of a draft release and sending it to a journalist who's not expecting it is not an agreement. They now have the news without having made a promise to honor the embargo deadline.

Pre-Briefing in the Online Era

Although pre-briefing the press is a time-honored tradition among publicists, the Internet complicates that process. In the pre-Web era, there wasn't much a weekly publication could do to scoop the story even if they wanted, as long as the publicist timed her briefing a week before your announcement date. Now, however, most publications are putting daily news on their Web sites in addition to their weekly print editions and are eager, therefore, for daily scoops.

In most cases, the risk is manageable. Mostly it comes down to being clear with the journalist that the NDA includes the Web site. If a journalist regularly goes around burning her sources, she'll soon have no leads for news, so the publicist can usually count on her word on NDAs. In some cases, however, the journalist might not have ultimate control over that process. A different team of editors might produce the Web site and sneak peaks at the material in the production cycle for the weekly print edition. The publicist should ask her journalist contact ahead of time if that's likely to be the case. (See Figure 8.9.)

Figure 8.9
Advertising Age prides itself on always respecting non-disclosure agreements, relying on companies to give it a heads-up on important announcements.

For some companies the risk of an early news break is too great, so they never pre-brief reporters. This is frequently the case with companies whose stock is publicly traded because they don't want to be accused of not sharing information equally with all investors. This is a viable position for companies prominent in their industries, such as Microsoft or Netscape. Journalists have no choice but to react to these companies' announcements, regardless of whether they were pre-briefed. For most smaller companies out there, however, this isn't a luxury they can afford.

Pitch on Fridays or Mondays

If the publicist's A-list includes weekly magazines, he should officially release his announcements on Mondays. Most weeklies begin their reporting cycle on Fridays and continue collecting news on Mondays and Tuesdays. Wednesdays and Thursdays are the deadline crunch and are the worst days to try to call them. By Friday the cycle starts over, with each edition hitting the streets on Monday. Some magazines come out on other days, such as *Business Week*, which is on news-stands by Friday (despite an official Monday cover date), but those are the exceptions.

When the publicist makes initial contact with his A-list reporters, he should ask them to clarify their deadline schedule and find out the best time to brief them. Again, he'll gain points for expressing consideration for their hectic jobs.

Understand News

The biggest challenge for most PR people is understanding what reporters consider genuinely newsworthy and what they consider fluff. This is generally due to a lack of perspective. Being as close as they are to their firms' daily struggles, many marketing directors, product managers, and CEOs think the whole world ought to care as much as they do about their company's every success. Save the self-congratulations for the weekly staff meeting. The press quickly learns to ignore a publicist if he issues fluff press releases too often.

What *Isn't* News?

All journalists are guided by what is called the "hype detector." With so many publicists trying to snow the press every day, this is a necessary defense mechanism. When a publicist is evaluating whether or not to issue a release, he should give it a thorough testing with his own hype-o-meter first.

If his is a publicly traded company, of course, even routine announcements about changes to his product line or company's online profile are always of interest to some business media. Entrepreneurial firms have a harder time getting ink generally, so a publicist should not waste too much time on corporate news that is journalistically small potatoes. The following are some common topics that companies think the press should care about, and are then disappointed when they don't.

New Web Sites, So What?

This one is a matter of spin. Of course, the launch of a new online service should be a significant news event for most companies. The point is that the novelty of simply launching a Web site hasn't been newsworthy in and of itself since early 1995.

The compelling news story is that the company's Web site provides a customer benefit or serves an unfulfilled need in the marketplace. What does the company offer that can't be found elsewhere on the Web? Until the publicist can answer that question, she shouldn't bother with a press release.

Redesigned Sites, Upgraded Products, Ho-hum

How compelling do you really find the words "new and improved" on a box of detergent or cereal? It's no more convincing as a news message than as an advertising pitch. Significant changes to a venture's business model might make interesting news, but cosmetic changes to its site design aren't even worth a media alert.

Similarly, if it's a software company, the publicist shouldn't count on the general media getting excited about its upgrade from a 2.0 product to version 3.0. Computer magazines might take notice of upgrades and duly report them, but a new version of the software rarely has the impact of a truly new product. If its customers are in a non-technical industry segment, the publications that serve them aren't likely to care about extra bells and whistles. Extolling theoretical benefits doesn't cut it. The press wants installed users who can talk about results, and not just about a few weeks of limited beta testing.

Staff Appointments, Big Deal

A new CEO is news, but it can be a signal that there was something wrong with the old one. It might not be the best news to crow about without a well-considered spin. Unless they're major industry celebrities, the vice presidents, directors, financial officers, and the rest probably don't merit more than a brief in the local daily paper. Some publications do have a "Movers and Shakers" column that a publicist can target, but her A-list reporters probably value new-hire releases only as background.

Customer Wins, Who Cares?

In a capitalist society, companies are in business to win customers. Failing to win customers and going out of business is news. Winning customers is business as usual, not news. Unless the likes of Intel, General Motors, the White House, or the People's Republic of China have standardized on the product, issuing a press release about a "customer win" is unlikely to spark the press's imagination.

What *Is* News?

A good news story needs a hook. It should contain some sense of drama, importance, or righteousness. It might appeal to human interest, local pride, or fascination with celebrity. Or it could click due to humor, surprise, or irony.

The following are some possible news hooks for Web ventures.

Embrace What's Topical

Stage an online event, or introduce a feature on the company's Web site focusing on something that's already prominent in the news or is destined to become so. The publicist could hold a forum on an important trial, congressional controversy, or foreign event. Every time a new virus hits Web email, for example, security companies such as MacAfee and e-Trust trot out statements, opinions, and recent product news in press releases.

Issue a Report

Find a topic related to the site's main theme, conduct a survey, and issue a report on the findings. Online media particularly love Internet surveys, as they're always desperate for statistics. Being the first to report which percentage of women executives are shopping online, for example, will certainly get the company immediate press exposure. Plus, the findings are likely to be cited repeatedly over time, and many other sites can link to the survey from their pages. Continue to update the research monthly, quarterly, or annually, and the report could become a "must visit" site for journalists, and a perpetual source of exposure for the company's site. Paying an outside consulting group to actually conduct the research would be money well spent, considering its genuine publicity value.

Rent a Celebrity

It's a sad comment on our society, but almost anything to do with a well-known personality is newsworthy enough to guarantee some press. Find some way to incorporate a big name into an event on the site, and it's worth a press release.

Form a Strategic Partnership

Unlike winning a customer, partnering with another company can be newsworthy if the union brings a new level of value to mutual customers or puts the company in a stronger competitive position against industry rivals. (See Figure 8.10.)

Figure 8.10

Ovum likes to make predictions that sometimes seem to run counter to the prevailing industry trends. In some quarters, that's news.

Buck a Trend

The press loves nothing more than controversy. If everyone in the industry is jumping on the same bandwagon, be the first to charge loudly in the opposite direction. The half-life of an online fad is normally a matter of weeks, so editors will tire of the latest overhyped trend quickly and be eager to give voice to someone who disagrees. Just be sure the company can stand by its convictions, and don't set a corporate strategy based on a publicity opportunity that later turns out to go against the company's best interest.

Celebrate a Milestone

Don't overdo this idea, but large round numbers are cause for attention. Celebrate the company's millionth customer, a million page views a month, $10 million in revenue a year, and so on.

Present an Award

Rise above being a mere player and become a judge of industry excellence. (See Figure 8.11.)

Do Public Good

Join a just cause, such as fighting a disease or raising money for a charity. Team up with organizations such as a mayor's office, a university, or, especially, other media outlets such as a newspaper or TV station, to champion a heart-warming cause. The company's contribution could be no more than online promotion, but the event could provide it with substantial goodwill exposure.

Figure 8.11
Punditry has paid off for Ovum, as this trade magazine article shows.

Take a Political Stance

Is there a legislative debate affecting the industry? Boldly declare a position. Become a leading proponent of one side.

Co-found an Industry Association

Does the industry need to agree on common standards, or lack a body to represent its interests? Don't let someone else steal the thunder. Act first to get the ball rolling. If the association already exists, run for its top office. Show leadership.

The Model Press Release

The three most important guidelines for writing an effective press release are:

1. Keep it short.

2. Keep it short.

3. Keep it short.

As any journalist can tell you, only one in 10 press releases actually manages to obey these three important rules. "Short" means a maximum of two double-spaced pages, *including* the "About Our Company" boilerplate. For an emailed press release, it means no more than one-and-a-half screens of text. That's about six or seven paragraphs, or 400–500 words.

If the publicist can't say it in those few words, she's not being clear about what she's trying to say. Imagine the journalist who only has room to report the announcement in a two-sentence brief. Is it possible to reduce the news to two sentences, or would the publicist rather not have a newsbrief at all?

If the announcement involves complexities that need a detailed explanation, relegate it to a *white paper* or other supplemental material. Focus on the customer benefit in the news announcement.

There's no question that writing so concisely is difficult. Henry David Thoreau said in a letter to a friend, "Not that the story need be long, but it will take a long while to make it short." All the more reason not to rush the press release process.

Consider that each journalist reading the release probably receives more than 100 email messages a day, the majority of which are other press releases. Every extra paragraph begs her to skip to the next email. If the release is short but compelling, she will call the publicist with further questions as necessary.

Death to Buzzwords

"Robust," "scaleable," "next-generation," "industrial-strength," blah, blah, blah. These sorts of terms are the bane of the high-tech industry. Jargon just makes the announcement sound unoriginal. Decide what is meant to be said and say it.

Similarly, resist hyperbole and superlatives, such as "the first," "the leading," or "revolutionary." Even if they're true, they sound insincere and invite challenge. And don't promise emotions, such as "exciting," "wonderful," or "incredible." Let the press, and ultimately your customers, be the judge of their reactions. Just the facts, ma'am. (See Figure 8.12.)

Figure 8.12
They're kidding, right? Crain's recent B2B trade magazine seems to have a hard time controlling the hype in its own online press kit.

Component Parts

In general, press releases follow a predictable formula. Unlike poets, publicists don't get much creative license. It seems stifling, but if the publicist wants to create art, he's in the wrong profession. If he gets too clever with anecdotal, feature-like copy, journalists may become confused and move on to the next release. Rules are made to be broken, of course, and should not inhibit the next William Faulkner of PR, but venture forth so advised.

The goal of a release is to communicate the news clearly and directly enough that the journalist can rewrite a short item based entirely on it. Or at least pique his interest enough to call. Leave the details to interviews, white papers, corporate backgrounds, and other follow-up material.

Headline

In the headline, state the news in as few words as possible, focusing on the customer benefit. Be straightforward, and leave the clever puns to the editors. Follow the Associated Press style rules on grammar, tense, and so on.

A sub-headline is optional. If one is needed, it should be used to express a secondary message, not simply to reiterate the same point as the main headline.

Date and Dateline

Don't forget to date the release. A reporter might reference it months from now to note when a certain company event occurred. The tradition of printing "For Immediate Release" at the top of a press release, on the other hand, is fairly redundant and can be ignored. Obviously it's for immediate release once it's made public.

A dateline—that is, the location from which the news was filed—indicates where the company is headquartered, although that same information should be contained at the bottom of the release in the contact information. Often, if a release is issued in conjunction with a conference, the dateline will reflect that location.

Issuing press releases at industry conferences, however, is rarely a good idea. Many other companies will do the same, and therefore most announcements are lost in the noise. Better to jump the gun and make announcements the week prior to a conference, so the story appears in the publications while all of the company's competitors are gathered at the event.

Lede

After the headline, the lede is the most important part of the release, perhaps the only paragraph the journalist will bother to read fully. Imitate news style. Be direct, immediately stating the news while emphasizing the customer benefit. Cover the news basics: who, what, where, when, why, and how.

Quotes

Quotes from the company's president, customers, or industry analysts are optional. Make quotes advance the story, not just reiterate what's already been said. Use them to express opinions. Avoid clichés and hollow claims such as, "Our service is a breakthrough that will revolutionize the industry."

Boilerplate

It's standard for a release to contain a brief description of the company and its positioning. This text remains the same for all the company's press releases. Keep it to one or two sentences.

Price and Availability

If applicable, the last section of a release before the contact information should note the price and availability of the product or service. Don't avoid the question of price; journalists will want to know this and won't appreciate having to call just to find out.

Lede means Lead

"Lede," by the way, is a peculiar spelling of the word "lead" that's traditionally favored by journalists in this context. The origin, like other strange journalistic spellings such as "graf," "hed," and "folo" (for "follow-up"), come from shorthand instructions to typesetters that were intentionally misspelled so they wouldn't accidentally get set into print.

Contact Information

Be sure to include contact information at the very bottom of the release. This should include the company's full address and URL, as well as a publicity contact. Include both email address and telephone number for the publicist. A sales department contact can be included as well as a publicist, given that press releases that are broadly issued are likely to end up directly on the screens of potential customers through Web news sites.

When this press release is posted on the Web site, don't neglect to include the contact information exactly as it appeared in print form. Long before a phone call is made, a journalist might research the Web site for background materials. Making contact information easily available can mean the difference between her calling this company, instead of another.

Page Numbers

Be sure to number each page on printed copies of the release, and print "- more -" at the bottom of each page. Remove these page markers when formatting the release for email, however.

Abstract

If it is impossible to limit the release to two pages, use an abstract at the top of the release. When alerting journalists by email, send only the abstract, with a URL where they can find the complete release if they desire.

Media Alerts

When the company feels compelled to make some official announcement for the record, yet it doesn't merit serious news coverage (such as a staff appointment), consider issuing a "media alert." This is a very short item of one to two paragraphs, sent out over PR Newswire or Businesswire, that is not pitched to any individual press.

An Example of an Effective Press Release

Here's a sample of an effective press release. The subject is genuinely newsworthy. The body of the release is under 500 words. The quotes advance the story and contain the only opinions in the release. The writing style is direct, newsy, and professional.

Contacts:	Jay Raymond	Greg Amrofell
	IMT Strategies, Inc.	IMT Strategies, Inc.
	203-705-6588	650-425-2427
	jay@imtstrategies.com	greg@imtstrategies.com

IMT Strategies Projects Marketers Will Spend $1 Billion by 2001 for 'Permission' to E-Mail Customers

Research indicates that permission email marketing is five times more cost-effective than direct mail, 20 times more than Web banners—and consumers like it

STAMFORD, CT – November 1, 1999 – IMT Strategies, Inc., a leading sales and marketing research and advisory firm, today released the findings of its groundbreaking study on permission email marketing. The study reveals that customers clearly distinguish between permission email and unsolicited commercial email (UCE), also known as "spam." Further, leading marketers that ask for and receive permission to email their customers are finding that their messages are not only welcome, but are greeted with response rates that far exceed other targeted marketing vehicles such as Web advertising and direct mail, as well as unsolicited commercial email.

The study methodology included a random phone survey of 403 adult U.S. email users and phone and Web surveys of more than 200 leading e-marketers.

According to IMT Strategies' research, more than half of all email users feel positively about permission email marketing, and nearly three quarters of users respond to permission email with some frequency. By contrast, the findings show that UCE can hurt the brand image of companies who use it: 67 percent of customers had "very negative" reactions to receiving spam.

Surprisingly, marketers have a hard time telling the difference between permission email and UCE. "The distinction between permission marketing and spam frequently appears gray to marketers," said Rick Bruner, IMT Strategies vice president. "Well-meaning but inexperienced marketers may acquire addresses through questionable means only to have their promotions equated in customers' minds with pornography, pyramid schemes, and con artists."

IMT Strategies predicts this will cause a "race for permission" over the next two years. "The window of opportunity is closing on marketers," Rick Bruner asserted, "when you combine rapidly growing email volumes with diminishing consumer tolerance for UCE." He believes "direct marketers will have a two- to three-year window to build permission relationships with customers and prospects before they shut the door on email solicitations."

In an effort to build vital "relationship share" with their target markets, companies will spend at least $1 billion on permission email marketing by 2001, according to IMT Strategies forecasts.

To Obtain Copies of the Report

Full copies of the report, "Permission E-mail: The Future of Direct Marketing," are available now by contacting IMT Strategies toll-free, at 877-566-7744, or visiting IMT Strategies' Web site at http://www.imtstrategies.com.

About IMT Strategies

IMT Strategies, Inc. helps organizations understand, anticipate, and capitalize on advances in marketing technologies and rapidly changing customer buying behavior. IMT Strategies is an affiliate and strategic partner of META Group, offering custom and syndicated research, consulting, and training services.

Disseminating Your Press Release

Now that the publicist has created a newsworthy event, written a short and to-the-point press release about it, and rigorously checked it for spelling, grammar, and writing style, he needs to get it into the hands of some journalists.

The Wire

When publicists speak of *dropping* a press release on the wire, they generally mean issuing it to PR Newswire and Business-wire, two subscription-based announcement services that have dominated the industry of disseminating press releases for decades (see Figure 8.13). Issuing a press release on one of these two services is synonymous with making the announcement public. The average fee for a basic wire announcement is around $500, depending on the length of the release and the breadth of the distribution.

These services provide at least two important benefits. First of all, thousands of news media outlets around the country and the world subscribe to them, and many editors scan them attentively according to their various topics of interest. News services such as Reuters and the Associated Press routinely rewrite press releases with no further research and forward them to thousands more outlets. A publicist is unlikely to find any other way to reach as many media outlets as quickly and efficiently.

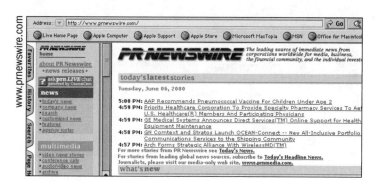

Figure 8.13

PR Newswire is one of the leading press announcement services, with thousands of media outlets worldwide subscribing to its feed of press releases.

Second, in the Internet age, releases from these wires are reissued directly for public consumption by many financial Web sites and other online services. (See Figure 8.14.) Whereas it used to be that only editors were likely to read press releases and decide whether or not to rewrite them for their readers, the Internet has cut out the middleman. Putting a release on the wire has effectively become a direct publishing channel between companies and potential stockholders or customers. Such online services also extend the life of a press release indefinitely through searchable databases.

Another class of press release distribution services has emerged recently that automates the distribution of releases directly to editors' email addresses. The benefit of such a service is marginal, at best. For one thing, PR Newswire and Businesswire offer the same added service. They will customize distribution lists for individual clients, or use their in-house lists that are specially tailored for narrow industry topics, for the same prices as the new breed of specialized Internet news wires. The new services don't offer the traditional wires' breadth of distribution, however.

More to the point, mass distribution of press releases to individual editors is far less effective than sending personalized messages.

Figure 8.14

Free online news services such as Yahoo!'s deliver news straight from Businesswire and PR Newswire to Internet readers at large.

Individual Distribution

As discussed earlier, the publicist should alert his key press contacts from your A- and B-lists before the actual release date of the announcement. He can send C-level contacts the release the same day it goes out over the wire.

In all cases, it's highly preferable to send the release to each journalist individually rather than placing all their names in the blind copy field. This conveys much more respect, indicating they are recognized as individual writers rather than a commodity. Add a sentence or two of introduction to the release, personalizing the message.

Of course, the publicist can cut and paste the release and the introduction into individual messages, typing in just the name of the journalist separately and making minor modifications to each introductory note as required.

Be sure to get the journalist's name right. It's an axiom of journalism that if the publicist can't get the names right, no one can trust the rest of the facts in the story. Don't assume a familiar name for the writer (such as "Kathy" for "Katherine") unless it's clear that's how she's known publicly. By default, use the same name the journalist does in her byline.

Any standard email program allows the publicist to keep an address book of contacts so he doesn't need to retype the email addresses every time he sends out a press release. The process of cutting and pasting and customizing each message obviously takes longer than copying a mass of addresses at once, but the extra half hour or so is time well spent. A good email program, such as Qualcomm's Eudora, makes creating form letters even easier with a "stationary" function (consult your software's Help or manual to see if it provides a similar feature).

If the publicist insists on copying multiple journalists with the same message, she should never add a mass of names to the To: or CC: fields. The result is a long, extremely tacky list of names dominating the first screen or more of the message. Instead, she should place all the addresses in the BCC: field (short for "blind carbon copy," from the days of typewriters and carbon paper). Address the message to herself or, in the case of Eudora, leave the To: field blank so the resulting message will automatically display "Recipient List Repressed" in the To: field.

Formatting for Email

Most journalists these days prefer to receive press releases through email, but the publicist should try to determine individual preferences ahead of time. Some traditionalists would still rather receive them by fax or snail mail and might react unkindly to email submissions.

When sending a release by email, *never* send it as a binary attachment. Always cut and paste the text of the release into the body of the email message. Unsolicited email attachments are an online no-no. Attached files can contain viruses (Microsoft Word files are notorious for them), frequently get garbled or deleted by corporate email gateways, take a long time to download (the writer might be checking email on her laptop through a long-distance phone connection), and so on.

60–65 Characters Per Line

When copying text from a press release into an email message, make sure the message is neatly formatted. The most important consideration is to put a hard return at the end of each line, creating relatively wide margins. Between 60 and 65 characters per line (including spaces) is ideal. More than that and the recipients' email software might cut off the ends of each line and leave just a few words dangling at the beginning of the next line. Use fewer characters than 60 and the release starts to look like a column of newsprint. (See Figure 8.15.)

Macintosh users have a rare occasion to gloat that a terrific application exists for their platform that makes text formatting a breeze, with no equivalent for Windows. Namely, it's Bare Bones Software's superb program, BBEdit.

In addition to line-wrapping, be sure to put a blank line between each paragraph to make the ASCII text much easier to read.

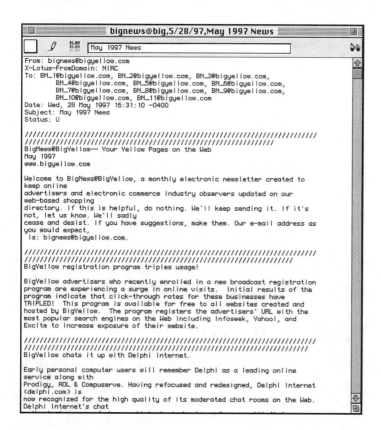

Death to Dumb Quotes

It's also important to eliminate all non-ASCII-standard characters, such as bullets, trademark symbols (replace with just "TM" in parentheses), em dashes (use two hyphens), and especially so-called "smart quotes," which are in reality dumb quotes. These insidious characters, which curl to the right at the beginning of a quote and to the left at the end, are supposed to be a clever enhancement to text. In the ASCII-based world of the Internet, however, smart quotes and all other non-ASCII-standard characters turn into accented i's, square blocks, or strings of gobbledygook.

Figuring out how to turn off smart quotes on a word processor can be a challenge. Consult the program's manual or online Help. (See Figure 8.16.)

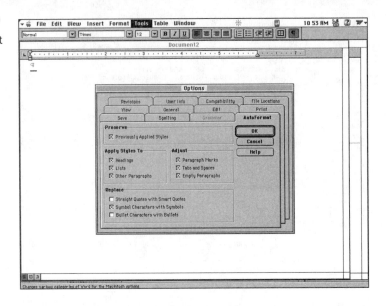

Figure 8.16

The dialog box with the smart quotes control is hidden in Microsoft Word 6.0, Tools/Options/AutoFormat. Die, dumb quotes, die, die, die!!

Press Kit Basics

With every announcement a publicist sends out, there should be an up-to-date press kit available for those journalists who request it. Don't send press kits unsolicited because reporters who didn't ask for them are liable to throw them away. A professionally packaged press kit isn't cheap to assemble, so save the company the expense and send them only when requested.

In addition to a *physical* press kit, every Web site should have a virtual press kit as well. This includes more than just recent press releases, which is all most sites seem to bother with, but also most of the items in the following list. This is a cost-effective alternative for smaller businesses for whom the production of professional physical press kits might be a prohibitive expense.

Corporate Fact Sheet

The corporate fact sheet is the chance to expand upon the standard boilerplate at the end of most press releases. It's a one-page summary of key company information for quick reference:

- Founding date

- Key executives' names and titles

- Product names and short descriptions

- Short mission statement and company history

- Corporate headquarters contact information, including directions by car or public transit

- PR contact information

Some companies also include in their press kits a several-page "corporate background" document, with more narrative extolling the company's vision and positioning. This is generally less useful to journalists. If a publicist chooses to include one, he should include a simple fact sheet as well.

Executive Biographies

Executive biographies should be limited to the top members of the executive team, the only people the press are likely to interview. Keep them as short as possible, one paragraph for each person if possible. More than one biography on a page is fine. Include hobbies as well, to round out the character of the individuals.

Press Releases Digest

Press kits typically include one or two recent press releases in addition to the current one being pitched. If the company has produced several press releases in recent months, it's useful to include a digest of one or two pages with a paragraph abstract for each press release. Refer to a URL where full copies of the releases are located.

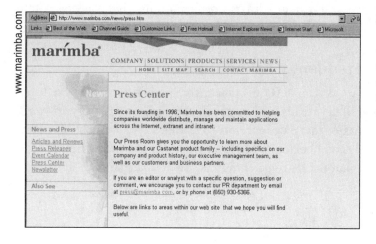

Figure 8.17
Marimba, Inc.'s Web site provides a good example of a simple but comprehensive online press kit. Screen shots are offered as pictures to go with product stories.

Graphics

Because the Web is increasingly a graphic, rather than text, medium, graphic images are extremely important in making the story attractive to a journalist or editor. A good downloadable image of the product in action can easily make the difference between a story being printed or not. In the online press room, provide at least a few screenshots of the site's home page or the company's products, as well as portraits of executives. Try to avoid overly corporate headshots of executives. Opt instead for more relaxed images.

Be sure to make the images available on the press area of the Web site in several digital image formats, including GIF and TIFF. In addition, be prepared to accommodate technophobic reporters by mailing the images on a disk, as well as making them available on an FTP server for the technophiles. Some editors prefer printed copies or slides of images.

Product Descriptions/White Paper

As necessary, a publicist might want to go into further detail about products and services in separate documents.

Customer/Analyst References

A publicist might want to provide customer and analyst quotes and contact information (with their permission, of course). Most journalists prefer the contact information to the canned quotes. Be prepared to surrender control of these interviews because a journalist is not comfortable interviewing a third party with a company publicist monitoring the call.

Frequently Asked Questions

A Q&A or FAQ document for journalists is only useful if a publicist truly anticipates the hard questions the press might ask or that past reporters have asked. Don't use this document as an opportunity to spoon-feed them marketing fluff. Keep in mind the BS-o-meter. Rather, use it as a chance to prepare the best spin for the difficult questions.

Reprinted News Stories

A reprinted news story as part of a press kit can be a double-edged sword. On one hand, a journalist might find a third-party report to be a more objective explanation of a company's positioning than the company's own marketing and PR material. On the other hand, the reporter might be turned off to see that the company has already been well-covered by her competition. Use no more than two or three of the best stories, if any.

Other Publicity Opportunities

Beyond print and the Web, there are still other ways to get the word out about the business and the site. Consider some of the following ideas.

Speaking Opportunities

Get the company's CEO or other top executives on the speaking circuit. Although maybe only a few hundred people will hear them speak on a given day, the caliber of audience reached through public speaking is valuable in influencing the rest of the industry. The "trickle-down effect" might be dubious in economics, but it's real in the world of publicity.

Keeping track of upcoming speaking opportunities can be difficult in this fast-paced industry. One of the better online resources is the Association for Interactive Media's Web site (see the "Resources" section at the end of this chapter for details). Speaking opportunities normally get booked months in advance, so look ahead. (See Figure 8.18.)

Opinion Pieces

Newspapers, magazines, and Web publications are often eager to receive opinion pieces for their editorial pages. Have the CEO write such a piece (or commission a freelancer to ghostwrite it), again discussing an industry trend without putting the company in the middle of the discussion. Having the company name and URL printed at the bottom of the piece is effective enough. Many of those who are inspired by a publicist's opinions will check out the company's site on their own.

Figure 8.18

SiliconAlley.com, a tabloid for the net set, maintains a comprehensive calendar of local, national, and international high-tech conferences and events.

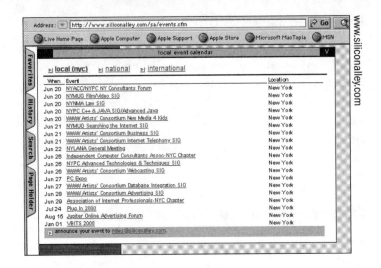

Similarly, writing letters to the editor is another option for publications that are more competitive in their opinion pages, such as the *New York Times*. Short letters under 300 words have a better chance of being published than longer ones, both on the Web and off.

Web 'Zines and Email Newsletters

From a PR perspective, the larger Web publications are generally not much different from traditional media, other than their immediate turnaround time is closer to radio, TV, news wires (like Reuters), or even newspapers, which require a day to turn news around.

Smaller Web publications, sometimes called *'zines*, as well as email newsletters, are often more malleable, however. Although many offer reasonably high quality information, particularly in narrow niches, they are almost all run on shoestring budgets. As a result, they might invite the CEO to become a regular columnist (pro bono, of course).

If a regular column is too much work, consider rewriting news releases to read like actual news stories. Try to copy the writing style of a targeted 'zine or newsletter, and be sure to present it to the editor in a text-only format as well as a double-spaced print press release. Editors of smaller news sites or newsletters will frequently reprint such offerings verbatim.

Call-In Radio Shows

If a publicist calls in to a talk radio program, the host will generally let him tell the audience the company's URL if his comments are on-topic.

Video News Releases (VNRs) and B-Roll

If a publicist has the budget for it, VNRs and *B-rolls* are a great way to get coverage on television. A video production company will charge in the neighborhood of $10,000 to prepare a mock TV news story about the company's latest announcement, which can be submitted to local TV stations. Some smaller stations are likely to broadcast the VNR in its entirety if it has been professionally produced. To find local video pros, look in the telephone book under "television production" or contact the state's film bureau for a list of companies. (Film bureaus, which administer shooting permits for film companies, are usually a division of the state's tourist office.)

Either as a separate undertaking or as part of the process of making the VNR, a publicist can produce B-roll. This is background footage of the company, showing employees at work, the executives answering general interview-style questions, footage of a computer screen with someone navigating the company's site, and so forth. A publicist can continue to submit B-roll material to TV stations long after any specific announcement, which the station's news team might edit together to make their own story. Most of the images could be used as background for the news reporter's original voice-over.

Small TV stations with limited resources for sending out their own crews are especially receptive to this technique, and are quite likely to follow through on a story once a publicist has made it this easy for them.

If a publicist is planning an IPO, or a major announcement that will impact the local community, he should make sure he has B-roll ready to go for the local TV news outlet. He should always have updated print press kits available in a file. These should include one-page summaries of product or site highlights, company history and background, and biographies and photos of key executives. This way, he's prepared for any event that might result in media coverage—from the unforeseen swell of word-of-mouth to the Web site, to an obituary of the beloved CFO. As they say in Hollywood, there's no such thing as bad publicity.

 **Resources**

Sites and Services

PR Newswire
http://www.prnewswire.com

- One of the two leading services for disseminating press releases worldwide. The Web site explains the company's services in detail and contains links to several valuable PR resources.

Businesswire
http://www.businesswire.com

- This is the other leading service for online press releases, with similar features and resources.

MediaMap
http://www.mediamap.com

- This online directory rents and maintains updated lists of press contacts. Other services include press material design and distribution. "Free" material on this site includes useful white papers on Web PR and two free, weekly email newsletters of interest to anyone working in Web PR.

Bacon's
http://www.baconsinfo.com

- Now a division of Primedia, Bacon's sells resource lists of media contact addresses, press release distribution services, and a clipping service to collect stories about the company.

Silicon Alley
http://www.siliconalley.com/sa/events.cfm

- The Web site for this online trade magazine displays free and extensive listings of upcoming Internet and related tech conferences, trade shows, seminars, and similar events.

Books

The Associated Press Stylebook and Libel Manual
- Available at any good bookstore, this is the bible of journalistic style and should be used for press releases as well.

continues

continued

Writer's Market

- An annual guide useful for hunting out niche consumer and trade publications that might be receptive to releases about a particular business-to-business or business-to-consumer Web site. Available in most libraries, in the reference section.

Elements of Style
By William Strunk, Jr. and E. B. White

- Every publicist should own a copy and reread it annually. Also available in part on the Web at http://www.columbia.edu/acis/bartleby/strunk/.

On Writing Well
By William Zinsser

- A better-than-average guide to good writing, useful to anyone writing a "white paper" or guest column or article.

IN THIS CHAPTER

Paid Media: Making Dollars and Sense with Web Advertising

MANY COMPANIES BEGIN WEB marketing by building a basic Web site and then they realize they need to promote the site. If million-dollar TV ad budgets are out of the question, they design some ad banners, buy several thousand impressions on some leading sites, and sit back and hope that 1 percent of those who see the ads click on them and come to the site.

And for a great many online ventures, that remains the extent of "Web marketing."

Now that you have read through to this last chapter, you should understand that online marketing is more complex and rewarding than simply putting up one Web site and a shower of ad banners. As described in Part I, your site needs to be extraordinary, representing real strategic goals for the company and true benefits for visitors. And as covered in the preceding four chapters of Part II, there are many other, more cost-effective ways to promote a site and develop a loyal audience than online ads. These methods include viral marketing, email lists, affinity site and affiliate site links, media relations, and more.

Why Advertise Online?

This is not to say that online advertising plays *no* part, of course. It can be very important for many sites. Our definition of *audience development* is made up of two key components—the audience creation techniques described in the previous four chapters of Part II, and paid media, also known as advertising. A two-pronged strategy that acknowledges the usefulness of paid promotions is necessary to create and sustain an active, engaged audience that drives repeat business to the Web site.

It is strategically important, however, to understand where the real benefits of online advertising lie and how to use ads in harmony with the less expensive media techniques we've been describing.

Impressions, Clicks, and Conversions: Conflicting Measures

Most mature sites have tried banners to drive inbound traffic. Although there are clearly cases where this makes sense, in B2B applications the kinds of audience creation techniques discussed in previous chapters are often more cost-effective for generating qualified, targeted traffic. While the strategic importance of banners for brand building should not be overlooked by both B2B and B2C Web marketers, banners alone cannot be expected to drive sales efficiently.

One reason more sites don't question the cost-effectiveness of using banners to drive traffic is a confusing incongruity between the two key measurements popularly used in Web advertising. For reasons of familiarity, online advertisers have accepted the cost per thousand measure (CPM) as the standard for banner pricing. CPM comes primarily out of the broadcast and print worlds, where branding is the prevailing advertising objective. Yet, at the same time, these advertisers deemed clickthrough rates (CTR), a clear extension of direct marketing goals to be the most common measure of advertising success.

In recent years the clickthrough rate has dropped as low as .03 to .05 percent. Small wonder that marketers have turned much of their attention, and budgets, to performance-based media, such as affiliate programs that pay per customer transaction, and email marketing, which currently sustains an average response rate (as measured by clickthroughs) of about 5 percent. Advertising rates haven't exactly plummeted in response to this competition, but advertisers now find it easier to purchase banner ads on pricing based not just on impressions or clickthroughs, but also on the rate of *conversion* (either a completed sale or other active customer transaction subsequent to a clickthrough).

Figure 9.1
Does IBM communicate much more about its brand message in its similar TV commercials? Seems like this animated Web banner ad more or less says it all.

Research by IMT Strategies, Adknowlege, and others has shown that there's more often an inverse relationship between clickthroughs and customer conversions. Banner campaigns with high clickthrough rates tend to have low conversion ratios, while banners with low clickthrough rates have higher conversion ratios. This is enough reason not to measure the effectiveness of a campaign simply by clickthrough ratios, but there are other good reasons as well. The first is that proxy servers, additional layers of servers that handle and shuffle traffic between sites at the Internet service provider (ISP) level, tend to lose or miscount clicks, to say the least. Plus, different advertising companies often count clicks differently, making a direct apples-to-apples comparison difficult when judging a campaign's worth. If the organizational goal is customer conversion, don't be swayed into buying media that is focused on counting clicks.

If you are buying banners for branding, it still makes sense to quantify the costs of banner ads in terms of sheer numbers of impressions registered with desired audience segments, as in offline media. If you're paying for branding but you're measuring for direct results, it's hard to know if you're getting what you're paying for. Measuring the success of branding is complicated, as discussed later in the chapter. Clickthroughs are a poor measure of branding success, and this measurement shouldn't be forced to fit this objective. If driving traffic is indeed the goal, on the other hand, it is useful to translate the CPM rate into a cost-per-click measure to make sure you're getting a fair price.

CPM rates online vary greatly, hovering from the $30 average found in rate cards, to the $1.50 CPM that many swear is what they're actually paying. But, for example, say an advertiser pays a typical $10 CPM and receives an approximate industry average of a .05 percent CTR. It makes for easy math—a total of five clicks per thousand means the cost is $2 per clickthrough (see "The Math" sidebar later in this chapter). At this fairly typical ad cost, a company would pay $10,000 to generate 50 visits to its home page.

Spending 10,000 on the type of unpaid audience creation techniques described earlier in Part II should render a lot more than 50 home page views. So why bother?

Scaleable and Complementary to Audience Creation

One way by which banner ads are clearly more effective than nonpaid audience creation techniques for driving traffic is their ability to scale their results proportionally to a company's spending. Marketers can try to target audience segments in only so many newsgroups without resorting to spamming. Companies such as IBM and Microsoft still commit multi-million-dollar budgets to online advertising. It would be hard to spend such amounts effectively just on search engine registration, sweepstakes, or even public relations, along with the other non-paid techniques discussed in earlier chapters. Successful banner campaigns, however, delivering better-than-average returns can easily be expanded to the purchase of more impressions across more sites, and theoretically continue to generate the same proportion of clickthrough traffic indefinitely. (See Figure 9.2.)

Web advertising is also an excellent strategic complement to the unpaid promotional strategies of audience creation. Advertising with a better-branded site opens the door for additional levels of cooperation, including exclusive sponsorships of select content, joint promotions, affinity links with top sites, affiliate partnerships, and so on. (See Figure 9.3.)

Figure 9.2
Microsoft and Visa can afford to spend whatever it takes to drive traffic. Presumably their crack marketing teams have taken the time to thoroughly analyze the cost of acquiring new customers and have found banners an effective means.

Furthermore, the $2 per clickthrough cost depicted previously is an oversimplification of the deeply nuanced strategies and rewards available in Web advertising today. That's what's covered in the rest of this chapter.

Online Ad Objectives

As in other media, there are two principal objectives in advertising online—branding and direct response. Both can be had online in a wide array of flavors and give much greater control than other media over market segmentation, performance review, speed to execution, and other advantages. Most online marketers benefit from a combination of the branding and direct-response characteristics of Web advertising, but it pays to appreciate the distinctions between the two.

Branding

By and large, marketers have been slow to embrace the brand-building potential of Web ads. It's not hard to see where some of that reluctance comes from. For one thing, page banners, the most common form of online advertising, are small. The most popular size, 468×60 pixels, fills about 10 percent of a Web browser window on a 14-inch or 15-inch monitor, and proportionally less on a larger monitor (see Figure 9.4). For advertisers accustomed to full-page newspaper ads, 17-foot-tall billboards, and 30-second TV commercials to achieve their branding objectives, a one-by-six-inch rectangle doesn't seem like much.

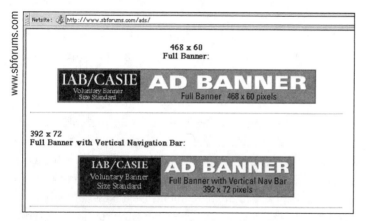

Figure 9.4

Two of the most popular banner sizes, standardized by the Internet Advertising Bureau (IAB) and the Coalition for Advertising Supported Information and Entertainment (CASIE), don't take up much real estate on a 14-inch monitor.

Add to this the easy-to-measure clickthrough ability inherent in the ads, and the appeal of a direct-response model have generally overshadowed branding as the key online advertising objective for many sites.

This is regrettable. Not to take anything away from the power of direct response online, but there's also real potential to achieve strong branding on the Web. The first evidence of this came from the Internet Advertising Bureau (IAB) and Millward Brown Interactive's 1997 Advertising Effectiveness Study.

IAB and Millward Brown Interactive's Advertising Effectiveness Study

Millward Brown, an international advertising research group, carefully designed a study to demonstrate how giving users a single exposure to a Web banner could have a significant positive impact on their recollection of the ad, affinity with the brand message, and even their intent to purchase the product. After surveying nearly 17,000 Web surfers' reactions to 12 real ad banners on 12 leading Web sites, the report concluded that after only one viewing of a banner ad, Web surfers were on average 5 percent more aware of the brand and 4 percent more likely to purchase the product over a competitor's product.

Some of the results were remarkable. In the case of Schick's Tracer FX razor, members of the test group shown the banner ad were 31 percent more likely to agree that it "meets your need for a men's cartridge razor" compared to the control group. And, the test group was 25 percent more inclined to believe that the product "is an acceptable price" compared to the control group. (See Figure 9.5.)

Among the 12 ads tested, average awareness of the brands increased 3 percent, from 61 percent to 64 percent, after just one additional exposure, the authors concluded. "Consumer loyalty" was up 26 percent for Volvo, 20 percent for Delta Business Class Air Travel, and more than 10 percent each for the Apple QuickTake digital camera, Deja News, and Toshiba. Across all 12 test banners, consumer loyalty rose by an average of 4 percent.

Figure 9.5

One showing of this Schick banner ad caused a dramatic brand benefit in the perceptions of those who saw it. (Data courtesy of Millward Brown Interactive and the Internet Advertising Bureau.)

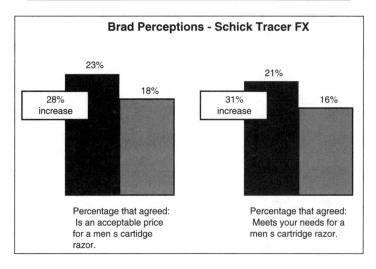

While the industry awaits a newer version of the Millward Brown study, some smaller tests continue to justify the money spent for banner branding efforts. A November 1999 survey by Andersen Consulting, which asked about 1500 Internet shoppers how they found their way to online stores, reported that 25 percent mentioned banner ads, compared to 14 percent who cited print ads; 11 percent cited TV commercials and 4 percent had noted radio spots or billboards.

Up Close and Personal

The most salient argument in favor of the Web's branding power, which many had made even before the IAB/MB interactive study, is that Web users are deeply engrossed in the medium and sit only inches from the monitor, unlike TV viewers who lounge halfway across the room and take bathroom breaks and snack runs during most commercials.

Banners still catch our attention as much as they did when they first appeared. They're often the only animation on otherwise static pages, and often the first elements to load. Early on, while a viewer waited for a page to finish downloading, she had little choice but to watch as the banner fills the top position of the page and runs through its animated message. (See Figure 9.6.)

Figure 9.6

A well-placed branding ad for Nepal.com, one of several destination sites managed by Virtual Countries.

But when it comes to clickthroughs, however, an active banner now vies for the viewer's next move with the rest of the jazzy activity on a Web page (rotating product shots, real-time stock quotes, recirculating news menus, livecams, and so on). In such an environment, the advertiser must rely more on frequency and familiarity to embed a brand message.

The average life of an effective banner branding campaign is five or six weeks. But many advertisers don't wait that long. According to a yearlong study by AdRelelevance that analyzed banners on the top 500 most-trafficked Web sites between July 1999 and June 2000, 23.7 percent of banner ads ran for only one week. In most cases, the short-run ads were for short-term, direct marketing promotions. When examining ad length by industry, AdRelevance found that automobile companies tended to run the longest campaigns (seven to eight weeks) followed by electronics companies (four weeks). Other brand-sensitive industries, such as financial services and travel companies, also ran longer campaigns.

For destination sites that use banners primarily to acquire "clickthrough" visitors, their branding potential over a long campaign should not be overlooked. A user might see a banner once and not click on it, but it leaves an impression, and this familiarity can lead the user to click on the banner later, after seeing it a second or third time. If the brand is familiar to the user, or the user occasionally visits the site, the exposure to the banner reinforces recollection of the brand name.

This is the rationale behind television advertising that repeated exposure creates a frame of mind—when faced with a buying choice at a later date, the user will choose the brand that has become familiar. The Web jargon for this is *mindshare*—a factor not to be confused with the often harsher realities of marketshare.

Click and mortar companies now use Web banners as if they were TV ads, reinforcing already-familiar logos and corporate color schemes in online variations. But in the case of pure-play Web businesses and Web-related industries, the most likely medium to reach a potential customer is through online presence. In some circles, having an online presence continues to have its own branding cachet. (See Figure 9.7.)

Another obvious benefit of online branding is the superb demographics of Web users. The latest data from the Web's largest demographic survey, conducted by the Georgia Institute of Technology, first indicated what has been confirmed more recently by other analysts—as more of the general population comes online, the average user's income and education levels are coming down while the average age goes up. But it's still the upper end of society leading the way.

In the U.S., more than two-thirds of Web users in 1999 reported household income of $50,000 or more, and when segmented into users who have already shopped on the Web the average goes up to $62,000, compared to the average U.S. household income of $35,000. Although companies might not yet reach all of their consumer audience online, they can potentially reach the most lucrative segment of that audience.

Figure 9.7
Levi's uses Web advertising to reinforce its hip, free-spirited image to the upscale digerati audience.

Direct Response Through Clicks and Conversions

One way to view the online advertising objectives of branding versus direct response is in terms of long-term versus short-term rewards. Although branding might translate into sales eventually, it's generally not an immediate cause and effect. Transactions, not clicks, are what count when trying to take advantage of the Web's capacity for instant results.

Online advertising offers direct marketers substantial advantages over traditional telemarketing and mailing campaigns, chiefly in terms of immediate feedback.

As discussed in more detail later in the chapter, a marketer can increasingly target banner ads to Web surfers by using the same demographic data used in traditional direct marketing—Zipcode, age, gender, income, and education, as well as shopping history and other known factors. He can further layer other targeting criteria on top of these demographics, such as clickstream profiles, time of day, and immediate user behaviors (for example, intercepting users as they search topical keywords or browse shopping directories).

Figure 9.8
In your face television commercials can now be downloaded in the short time it takes for a user to dial-up his Internet connection.

www.1stup.com

When a Netizen clicks on an ad banner, what happens next? Making the company's home page the destination is not just old-fashioned, but neither the most evaluative or useful option. Smart Web marketers channel their clicks into a microsite—a temporary Web page that supports and enhances the promotion.

When a user clicks on a specific ad and is transported to a home page, the array of options might be confusing, "Oh, it's just an ad," says the user, reflexively punching the "back" button. End of interaction. The same user transported to a microsite that details and expands the message in the banner often lingers. Interaction continues, the user becomes more engaged or at least becomes more familiar with the online brand.

Microsites work by stretching the visitor's latitude of acceptance, or what salespeople call "getting a foot in the door." A user sees an ad banner referencing cowboy boots. Liking either cowboys or boots, he then clicks through to a microsite that's all about cowboy boots. The microsite invites the user to further action. The user can get more information about cowboys (updated rodeo schedule) or more information about boots on sale (sales promotion). Either path creates an ever-deepening excursion into the pages of the Billy Bob Tack and Rack Emporium Web site, lead the user to a sign-up page for further promotions, or makes a direct sale.

Billy Bob gleaned useful information. Server logs will reveal not only how many users clicked on the ad, but also how many are interested in cowboys and how many are truly interested in boots. If the focus of the promotion is not sales but market research, microsites can provide an environment for even higher levels of consumer testing.

The technical parameters of microsites are not daunting. Once a company already has Web pages on its domain name server, adding new pages is like adding telephone extensions to an existing telephone line. A temporary Internet protocol (IP) page address can be appended to the home page address with a slash mark (www.billybob.com/cowboymania) but designers and domain name servers seem to prefer that temporary pages be prepended with a period mark (www.cowboymania, billybob.com). Listing the new address is done by the domain server host, and if the company has good relations with the hosting ISP, the process of getting a microsite extension added to the server file usually takes a day or two at most. When the promotion is over, a request is again made to the host, this time to "disconnect" the extension address.

continues

continued

Microsites work well for contests and sweepstakes, seasonal sales, and promotions that exploit events (trade shows or news trends) or limited-term partnerships ("Welcome AOL member!"). Email marketers also channel clicks to microsites, but their potential for creating flexible and user-personalized pathways within and between commercial Web sites has yet to be fully explored.

Quantifying Clicks

More and more sites are giving in to pressure to charge for advertising not only on a CPM basis of impressions shown to visitors but also on a cost-per-click or cost-per-transaction basis. Our favorite jargon for this type of pricing, be it cost-per-click, cost-per-lead, or cost-per-sale, is *cost-per-whatever* (CPW).

Publishers are frequently reluctant to fix the pricing of a banner to its performance, which is understandable. They argue that many factors that might impact the response are out of their control, such as the quality of the banner's design and copy writing or the promotion on offer. It's a bit like a department store paying a newspaper for advertising based on how many sales the ad generates.

The dark secret, however, is that few Web sites are actually selling anywhere near their total inventory of available impressions. Reliable numbers suggest that the amount of unsold inventory is as high as 70 to 80 percent. House ads, barter, and freebies frequently fill up the majority of ad impressions served at all but the top handful of sites. For this reason, many sites will negotiate CPW ad deals (although most try to keep the availability of such pricing models quiet, as they might be perceived to weaken the site's ability to ask high CPM rates).

Ad-supported sites ultimately recognize that getting something for that excess ad inventory (even if at fire-sale prices) is better than nothing. A few networks already offer performance-based pricing over the table, including DoubleClick Direct, Engage, Petry, and PointCast Direct.

Do the Math for CPW

When measuring the success of advertising by a CTR or other CPW criteria, it is critical to do the math on the bottom-line worth of the "whatever" in "cost per whatever" to calculate the return on the investment of marketing expenses.

An online commerce site, for example, might be paying the equivalent of $2 per clickthrough, either on a straight CPW basis or as $10 CPM with a 0.5 percent CTR. By tracking visitors over time with cookies, the site can calculate that, on average, 2 percent of those who hit the home page make a purchase worth $50 within a year. That means it costs the site $100 to acquire a $50 purchase. Considering that the customer might become a regular shopper, over the course of several years and balancing that against other overhead, marketers at such a site might decide that's a profitable acquisition cost, if it projects a "customer lifetime value" (LTV) of several hundred dollars.

On the other hand, if visitors finding the site make a purchase of $1,000, the site has made $900 in revenue on a $100 ad expense.

Unless the site has a high-end product or service to sell, justifying this math is a tall order. Put yourself in the Web surfer's place. When you click on a banner, how likely are you to become a loyal user of that site and to visit it again 50 times over the course of several months? Probably not that likely. Most of the time you click a banner, take a quick look at the home page it leads to, decide you're not interested, and never go back again. Right? (See Figure 9.9.)

The Math:

0.5 percent CTR of 10,000 impressions = 50 visitors.

50 visitors divided by the expense of $100 per ten thousand ad impressions = $2 per visitor.

2 percent of those 50 visitors (= 1 person) spend $50 a year.

Your acquisition cost = $100 per customer

Bottom line = $50 net loss per acquisition.

Sadly, this was a typical customer acquisition cost analysis for many e-commerce companies through 1999.

The One-Two Punch

One solution for this cost dilemma has been to price advertising based on a two-tiered measurement—one fee for impressions, at a figure below $10 CPM, and a higher fee for successful transactions, not just clickthroughs. Web sites that rely on ad revenues for support have tried to resist pay-on-performance pricing, arguing justifiably that impressions have an inherent branding benefit. With this in mind, a two-tier system of payment seems reasonable. And, according to the Internet Advertising Bureau (IAB), most deals today involve a hybrid pricing model of CPM and CPW.

Figure 9.9

A picture might be worth a thousand words, but is it worth the price of CPM when generating traffic is the goal? Marketers who are measuring results by clickthroughs better do the math.

But this works only when advertisers anticipate the latent branding benefit and promote the brand.

"It astounds me how many ad banners don't even have a company's name on them," said Kent Valandra, executive VP and director of New Media at Western International Media. An online advertising veteran, Mr. Valandra spent 20 years in the print magazine world before he started working with Prodigy's ad department in the late '80s.

"It's obvious that banners have a branding value," he continued. "A salesman from *Time* magazine doesn't say to an advertiser, 'I can give you 50 million readers, of whom maybe 3 million are going to care about your ad.' If it's worth money for a company to put its name on a basketball court or a rodeo fence or the side of a bus, it's worth putting a name on a Web banner. You never see a billboard for cigarettes at a rodeo without the name of the cigarette."

The IAB/MB interactive study further makes the point that a CTR is not an effective measure of the branding power of an ad. On average there was a less than 1 percent difference between people who did *not* click on an ad but who still recalled its message (43.7 percent) and those who had seen the ad, *including* those who had clicked on it and who recalled its message (44.1 percent).

In the case of the Schick razor ad mentioned earlier, a single exposure of the ad banner boosted by 31 percent the number of people who agreed that it "meets your needs for a men's cartridge razor." Yet the ad had a lowly 0.5 percent CTR. Clearly, the CTR alone is a poor measure of that ad's branding success.

The moral of the story is that although a cryptic banner that doesn't reveal the name of the company or product might marginally raise the CTR, the sacrifice of branding is usually a net loss. MCI's memorable "Shop Naked!" banner campaign for its online shopping mall, Marketplace MCI, generated a lot of clicks, upwards of 50 percent, but not many shoppers. The mall is now defunct. (You might wonder what a telecommunications company was doing in the consumer e-tail business in the first place, but that's a different question.)

Good Banners and Buttons

In cases where clickthroughs are an important and well-considered objective, there are a few rules of thumb for design and ad management in addition to the most critical factor of targeting the right audience:

- Bold colors

- Top of page placement

- Animation

- Call to action (for example, "click here," "buy one, get one free," or even the standard blue hyperlink border around the banner)

Most of these fall in line with the classic direct-marketing mnemonic of *AIDA*—a promotion should grab *attention*, rouse *interest*, stimulate *desire*, and call to *action*. (See Figure 9.10.)

Marketers have begun to measure user interest by the length of time spent viewing an ad; once engaged, a user might spend several minutes exploring an interactive, rich-media advertisement. If the purpose of the ad is direct response, richly interactive media might be worth the extra fuss.

If branding is the point of the banner campaign, keep creative elements to a minimum. A logo image, one graphic, and a three word tagline is six elements, for example, and is easy to recall. One survey of 33,000 users by Dynamic Logic in the spring of 2000 found that brand recall of simple ad (six elements or less) was more than four times that of a complex ad (sixteen elements or more). Clearly, the challenge for creative and cost-conscious advertisers is a direct-response ad that still packs a branding punch.

Figure 9.10

This SmartMoney banner demonstrates the AIDA direct response advertising principle. Its animation grabs attention, its changing message rouses interest, its advice for making money stimulates desire, and its offer of a free product to those who "click here" calls to action.

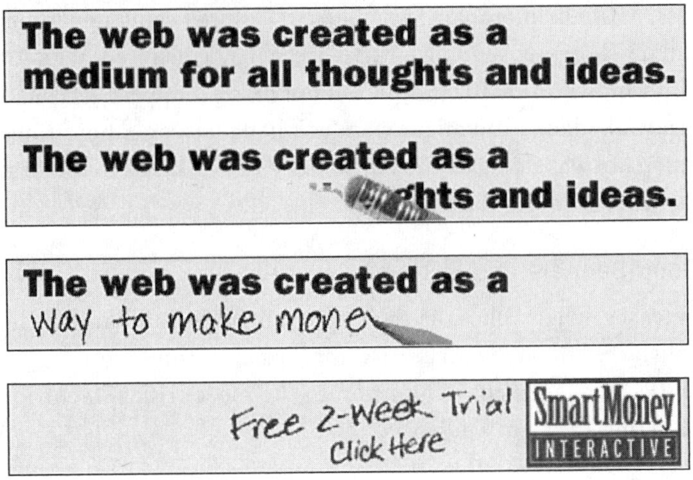

Boosting frequency of exposures, instead of extending the length of a campaign over time, seems to work less successfully for direct response ads than for branding ads on the Web. When it comes to clickthroughs, the law of diminishing returns seems to apply.

In mid-1996, the DoubleClick network conducted an oft-cited study regarding the effects of ad frequency on CTRs. It concluded that after a typical Web surfer had seen the same ad more than three times, the likelihood he would click on it dropped below 1 percent. DoubleClick dubbed this phenomenon "banner burnout."

The current low level of clickthrough rates—a dismal .03 percent to 0.5 percent—suggests a general trend of "banner fatigue" among users in general. Netizens are simply tuning banners out, while advertisers strive to fight back with ever-more antic animation and attention-grabbing art.

Many sites use cookies to track how many times any given Web surfer sees the same ad, and can automatically control the frequency of specific ad exposures. Of course, Web surfers can encounter the same ads running on other sites. Therefore, advertisers are advised to creatively change their direct-response banners often, and give more consideration to tailoring, or "personalizing" banners to the site or even to the user.

But if the goal is branding, beware of the "frequency cap." Some recent studies suggest that it might not be wise to limit the times a particular ad is fed to the same browser. An analysis by Dynamic Logic based on 24,000 interviews, and covering many different product categories, found that branding awareness could be lifted by slightly less than 6 percent with a banner ad, but the awareness level jumped to over 10 percent when the same banner was shown four times to the same user.

Frequency caps and the ability to create multiple versions of a single campaign might make ad testing easier, but it should not hurt branding efforts. Even if creative elements are changed frequently, keeping logo and tagline placement in the same place on the banner each time is recommended.

Types of Online Ads

Because the Internet is an amalgamation of several media experiences (text, images, sound, video, 3D, chat, and so on) online ads also come in many varieties. The creativity behind the use of new technology is one of the most exciting aspects of Web marketing today.

Within the Banner

Before moving "beyond the banner," an almost meaningless buzz phrase so many online advertisers love to talk about (but seemingly rarely act upon), there is much to consider within the realm of those lovable, ubiquitous hyperlinked rectangles.

When HotWired introduced the first ad banner for AT&T in 1994, it was simply a static graphic image fixed at the top of the page. No particular targeting, no rotation, no animation, *nada*. Pretty crude by today's standards. Now banners do more than act as static, two-dimensional logos fixed on every page. In addition to advanced technical targeting techniques discussed later, banners have become dramatically more flashy and functional, thanks to Shockwave, Java, compressed audio and video formats, and other hot technologies.

Horizontal or Vertical?

Roughly 90 percent of U.S. commercial Web sites accept the IAB's "standard" banner of 468×60 pixels—that horizontal tube seen at the top of a screen. Recently, bigger vertical ads, about 120 pixels wide and typically 800 pixels deep, have shown up on premier ad sites such as the New York Times' online edition. The larger format often mimics a print ad, and can carry the weight of more copy or an interactive element (see Figure 9.11).

Figure 9.11

Horizontal banners that mimic print ads are popular on content sites such as the New York Times.

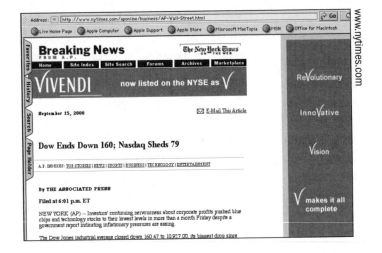

Animation

One drawback to using the "rich-media" formats (jargon for anything much more exciting than static graphics) in ad banners is that some users with slower modems might have trouble viewing or even downloading the artwork. For example, although Java is by now a fairly reliable technology on most browsers, Shockwave animation is limited by whether Web surfers have downloaded and installed the required plug-in.

The most common type of banner animation still uses the GIF89 technique. Its popularity stems from its near-universal browser support (including the 2.0 versions of the "big two" browsers), smaller file sizes than other animation types, and the relative simplicity of creating the animation. The name derives from a 1989 adaptation of the graphic interchange format (GIF) that CompuServe developed a few years earlier.

Basically, GIF89s aren't much different than the penny-arcade kinetoscopes that so charmed folks 100 years ago—a series of images that flip past each other in quick succession. Most of the banner ads that endlessly cycle through the same four frames of clever text ending in "Click Here!" are GIF89s.

Rich-Media and ROI

A technology named for the year 1989 is ancient history in Web terms, of course, and innovative companies have since introduced more compelling techniques such as Flash animation and RealAudio. Cartoons, lifelike video, and "speaking" ads add a novelty factor shown to boost clickthrough rates.

Rich-media of audio, video, and animation definitely costs more. The research firm eMarketer puts the current price of a typical banner ad at $4,000, and estimates the average fee for a rich-media version of the same ad hovers around $33,000. Creative costs for a Flash pop-up are roughly four times the price of creating a simpler animated GIF, for example, Java creativity often requires large file sizes and hand coding. To deliver rich-media smoothly, additional development and fees on the server level can add between $2 to $10 to the CPM price of the campaign.

But online advertising agencies, such as Lot 21, Modem Media, and iFrontier, counter with statistics showing that the novelty of rich-media engages the viewer more fully, with some users spending as long as five minutes interacting with the ad materials. Conversion rates (the ratio of ad viewers who have completed an interaction goal) are cited as high as 30-35 percent, far higher than the response rates of banners using older techniques. (See Figure 9.12.)

Figure 9.12

This interactive, large format banner designed by Lot 21 for Bank of America has four different video stories, created with Flash and Enliven software.

Interactivity

Realizing that about 99 percent of the time Web surfers don't want to click ad banners because they're happy with the site they're on, some marketers have begun creating ads in which Web surfers perform functions within the banner without needing to clickthrough to another destination.

Jazzing Up Ads with Java

Enliven, owned by Excite@Home, is an example of a basic yet effective software system to produce interactive banners. Enliven ads are created as Java files, so they don't require any special plug-ins on standard browsers, yet they deliver smooth animation and sound effects sure to grab a Web surfer's attention. Using streaming technology, the ads download additional data from the server only when the user interacts, creating an experience of seemingly endless new content without excessive delays. (See Figures 9.13 and 9.14.)

The result is arguably a more powerful ad experience than possible on TV or in print. The user truly interacts with the brand as she clicks on icons, selects choices from pull-down menus, drags and drops items across the screen, and otherwise immerses herself in the ad. While expensive to produce, the ads are fun and typically absorb users for five minutes or more.

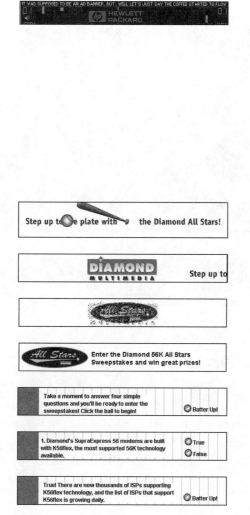

Figure 9.13
Hewlett-Packard's clever Pong banner, designed by Red Sky Interactive with Shockwave technology, set new standards for creativity in banner design back in 1997. The banner let netizens relive the '70s by playing the world's first video game again, within the banner itself.

Figure 9.14
This banner for Diamond Multimedia uses Narrative's Enliven technology to rousing effect. The ad starts with a bat swinging at a ball and making an audible crack, followed by a crowd's cheers. It then offers some true/false questions and a chance to win prizes.

Advertisers such as Citibank, New Balance, and L.L. Bean have used Enliven in ads to demonstrate product features, collect sweepstakes entries, provide useful consumer information, and more, all within standard-size banner ads. Companies are also taking advantage of enlarged ad windows, and new interactive technologies that also do not require plug-ins. Examples of hardware-software solutions include Control Commerce's Virtual Kiosk, which opens a "daughter window" that allows purchase transactions or delivers enriched content within a pop-up frame, and E-Pod. (See Figures 9.15 and 9.16.)

Figure 9.15

Clicking on a banner advertising classical music brings the viewer to this Virtual Kiosk site, which offers branching pathways to opera news, recorded audio demos, and CD shopping, within the confines of a "daughter" site.

Figure 9.16

This multiple-choice pitch for term insurance isn't flashy, but its interactive, pull-down menus help qualify the user before the point of clickthrough.

Interstitials

If ever a piece of computer jargon deserved to be hung up by its thumbs, it has to be the abominable *interstitials*. These are the full-screen ads that occasionally pop up between pages on cutting-edge sites. Unfortunately, *interstitial* is indeed a genuine, if somewhat obscure dictionary word meaning "situated in the space that intervenes between things."

Interstitials are what TV advertisers have been waiting for on the Web. They get in the user's face, can take up the full browser screen, and don't go away until the user clicks on them or they're done with their animation. The latest generation interstitials persist on a user's computer screen, even after the user has quit the browser application. A variation known as *splash screen* ads are simply static ad pages that the user has to click to go to the next page. True interstitials are animated, lasting 5 to 15 seconds. (See Figure 9.17.)

Sponsorships

Sponsorships are popular across the Web in a variety of forms. With the boundaries between online editorial and marketing still maturing, it's sometimes difficult to tell where the content ends and the advertising begins. But research shows that URLs imbedded in editorial text (with the familiar blue underlining) are clicked through more often than URLs in ads on the borders surrounding page content. This makes a lot of marketers feel confident in exploring sponsorships.

Although in most forms of sponsorship Web surfers are encouraged to clickthrough to the sponsor's site, the goal of this model is principally brand-building. Advertisers and publishers are still playing with the definitions of sponsorship on the Web, and so far the results have taken many different forms. Based on current trends, here are five basic types of sponsorships:

- Branded content
- Event promotions
- Chat Promotions
- Advertorials
- Paid Partnership/Portal Deals

Branded Content

Branded content most closely follows the "brought to you by" model of early television and today's public television. Think of yesteryear's "Mutual of Omaha's Wild Kingdom."

In the branded content model, the advertiser has no hand in creating or shaping the content. Editorial control is left entirely to the publisher, while the brand benefits from the association with the quality content. These kinds of deals are frequently negotiated as long-term contracts, normally in an exclusive arrangement so that no other advertiser, particularly a competitor, is associated with the content.

In such cases, an advertiser might sponsor a regular section of a site, or the entire site in some cases. In the business-to-business environment, a long-running sponsorship on a business information site helps legitimize a brand in short order. Adding an interactive element, such as a yes-or-no industry "poll," is one of several common tricks to help qualify readership of the sponsored material. (See Figure 9.18.)

Event Promotions

Event promotions involve a closer integration of publisher and advertiser content. These promotions last only a short period, normally from one to several weeks, and highlight a special offer, contest, or event. They're frequently given great prominence by the publisher, often at the top of the home page. (See Figure 9.19.)

Figure 9.18
DoubleClick.net sponsors a reader's forum on ClickZ.com, a Web site for the online marketing community. The audience-research poll adds ROI value to the sponsorship buy.

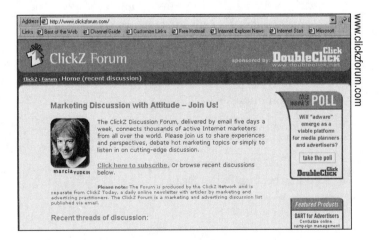

Figure 9.19

Yahoo! regularly hosts event promotions, such as this contest sponsored by Volvo.

Chat Promotions

In early 1997, AOL led the charge in chat advertising, enabling marketers to display ads to the millions of users of its more than 15,000 chat rooms. In the same year, Web-based chat software hit its stride, and now nearly every vertical or horizontal portal offers chat communities as exclusive site services or as enhancements to other content.

More recently, chats involve live Web audio from participants who are simultaneously viewing the same screen image. Although that image happily contains an advertisement or other promotional images for the Web site, the driving force behind the medium, however, remains flirtation and other social interaction.

Advertorials

Further blurring the line between ad and editorial content online are *advertorials*. They're a familiar tradition in print journalism, where publishers normally make it clear that they're paid advertisements. Typically they do this by setting the type in a distinct font, surrounding the item in a border, and prominently labeling it "Paid Advertisement." Web publishers aren't always so fastidious.

Many smaller publishers struggling to stay afloat are willing to cut corners on such formalities and display material in whatever way makes advertisers happy. Surprisingly, even established media companies have shown a willingness to blur this line in their online ventures. (See Figure 9.20.)

Figure 9.20
The whole right-hand column of this page is an advertorial, although Forbes doesn't make this clear until the bottom of the column.

Paying Partnerships and Portal Deals

Promotional arrangements with *portals* and *vortals* (as described in Chapter 6) are the murkiest category of sponsorship. Here, the distinctions between advertising, syndication, revenue sharing, and other online promotional and money-making strategies begin to meld completely.

A portal sponsorship, by our definition, is where one site agrees to integrate the content of another site as a service to Web surfers and a branding value to the content provider. Examples include a news site incorporating the functions of a leading search engine, or a business magazine offering up-to-the-minute stock quotes from a specialized stock service.

When portal deals are expected to lead to e-commerce transactions, the stakes get higher and competition for screen space intensifies. For years, **Amazon.com** and **BarnesandNoble.com** have been in pitched battle to secure exclusive linking arrangements with leading sites as the preferred online bookstore. But **Amazon.com** recently declined to renew a three-year contract with AOL, to the amazement of its industry, and **BarnesandNoble.com** leaped quickly into its expensive keyword slot. (See Figure 9.21.)

Figure 9.21
Once Amazon.com yielded its position as the preferred bookseller on AOL and Yahoo! to rival BarnesandNoble.com, the value of such placements appeared in doubt.

Amazon.com officials cited cost cutting as the reason for the move. Other e-commerce companies might follow its lead, as indicated by a Jupiter study among online advertisers that showed nearly half were "unhappy" with the CTRs they were getting through high-priced portal placements. In the near future, look for portal fees to go down, or become more performance-based and look more like affiliate programs.

The **Amazon.com** Associates Program, for example, encourages smaller sites to post an **Amazon.com** logo with recommendations of specific books, rewarding the sites with up to a 15 percent revenue share on any subsequent sales through the link. Is that an ad fee or an affiliate sales commission? The distinction probably doesn't matter to the sites getting paid to host the link. Yet **Amazon.com** wins either way, and receives free branding even if the link generates no sales.

In some portal arrangements, no money ever changes hands. **ABCNews.com**, for example, links to Mr. Showbiz for its entertainment news, and likewise Mr. Showbiz links to **ABCNews.com** on its home page. Because both sites are properties of ABC, it's a pure cross-promotion deal.

Figure 9.22

DLJdirect pays the *New York Times* for the publicity it receives on NYTimes.com by providing the news giant with a stock quote service for free. A classic portal sponsorship.

Synergies with TV and Print

Megamedia conglomerates are still trying to figure out the Web's cross-promotion possibilities. Disney's empire, for example, discovered it could not plaster reciprocal links for its broadcast, cable TV, and movie divisions all over its own search engine site, **Go.com**, without alienating other advertisers and diluting the value of **Go.com** as a search site.

Simultaneous campaigns that run in print, street media, and online at the same time require a lead time of several months to coordinate. And at least up until now, combined rate cards for package deals including online and print combos, or online and broadcasting, have to be compared carefully to separate buys to determine real bargains.

The obvious answer, hiring a large, traditional advertising agency to handle a national roll-out, can cost millions and might in fact not be the most cost-effective way to launch a Web campaign. One online retailer advises purchasing offline media for branding during the summer and other slack periods when prices are low, and then moving into direct-response, performance-based online advertisements during the holidays or other busy shopping seasons, when magazine and broadcast rates soar.

Personalization Technologies and Target Marketing

The battle cry of Internet marketing has long been "one-to-one marketing." Although the phrase has fast become a cyber-cliche, the message behind it is real. In the world of online advertising, the operative word is *targeting*.

Imagine if television sets were two-way communication devices that could stare back at their viewers and relay information about them to the broadcast station. For example, one TV set could see that its viewer was a woman in her mid-40s. In fact, it knew her name was Mary Wilson. She was fairly affluent, judging by the furnishings in her living room, yet she was single. According to her viewing habits, the TV surmised that she was interested in sports, cooking, and celebrity entertainment news. It knew that Mary lived on the lower-east side of Manhattan. It also had a sense of self, aware that it was a six-year-old Sony and that soon she would be in the market for a replacement.

The TV dutifully sent all this information back to the broadcaster, who accordingly targeted her with ads suited just for her—running shoes, New York singles bars, cooking classes, and new TVs. Her neighbor in the apartment next door watched the same shows at the same time, but saw a completely different set of ads.

It sounds like an Orwellian nightmare. But while something not far from this scenario has been initiated by television technology pioneers such as TiVo and ReplayTV, it's already taking place on the Web today, whether the majority of netizens realize it or not.

Rotating advertising according to sales commitments is no mean feat for any site, and targeting those ads to individual users based on their unique characteristics, all within a fraction of a second, seems impossibly complicated. Yet several specialized companies provide software packages and services to do exactly that, including DoubleClick, Engage, MatchLogic, Real Media, 24/7 Media, L90, and others. Although these companies take care of the under-the-hood technical aspects of ad targeting, it behooves you to understand the general strategies for audience segmentation online. These include content, technographic, demographic, geographic, and psychographic/behavioral targeting.

Figure 9.23
A banner for office supplies on a Goto.com page devoted to lingerie shopping illustrates the difference between targeted content and run-of-site ad placements.

Content

The most basic form of online ad targeting, and also one of the most effective, is content affiliation. Just as a running shoe manufacturer would advertise in Sports Illustrated magazine and an investment service would advertise in Money magazine, advertisers online generally seek their target audiences according to the editorial themes of specialized sites. A marketer could do this kind of targeting in her sleep. In fact, the vast majority of ad targeting on the Web today is done this way.

Content targeting, generally, doesn't necessarily exploit much technical sophistication. Rather, it's done through familiar, manual means. Media buyers analyze which sites are suitable venues for their marketing objectives, and the ads are then placed in general rotation across the site or within particular site sections. One of the advantages, and difficulties, of targeting by content is the incredible breadth and diversity of Web sites out there. For advertisers in search of niche markets, no other medium comes close to the Web's minute categorization.

Technographic

Also called *environmental* targeting, aiming ads to users according to the technographic information volunteered by every browser is the most basic form of dynamic ad targeting. In the back-and-forth chatting of the HTTP Web protocol, the browser gives the server various information about the Web surfer's computer and network, such as what kind of browser and operating system he uses, his ISP, what URL he linked to the site from, what time of day he visited, and other data.

With the appropriate server software, sites can target ads to individual users based on all these criteria. Many sites that brag about being able to target ads to users "dynamically" or in "real-time" are targeting according to such technographic variables, mainly because it's the easiest data about users to collect.

Unfortunately, technographic targeting is of limited benefit to most non-technology advertisers. If the site is selling beer, mutual funds, or cars, it probably doesn't make much difference whether Web surfers use Netscape or Microsoft browsers on Macs or PCs.

Perhaps a product particularly geared towards students could target according to .edu domains. Or, it could target Web surfers with AOL accounts on the broad assumption that they represent typical Middle American consumers (and presuming there's some advantage to targeting them on a particular Web site instead of directly within AOL's network).

Time of day is another data point that sites extol as a target for advertisers. They cite examples such as a TV program that's promoted an hour before showtime or a snack maker that runs banners around lunchtime. The problem with targeting by time, however, is time zones. Although it might be TV primetime according to the site's California-based servers, it would already be pushing midnight for a New York Web surfer. Judging the users' geographical location by technographic information is a much trickier proposition, as discussed shortly.

On the balance, although technographics can be very important for software vendors and other technological companies, non-tech advertisers need to scrutinize the purported benefits of this kind of ad targeting.

Demographic

Demographic targeting is "the beef" of the "one-to-one marketing" hype, and its techniques are familiar fare to anyone who has worked in direct mail. Demographics weed out the pimple-faced teenage burger-flippers surfing in mom's basement from the males aged 35 to 45 in the Bay Area who earn over $100,000 and are interested in fast cars.

Much of the demographic information about Web users that is valuable to marketers can be gleaned from Web surfers directly. This generally involves requesting visitors to fill out site registration data, and many of them are still happy to do so. (See Figure 9.24.)

Figure 9.24

Free email services such as Hotmail ask users to fill out a demographic survey, allowing the site to target ads more directly to their screens.

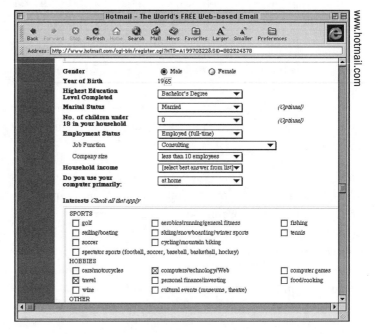

Many sites out there manage to do so, offering advertisers powerfully advanced targeting abilities. But even the *Times* they are a-changin'. That would be The *New York Times,* one of the few sites that, up until mid 2000, demanded that all users register to gain access. Due to its highly desirable content, this was a trade-off that more than two million registered users were willing to make, even though the registration process once asked the readers to fill out more than two screen-pages of personal data, including street address and household income. This enabled the *Times* to sell targeted ads to the demographic "golden triangle" of *ZAG (Zip code, age, and gender),* plus income brackets. (See Figure 9.25.)

Figure 9.25
CellularVision used the *New York Times'* ZIP code demographic to target ads to users in particular New York neighborhoods, such as the fashionable downtown Chelsea district. Acquisition rates outperformed the company's ads in all other media on a cost basis.

Perhaps in response to privacy issues, the *Times* has simplified its registration, and now lets its subscribers alter or update their preferences for receiving junk email. More recently, **EdificeRex.com,** which caters to urban apartment dwellers, has been experimenting with neighborhood-specific content and ads.

Cookies

Probably the most misunderstood, maligned, and punned-upon Internet technology is the so-called cookie file.

Originally dubbed magic cookie by its inventors at Netscape, a cookie is nothing more than a text file that resides on the user's hard drive, into which sites can record a short string of data about the user for future reference. Without cookies, the HTTP protocol of the Web doesn't provide any easy way to recognize the same user from one click to the next.

continues

continued

Typically, a site uses a cookie to assign a serial number to an individual user, against which it can cross-reference data stored on the site's own database regarding the user's previous interactions with the site.

Common uses for cookies include the following: Enabling a user of a commerce site to carry a virtual shopping basket from page to page so the site can keep track of what items the user selected for purchase on earlier pages, recognizing a registered member at the home page so he doesn't have to always enter his password and ID, tracking how many times a Web surfer has seen a particular ad banner to avoid showing him the same one too many times, and matching a user to his profile of observable surfing behaviors.

Despite hysterical media reports, cookies cannot "learn" anything about Web surfers. They're simply repositories for data, not agents that sniff anything out. They most certainly can't determine a visitor's email address, bank account number, or any other personal information, unless he volunteered that information to the site in the first place. In that case, the cookie simply allows the site to cross-reference the ID of the browser against the user's personal information in the site's database.

Because sites don't actually store much more than a serial number on the user's hard drive, an unrelated site can't use the cookie to gain access to any personal information that the user might have divulged. If sites belong to the same network, however, the network can cross-reference the shared data about individual users from one site in the network to the next through cookies.

Most of the ad networks, for example, such as DoubleClick, Engage, and MatchLogic, use cookies to track users across sites within their networks. When a visitor shows up at Site A, the network serves him an ad, slipping him a cookie marker when doing so. When the same user shows up at Site B in the network, the network recognizes him and manages its ad targeting accordingly.

The idea of third-party cookies bothers many privacy advocates, since it would be quite easy for sites to team together to track users across multiple sites. Marketers, technologists, and user advocates have debated for the past few years on a solution. The best hope was a protocol known as P3P, which would have given surfers a greater control over their privacy preferences through their browsers. That initiative has been mired in patent disputes, and for the near term the fine line between personalization and privacy invasion will remain a vexing issue.

Geographic

Many marketers are realizing that the Web can be used effectively for local marketing. So how can you target geographically? The most reliable way is, again, demographic data supplied by the users. Privacy concerns, however, might make it difficult to ascertain *real* demographics. Fortunately, there are several alternative ways you can target by geography.

One method that can geographically locate perhaps 10 to 20 percent of site traffic from server logs is known as *reverse IP look-up*. Sites and networks attempt to recognize visitors by their assigned IP address—a unique string of numbers assigned to every host computer connected to the Internet—and determine where that computer resides physically. This works with many corporate Internet users, whose desktop computers are constantly online and are assigned fixed IP addresses that never change.

The drawback is that the majority of Internet users are connecting from home through ISPs that assign different IP addresses to users each time they connect. The problem is particularly acute with AOL's 20 million-plus users, who are all routed through a handful of external gateways to the Internet. So according to their IP addresses, they almost all appear to be residents of Vienna, Virginia. The same might be true of employees of large national corporations, all of whose IP addresses can be routed through one gateway.

Street-Level Marketing

The advent of wireless Web remote services, such as AvantGo and Vindigo, presents a far more interesting opportunity to reach users not just where they live, but where they're standing at any given moment in time. Using the same geopositioning technology used by airline pilots and car rental companies, such services, accessed by hand-held, wireless Web remotes, offer city guides that can call up shops, restaurants, weather, and nightlife events within a few square blocks of the user.

For example, if the user wants to see a movie, Vindigo displays show times and walking directions for the nearest movie theater. Like AvantGo and similar services, Vindigo is a free download and a free service (tiny advertisements appear among the listings) (see Figure 9.26). A restaurant located close to the movie theatre might run an ad with a "pre-theater special" on such a service. Current technology enables these early adapters to make a dinner reservation through the Web remote.

Figure 9.26

Handheld wireless Web access suggests a future of ads targeted to an individual's time and place.

Psychographic/Behavioral

Arguably the most effective means of ad targeting is based on reading people's behavior. Psychologists and market researchers agree that in order to reliably predict what people will do in the future, a marker should pay more attention to what they have done in the past than to what they say they'll do.

Already among the most valuable kinds of ad targeting is catching Web surfers as they're searching for somewhere else to go online. The most obvious form of this is through keywords on search engines. The search engines sell banner ads that come up on the results pages in response to surfers searching on popular keywords. Most prime words associated with big-ticket items, such as "travel," "cars," and "computers," are sold out months or years in advance on the leading search engines.

The recent emergence of *neural networking* technology on the Web is likely to have an important impact on ad targeting in the near future. Originally designed for military use in pattern recognition, such as the modus operandi of terrorists, this kind of software is already providing remarkable results on the Web, recognizing patterns in how users interact with Web pages and serving ads accordingly. In short order, the software can get the gist of what kind of content a Web surfer is browsing and anticipate which ad would best catch his attention.

Into the Future

The golden age of Web advertising has yet to arrive, but it's coming soon. Early adventurers, along with the agencies and service companies that help them spend their money, have discovered that paid media on the Internet is not TV, nor is it radio, or print, or even junk mail. It can use elements of all of these, and it is beginning to explore some media of the past it had ignored. For example, the arresting impact of a sharp and passionate visual image, comparable to the drawn posters of the 1800's and the photographed magazine campaigns of the mid-1900's, is returning as computer monitors gain in size and clarity.

What's heartening is that the learning curve in Web media is pretty damn fast. A site thrives or gets the plug pulled in short order. What's daunting is that while well-publicized failures can put a crimp on creativity, the Web is not friendly to timid market efforts. If little was said about creativity in design or prose it's because the readers have the potential to wow us in that regard. If our years in Web marketing have taught us anything, it's that good ideas come from everywhere. We can't wait to see what happens next.

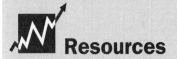

Resources

Also see the Appendix, "Internet Resources," for more online resources related to Web advertising.

Associations

The Internet Advertising Bureau (IAB)

http://www.iab.net/

- The IAB is the leading association for companies concerned with Web advertising, whose members include leading online publishers, advertisers, software makers, ad agencies, and others. The site offers a wealth of free resources and even more to paying members.

The Coalition for Advertising Supported Information and Entertainment (CASIE)

http://www.casie.org/

- Best known by its acronym, CASIE represents mostly ad agencies. The site offers some useful resources.

The Direct Marketing Association

http://www.the-dma.org/

- The Direct Marketing Association doesn't have a particularly strong Web site yet, but it's a leading association for direct marketing in the real world, so maybe it will become a better resource with time.

American Association of Advertising Agencies (AAAA)

http://www.aaaa.org/

- "The Four As," as it's known, is a leading association in the traditional advertising world. Drill down a bit, and the site offers many useful links and services.

Online Advertising News

Advertising Age

http://www.adage.com/

- *Ad Age*, the bible of the real world ad trade, was quick to get hip to the Net, both with its own site and a dedicated section covering Internet advertising (to which your author is a regular contributor). The Interaction section of the site is a bookmark for most who follow online advertising.

Adweek

http://www.adweek.com/

- *Adweek*, *Ad Age's* historic rival, also has a site featuring online ad news.

ClickZ

http://www.clickz.com/

- This regularly updated site features vendor information for many current players in the online advertising business, plus news, useful online forums, links, and other resources.

ChannelSeven

http://www.channelseven.com/

- The site reviews online ad campaigns and offers other services.

Internet Advertising Report

http://www.internetnews.com/iar/

- One of the many properties of Mecklermedia's **Internet.com** site, the Internet Advertising Report also covers the online industry closely.

Iconocast

http://www.iconocast.com/

- This email newsletter is a valuable insider report of behind-the-scenes deals in the online ad space. It is written with wit by Michael Tchong, founder of *MacWEEK* magazine and former executive at the Chiat/Day ad agency. The Web site provides subscription information and archives.

Microscope

http://www.microsope.com/

- Purchased by ClickZ in late 1997, Microscope reviews ad campaigns and invites media buyers to write about their experiences.

Ratings and other Services

Adknowledge

http://www.engaged.com/adknowledge

- Now a subsidiary of Engaged, AdKnowledge tracks and researches online media effectiveness. Recent studies are abstracted as news releases on the Web site, while full reports and customized research is for sale.

continues

---

continued

Media Metrix/AdRelevance

http://www.jup.com

- The current leaders in online ad tracking and ad research, Media Metrix and AdRelevance are now part of Jupiter's research group. Published reports on banner purchasing trends, rich-media effectiveness, and new technologies are available as abstracts or news releases on the Web pages; full reports can be purchased individually or by subscription.

NetRatings

http://www.netratings.com

- Founded in 1998, this ad tracking and ad research firm is partially owned by ACNielson,which recently launched a joint venture called **e.Ratings.com**, to study online advertising in European and Pacific rim markets.

Net Value

http://www.netvalue.com

- A ratings firm based in France, useful for international research.

Discussion Groups

The Online Advertising Discussion List

http://www.o-a.com/

- The Online Ads email list is generally thought of as the best forum for the wide range of companies trying to make a buck or promote a product with Web advertising. Newbies and old hands are in equal measure. Sign-up is easy at the site.

ClickZForum

http://www.clickZforum.com

- A new ClickZ property, this forum was launched by Online Ad's longtime moderator Richard Hoy.

Internet Advertising Discussion List

http://www.exposure-usa.com/i-advertising

- This is a near facsimile of the Online Ads list.

Other Resources

The Online Advertising Forum

http://www.olaf.net/

■ This site is a collection of lots of good online ad-related links and content.

SRDS

http://www.srds.com/

■ This service is a staple in traditional advertising for providing data on ad outlets ranging from consumer magazines and newspaper to direct marketing lists, radio, and TV. Like everyone else, it's moving online. Although its best services are available only to subscribers, the site does have an excellent list of other online advertising and marketing resources.

DoubleClick Resource Center

http://www.doubleclick.net/nf/general/resouset.htm

■ This ad network offers lots of free advice, including its tips for effective banners and the "Banner Burnout" study mentioned earlier in the chapter.

Yahoo! on Web Advertising

http://www.yahoo.com/Computers_and_Internet/Internet/Business_and_Economics/Advertising_on_Web_and_Internet/

■ This page links to many more sites covering the topic of online advertising.

Internet Resources

Disclaimer

The following URLs aren't meant as endorsements of any products or services, nor are they meant to be comprehensive lists of the services in any categories. They're either useful resources or examples that were cited in this book. A listing of these URLs can also be found at **newcanoe.com.**

Internet Guides, Histories, and Glossaries

Intenet Society on Internet History
http://www.isoc.org/internet-history/

Learn the Net
http://www.learnthenet.com/

Netscape on Netiquette
http://www.home.netscape.com/menu/netet/

Yahoo! on Internet Beginners Guides
http://www.yahoo.com/Computers_and_Internet/Internet/
Information_and_Documentation/Beginner_s_Guides/

and

http://www.yahoo.com/Computers_and_Internet/Internet/
Information_and_Documentation/Internet_Glossaries/

Growth and Usage of the Web and Internet

Internet Advertising Bureau/Millward Brown Interactive Advertising Effectiveness Study
http://www.mbinteractive.com/site/iab/study.html

The Internet Index
http://www.openmarket.com/intindex/

Mediamark Research, Inc.
http://www.mediamark.com/

University of Illinois Browser Statistics Survey
http://www.cen.uiuc.edu/bstats/latest.html

USA Data
http://www.usadata.com/

Yahoo! on Net statistics
http://www.yahoo.com/Computers_and_Internet/Internet/World_Wide_Web/Statistics_and_Demographics/

Search, Directory, and Listing Services

Unless otherwise noted, the following services are general Web search tools.

AltaVista
http://www.altavista.digital.com/

Ask Jeeves! (Ask.com)
http://www.askjeeves.com

CataList (mailing lists)
http://www.lsoft.com/lists/listref.html

Deja News (search engine for Usenet newsgroups)
http://www.dejanews.com/

Dogpile
http://www.dogpile.com

Excite
http://www.excite.com/

Four11 (people search)
www.four11.com/

Google.com
http://www.google.com

HotBot
http://www.hotbot.com/

Huron Online (sweepstakes listings)
http://www.huronline.com/

Infoseek (Go Network)
http://www.go.com/

Liszt (mailing lists search)
http://www.liszt.com

LookSmart
http://www.looksmart.com/

Lycos
http://www.lycos.com/

MetaCrawler
http://www.metacrawler.com/

Netguide (online events)
http://www.netguide.com/Happenings/

Search.com
http://www.search.com/

WebCrawler
http://www.webcrawler.com

WebTaxi
http://www.webtaxi.com/

WhoWhere (people search)
http://www.whowhere.lycos.com

WorldPages (business directory)
http://www.worldpages.com/

Yack (chat event guide)
http://www.yack.com/

Yahoo Net Events
http://events.yahoo.com/

Yahoo!
http://www.yahoo.com/

Official Internet Bodies and Lobby Groups

The Domain Name Right's Coalition
http://www.domain-name.org

Electronic Frontier Foundation
http://www.eff.org/

Internet Engineering Task Force
http://www.ietf.org/

Internet Society
http://info.isoc.org/

InterNIC
http://www.internic.net/

InterNIC "WhoIs" domain registration
http://rs.internic.net/cgi-bin/whois

The Internet Council of Registrars
http://www.corenic.org.

The Internet Corporation of Assigned
Names and Numbers (ICANN)
http://www.icann.org

ICANN Watch
http://www.icannwatch.org

Policy Oversight Committee (Generic
Top Level Domain Memorandum
of Understanding)
http://www.gtld-mou.org/

Online Marketing Resources

Advertising Law Internet Site
http://www.arentfox.com/quickGuide/
businessLines/advert/advertisingLaw/
advertisinglaw.html

Advertising Media Internet Central
http://www.amic.com/

American Advertising Federation
http://www.aaf.org/

American Association of Advertising
Agencies (AAAA)
http://www.aaaa.org/

American Demographics
http://www.demographics.com/

American Marketing Association
http://www.ama.org/

Association of Direct Marketing Agencies
http://www.cyberdirect.com/ADMA/

Association for Interactive Media
http://www.interactivehq.org/

Audit Bureau of Circulations
http://www.accessabc.com/

Bacon's
http://www.baconsinfo.com

BPA International
http://www.bpai.com/

Bruner Communications
http://www.bruner.net/

Business Marketing Association
http://www.marketing.org/

Businesswire
http://www.businesswire.com/

Coalition for Advertising Supported
Information and Entertainment (CASIE)
http://www.casie.org/

CommerceNet
http://www.commerce.net/

Direct Marketing Association
http://www.the-dma.org/

Forrester Power Rankings
http://www.forrester.co/ER/PowerRankings/

Internet Advertising Association
http://www.internet-association.org/

Internet Advertising Bureau
http://www.iab.net/

Internet Press Guild
http://www.netpress.org/

John Marshall Law School Index
of Cyber Legal Issues:
http://www.jmls.edu/cyber/index/

JunkBusters
http://www.junkbusters.com/

LinkPopularity
http://www.linkpopularity.com

Magazinedata
http://www.magazinedata.com/

Marketing Research Association
http://www.mra-net.org/

The Online Advertising Discussion List
http://www.o-a.com/

Online Advertising Forum (OLAF)
http://www.olaf.net/

Oppedahl & Larson
http://www.patents.com/

Position Agent
http://www.positionagent.com

PR Newswire
http://www.prnewswire.com/

Publicity.com
http://www.publicity.com/

SRDS
http://www.srds.com/

Tenagra Corporation
http://tenagra.com

Thunder Lizard Download Handouts
http://www.thunderlizard.com/dwnld_hand-
out.html

TRUSTe
http://www.truste.org/

WilsonWeb
http://www.wilsonweb.com/

Yahoo! on Best of the Web Directories
www.yahoo.com/Computers_and_Internet/
Internet/World_Wide_Web/Best_of_the_Web/

Yahoo! on Domain Brokers
http://www.yahoo.com/Business_and_
Economy/Companies/Internet_Services/
Domain_Registration/Brokerages/

Yahoo! on Domain Controversies
http://www.yahoo.com/Computers_and_
Internet/Internet/Domain_Registration/
Domain_Name_Controversies/

Yahoo! on Spam
http://www.yahoo.com/Computers_and_
Internet/Internet/Policies/Abuse/

Yahoo! on Specialized Search Services
http://www.yahoo.com/Computers_and_
Internet/Internet/World_Wide_Web/
Searching_the_Web/

Yahoo! on Web Advertising
http://www.yahoo.com/Computers_and_
Internet/Internet/Business_and_Economics/
Advertising_on_Web_and_Internet/

Internet and Online Marketing News

Advertising Age
http://www.adage.com

AdWeek
http://www.adweek.com/

BoardWatch
http://www.boardwatch.com/

Browsers.com
http://www.browsers.com/

ChannelSeven
http://www.channelseven.com/

ClickZ
http://www.clickz.com/

CMPnet
http://www.cmpnet.com/

CNET
http://www.cnet.com/

Colloquy
www.colloquy.org/

Direct Marketing News
http://www.dmnews.com/

Fast Company
http://www.fastcompany.com/

Forbes Digital Tool
http://www.forbes.com/

HotWired
http://www.hotwired.com/

Iconocast
http://www.iconocast.com/

InfoWeek
http://www.infoweek.com

Internet Industry Standard
(The Industry Standard)
http://www.thestandard.com/

Internet SourceBook
http://www.internetsourcebook.com/

Internet.com
http://www.internet.com/

Marketing Computers
http://www.marketingcomputers.com/

MarketsResearch.Com
http://www.marketsresearch.com/

MediaCentral (Direct Marketing News)
http://www.mediacentral.com/

MediaPost
http://www.mediapost.com

Microscope
http://www.microscope.com/

NetMarketing
http://netb2b.com/

News.com
http://www.news.com/

Red Herring
http://www.redherring.com/

Sales and Marketing Management
http://www.smmmag.com/

Silicon Alley Reporter
http://www.siliconalleyreporter.com/

TechWeb
http://www.techweb.com/

Upside
http://www.upside.com/

Web Digest For Marketers
http://www.wdfm.com/

WebWeek
http://www.webweek.com

Who's Marketing Online
http://www.wmo.com/

Wired News
http://www.wirednews.com/

ZDNet
http://www.zdnet.com/

Software and Online Service Companies

AdForce
http://www.adforce.com

Associate-It
http://www.associate-it.com/

Accrue Software
http://www.accrue.com/

AdKnowledge
http://www.adknowledge.com/

Affiliate Shop
http://www.affiliateshop.com/

Affiliate Zone
http://www.affiliatezone.com

Apple Computer
http://www.apple.com/

Aptex
http://www.aptex.com/

Auraline
http://www.auraline.com

Autonomy
http://www.autonomy.com/

BackWeb Technologies
http://www.backweb.com/

Be Free
http://www.befree.com/

Broadvision
http://www.broadvision.com/

Cisco Systems
http://cisco.com/

ClickTrade
http://www.clicktrade.com

Commission Junction
http://www.commissionjunction.com

Did-It
http://www.did-it.com

DoubleClick Network
http://www.doubleclick.net/

eGain
http://www.egain.com

eMarketer
http://www.emarketer.com

Engage
http://www.engage.com

ePrize
http://www.eprize.net

Firefly
http://www.firefly.net/

FlyCast
http://www.flycast.com/

Hotmail
http://www.hotmail.com/

ichat
http://www.ichat.com/

Imgis
http://www.imgis.com/

Internet Profiles (I/PRO)
http://www.ipro.com/

JavaSoft
http://www.javasoft.com/

Juno Online
http://www.juno.com/

LinkExchange
http://www.linkexchange.com/

LivePerson
http://www.liveperson.com

Lot 21 Interactive
http://www.lot21.com

Macromedia
http://www.macromedia.com/

Marimba
http://www.marimba.com/

MatchLogic
http://www.matchlogic.com/

Microsoft Corporation
http://www.microsoft.com/

MyPoints
http://www.mypoints.com/

Narrative Communications (Enliven)
http://www.narrative.com/

Net Perceptions
http://www.netperceptions.com/

Netcentives
http://www.netcentives.com/

NetGravity
http://www.netgravity.com/

Net Perspectives
http://www.netperspectives.com/

Netscape Communications Corporation
http://www.netscape.com/

Network Solutions
http://www.netsol.com

New Canoe
http://www.newcanoe.com

Network Solutions
http://www.netsol.com/

Personify
http://www.personify.com

Poppe Tyson
http://www.poppe.com/

Qualcomm
http://www.qualcomm.com/

Real Media
http://www.realmedia.com/

Real Networks
http://www.real.com/

Red Sky Interactive
http://www.redsky.com/

Refer-It
http://www.refer-it.com

Silicon Graphics
http://www.sgi.com/

Sun Microsystems
http://www.sun.com/

Thinking Media
http://www.thethinkingmedia.com/

24/7 Media
http://www.247media.com/

Visibility Index
http://www.visibilityindex.com/

YesMail
http://www.yesmail.com

General News, Business, Entertainment, and Culture

ABC.com
http://www.abc.com/

ABCNews
http://www.abcnews.com/

America Online
http://www.aol.com/

CBS.com
http://www.cbs.com/

CNN Interactive
http://www.cnn.com/

Disney
http://www.disney.com/

E!Online
http://www.eonline.com/

ESPN SportZone
http://www.espn.sportszone.com/

Icebox
http://www.icebox.com

MapQuest
http://www.mapquest.com/

Mercury Center
http://www.mercurycenter.com

Microsoft Network
http://www.msn.com/

MP3.com
http://www.mp3.com/

MSNBC
http://www.msnbc.com/

MTV
http://www.mtv.com/

NBC.com
http://www.nbc.com/

New York Post
http://www.nypost.com

New York Times
http://www.nytimes.com/

Salon.com
http://www.salon.com

USA Today
http://www.usatoday.com/

Wall Street Journal
http://www.wsj.com

Examples of Marketing and E-Commerce Sites

Amazon.com
http://www.amazon.com/

Barnes & Noble
http://www.barnesandnoble.com/

Butterball Turkey Online
http://www.butterball.com

Corcoran Group
http://www.corcorangroup.com/

Coca-Cola
http://www.coke.com/

Crest
http://www.crest.com

eBay
http://www.ebay.com

MSCSoftware
http://www.engineering-e.com

Federal Express
http://www.fedex.com/

Fingerhut Companies
http://www.fingerhut.com/

Ford Motor Company
http://www.ford.com/

The Gap (Levi Strauss)
http://www.thegap.com

General Motors
http://www.gm.com/

GiftCertificates.com
http://www.giftcertificates.com

Hershey's
http://www.hersheys.com/

Intel
http://www.intel.com

Kotex Girlspace
http://www.kotex.com/girlspace

LandsEnd
http://www.landsend.com/

Levi Strauss
http://www.levi.com/

Nike
http://www.nike.com/

Nordstrom's
http://www.nordstroms.com

Office Depot
http://www.officedepot.com

Priceline
http://www.priceline.com/

Ragu
http://www.ragu.com/

Small Business Depot
http://www.smallbusinessdepot.com

Spam (Hormel)
http://www.spam.com/

Staples
http://www.staples.com/

TV Guide
http://www.tvguide.com/

Internet Market Research Groups

Burke
http://www.burke.com/

Forrester Research
http://www.forrester.com/

Gartner Group
http://www.gartner.com/

Greenfield Online
http://www.greenfieldcentral.com

IMT Strategies
http://www.imtstrategies.com

Jupiter Communications
http://www.jup.com/

NetValue
http://www.netvalue.com

Media Metrix (formerly PC Meter)
http://www.mediametrix.com/

Nielsen Media Research
http://www.nielsenmedia.com/

Millward Brown
http://www.millwardbrown.com/

Relevant Knowledge
http://www.relevantknowledge.com/

NetRatings
http://www.netratings.com/

YankeeGroup
http://www.yankeegroup.com/

Index

Butterball Turkey, 23

buying positions, optimizing search engine rankings, 146

bytes, 76

C

cashpile.com, 214

CASIE (Coalition for Advertising Supported Information and Entertainment), 279, 312

CDNow.com, 172

CellularVision, 307

ChannelSeven, 313

chat promotions, sponsorships, 299

choosing domain names, unique domain names, 103-110

Claritin, 172

ClickAction, 191

clicks, quantifying, 286-287

clickthrough rates. *See* CTR

ClickZ, 298, 313

ClickZForum, 314

CNET
  domain names, 112
  links, 200
  personalization, 43

CNET Builder.com, 88

Coalition for Advertising Supported Information and Entertainment (CASIE), 279

cobwebs, 38

collaborative filtering, 17, 45-46

color palettes, rich media, 71

commercial online services, 186
  AOL, 184
  Microsoft Network, 186
  portals, 187
  viral marketing, 184-186, 188-189

commercials, television commercials, 284

commision, affiliate sites, 215

Commission Junction, 219, 222

Commodore64, 29

competing with better-branded competitors, affiliate sites, 216-218

CompuServe, 186

consumers, statistics for, 54

contact information, writing press releases, 254

content, target marketing, 304

content services, ROI models, 26-28

conversions, 275

cookies, 290, 307-308

Cool Site of the Day/Week award, 206

Corcorangroup.com, 23

corporate fact sheets, press kits, 262-263

cost of direct response online advertising, different prices, 287-288

cost comparisons, email versus snail mail, 159

cost per thousand measure (CPM), 275

cost-per-whatever (CPW), 286

Council for Responsible Email, 170-171

CPM (cost per thousand measure), 275-276

CPW (cost-per-whatever), 286
  direct response online advertising, 287

crateandbarrel.com, 174

crawlers, 133

creating email campaigns, 168-171
  media, 171-172

CRM (customer relationship management), 12

cross-promotion possibilities, online ads, 302

CTR (clickthrough rates), 275
  brand-building, 288

press releases, 241
  disseminating, 257
    distributing by email, 260-261
    *distributing to individual
      journalists, 259*
    dropping on the wire, 257-258
  embargoes, 242, 244
  example of, 255-256
  NDAs, 242, 244
  pre-briefing the press, 244-245
  timing of, 241-242, 245
  writing, 250-252
    abstracts, 254
    availability, 253
    boilerplates, 253
    contact information, 254
    datelines, 252
    dates, 252
    headlines, 252
    lede, 253
    page numbers, 254
    prices, 253
    quotes, 253
press releases digests, press kits, 263
Priceline.com, 16, 100
prices, writing press releases, 253
privacy
  personalization, 46-47
  reel.com, 46
  TRUSTe, 47
Procter & Gamble, 100
  domain names, 101
product descriptions, press kits, 264
product names, registering as domain
  names, 114-115
Productopia.com, 176
products that sell on the web, 21
protecting assets
  domain names, 110-112
  registering product names, 114-115
  registering variations of your domain
    names, 112-113
  renewing domain names, 116

psychographic, target marketing, 310-311
publicists. *See also* PR firms
  becoming a source, 235
    editorial calendars, 240
    face to face meetings, 239
    finding contact addresses, 236-237
    media directories, 238
    telephone etiquette, 239
    use a personal touch, 236
  deciding what is news, 247-250
  deciding what is NOT news, 245-247
  journalists' complaints about, 234
  press releases. *See* press releases
  relationship with journalists, 231-232
publicity
  email newsletters, 266
  opinion pieces, 265
  radio shows, 267
  speaking opportunities, 265
  VNRs, 267-268
  'zines, 266
Publishers Weekly, 237
purchases, researching infocentric designs,
  49-50
pure play sites, 28

Q

quality search engine rankings, 153
quality banners, creating, 289, 291
quality time, spending time with
  journalists, 239
quantifying clicks, 286-287
quotes, writing press releases, 253

R

radio shows, publicity, 267
rankings. *See* search engine rankings
real-time, 52-54
real-time video, 71. *See also* rich media

Red Sky Interactive, 295

reel.com
    collaborative filtering, 46
    privacy, 46

refer-it.com, 214

Register.com, 205

registering
    product names as domain names,
      114-115
    variations of your domain name,
      112-113
    web sites, 135-137

renewing domain names, 116

reporters. *See* journalists

reprinted news stories, press kits, 265

researching
    domain names, 103
    products, infocentric designs, 49-50

resources
    CNET Builder.com, 88
    Useit.com, 88
    Web Pages That Suck, 88
    WebMonkey, 88
    Yahoo! On Design Guides, 88

response management, email, 174-175

Return on Investment. *See* ROI

revenue streams, 209

reverse IP look-up, 309

rich media, 71-72
    browsers, 78-79
    color palettes, 71
    modems, 73-74
      56KBps, 74-75
      size of web pages, 76
    monitors, 76-77
    navigation, 82, 84-85
    need for, 85-87
    plug-ins, 79-81
      interface options, 81-82

Ring of Fire, 202-203

Robot Exclusion, 155

robot exclusion, optimizing search engine
  rankings, 148-149

robots, 133

Robots Exclusion Protocol, 149

RockNet, 122

ROI (Return on Investment), 10
    media rich banners, 293
    models of, 13-14
      brand-building, 14-16
      content services, 26-28
      customer suppoort, 22-23
      lead generation, 17-18
      market research, 24, 26
      online sales, 20
    traditional business models versus
      models, 11-13

S

Schick's Tracer FX razor, 279

search engine rankings, 137
    importance of, 146
    optimizing, 138
      buying or bidding on positions, 146
      dead-end links, 147
      dynamic pages, 148
      following other sites strategies, 144
      frames, 147
      headlines and body text, 141
      image maps, 147
      keywords, 139, 142-143
      meta tags, 141-142
      page title tags, 139-140
      password-protected pages, 147
      pointer pages, 145
      popularity, 143
      robot exclusion, 148-149
      spamdexing, 144
    quality, 153
    Yahoo!. *See* Yahoo!

Search Engine Watch, 135, 154, 221

FOR MORE ABOUT E-COMMERCE AND WEB USABILITY, CHECK OUT...

Designing Web Usability:
The Practice of Simplicity

Jakob Nielsen
ISBN: 1-56205-810-X
$45.00 USA

Read what the world is reading. Over 250,000 copies in print, in over 11 languages, and growing every month. In this landmark design reference, the world's acknowledged authority on Web usability, Jakob Nielsen, shares the full weight of his wisdom and experience. From content and page design to designing for ease of navigation and for users with disabilities, Jakob Nielsen delivers complete direction on how to connect with any Web user, in any situation.

For more information and how to buy this and other New Riders titles, contact us at:
201 W. 103rd St.
Indianapolis, IN 46290-1097
Toll-free (800) 571-5840 + 9 + 7477
If outside U.S. (317) 581-3500. Ask for New Riders.

www.newriders.com

New Riders Professional Library

**Adobe Photoshop 5.5 Fundamentals
with ImageReady 2**
Gary Bouton
0-7357-0928-9

**Bert Monroy: Photorealistic
Techniques with Photoshop &
Illustrator**
Bert Monroy
0-7357-0969-6

**CG 101: A Computer Graphics
Industry Reference**
Terrence Masson
0-7357-0046-X

<coloring web graphics.2>
Lynda Weinman and Bruce Heavin
1-56205-818-5

**Creating Killer Web Sites,
Second Edition**
David Siegel
1-56830-433-1

<creative html design>
Lynda Weinman and William
Weinman
1-56205-704-9

<designing web graphics.3>
Lynda Weinman
1-56205-949-1

Designing Web Usability
Jakob Nielsen
1-56205-810-X

E-Volve-or-Die.com
Mitchell Levy
0-7357-1028-7

Flash 4 Magic
David Emberton and J. Scott Hamlin
0-7357-0949-1

Flash Web Design
Hillman Curtis
0-7357-0896-7

HTML Artistry: More than Code
Ardith Ibañez and Natalie Zee
1-56830-454-4

HTML Web Magic
Raymond Pirouz
1-56830-475-7

Inside Adobe Photoshop 6
Gary David Bouton, et. al
0-7357-1038-4

Photoshop 5 & 5.5 Artistry
Barry Haynes and Wendy Crumpler
0-7457-0994-7

Photoshop 6 Effects Magic
Rhoda Grossman, et. al
0-7357-1035-X

Photoshop 6 Web Magic
Jeff Foster, et. al
0-7357-1036-8

Photoshop Channel Chops
David Biedny, Bert Monroy, and
Nathan Moody
1-56205-723-5

Secrets of Successful Web Sites
David Siegel
1-56830-382-3

1379